Multi-party politics and the Constitution

Multi-party politics and the Constitution

VERNON BOGDANOR

Fellow of Brasenose College, Oxford

CAMBRIDGE UNIVERSITY PRESS

Cambridge

London   New York   New Rochelle
Melbourne   Sydney

Published by the Press Syndicate of the University of Cambridge
The Pitt Building, Trumpington Street, Cambridge CB2 IRP
32 East 57th Street, New York, NY 10022, USA
296 Beaconsfield Parade, Middle Park, Melbourne 3206, Australia

First published 1983

Printed in Great Britain at
the University Press, Cambridge

Library of Congress catalogue card number: 83–1901

British Library Cataloguing in Publication Data
Bogdanor, Vernon
Multi-party politics and the constitution.
1. Political parties – Great Britain
I. Title
329.941 JN1117
ISBN 0 521 25524 4 hard covers
ISBN 0 521 27526 1 paperback

For

R.B.   J.E.B.

P.S.R.B.   A.M.D.B.

With thanks

Contents

Tables

Acknowledgements

I should like to acknowledge the gracious permission of Her Majesty the Queen for allowing me the privilege of using the Royal Archives at Windsor Castle, and for granting me permission to quote from the papers of King George V. I am grateful, also, to Sir Robert Mackworth-Young, KCVO, Librarian, Windsor Castle, for the help he gave me. I should like to thank Brigadier A. W. A. Llewellen Palmer for allowing me to quote from the diary of the Marquess of Lincolnshire, and Lord Simon for allowing me to quote from his father's papers.

I am deeply grateful for the generosity of the Nuffield Foundation and the Parliamentary Democracy Trust in providing me with financial assistance which enabled me to study the working of multi-party politics in Scandinavia.

I owe a great debt of gratitude to David Butler for arranging two conferences at which working papers for this book were discussed. David Butler has himself been investigating the problems arising out of *Governing Without Majorities*, the title of his book published by Collins in 1983, and I have benefited considerably from exchanging ideas with him, although our approaches and conclusions are somewhat different.

I should like to thank Anthony Teasdale for the meticulous care with which he read an earlier draft of the manuscript, and for many stimulating discussions on the topics with which this book deals. Earlier drafts have also been read, in whole or in part, by Sir John Herbecq, Barry Nicholas, Peter Pulzer and Philip Williams, and I am most grateful to them; but, of course, they are not to be implicated in my conclusions.

But my greatest debt, as always, is to my wife for encouraging my work in a field of interest far removed from her own; and to my sons, Paul and Adam, who prefer kings to governments.

Brasenose College, Oxford   VERNON BOGDANOR
October, 1982

ix

Note on sources

The following manuscript collections were consulted in the preparation of this book:

Royal Archives, Windsor Castle (RA)
Addison Papers, Bodleian Library, Oxford
Dalton Diary, Library of London School of Economics and Political Science
Diary of Marquess of Lincolnshire, on microfilm at Bodleian Library, Oxford
Samuel Papers, House of Lords Record Office
Simon Papers, Bodleian Library, Oxford
Strachey Papers, House of Lords Record Office

Introduction

The purpose of this book is to chart the course of multi-party politics in Britain and to trace the likely consequences of multi-party politics for the political system and the Constitution. The first part of *Multi-Party Politics and the Constitution* considers why the two-party system came under challenge in Britain in the 1970s, and analyses the character of the latest challenger to the hegemony of the major parties, the Liberal/SDP Alliance with its commitment to electoral reform. Proportional representation would make it unlikely that Britain would ever again return to a two-party system such as existed during the 1950s and 1960s. It would be a transformation which, if not irreversible, would be extremely difficult to reverse.

It is particularly important, therefore, that we should be aware of the consequences of multi-party politics, whether we regard these changes as desirable or not. In a previous book – *The People and the Party System* (Cambridge University Press, 1981) – I argued strongly for the introduction of proportional representation in Britain. This book, however, deals less with the *arguments* for proportional representation, than with its likely *consequences*. It is to be hoped that some consensus can be reached on what these consequences might be and how the constitutional problems which will arise should be resolved, even amongst those with differing views as to the desirability of proportional representation.

The political consequences of a multi-party system are likely to affect the *role* of parties as much as their relative strength. As in many other industrial societies, parties may come to lose the central role in political life which they have enjoyed since the dawning of the age of mass suffrage. If that happens, Britain may undergo a period of considerable political volatility and instability and will be forced to consider the question of how democracy is likely to work in the absence of strong parties. History can offer little guidance in answering this question.

The second part of *Multi-Party Politics and the Constitution* analyses the constitutional consequences of multi-party politics. Here, historical precedents do offer a clue as to the principles which might be followed to resolve constitutional problems. In particular, the experience of the 1920s, which was also a period of multi-party politics in Britain and of the years 1974–79 which again gave Britain the experience of minority government, is of some value in analysing how the constitution might work in the future. However, the value of these precedents is limited by the fact that, after a brief period of multi-party politics, the two-party system was restored on each occasion; and, even more important, most politicians acted under the assumption that the two-party system *would* be restored, and so they did not feel the need to accommodate hitherto unchallenged practices to the exigencies of a new political system. With proportional representation, however, this expectation would disappear, and habits would begin to change. They would change not suddenly but gradually as a new generation of politicians came to appreciate that they were working under different constraints from those of their predecessors. For, as Bagehot noticed, over a hundred years ago, 'What we call the "spirit" of politics is more surely changed by a change of generation in the men than by any other change whatever.'[1]

Some of the likely effects may not occur until the quite distant future and can at present be perceived only 'as through a glass darkly'. Nevertheless, since a number of the supposed principles and conventions of the British Constitution are in reality conventions of the two-party system and depend upon the assumption of an alternating single-party government and opposition, *Multi-Party Politics and the Constitution* seeks to answer the question whether existing conventions relating to Cabinet government, collective responsibility, the choice of Prime Minister and the dissolution of Parliament can survive the entrenchment of a multi-party system. The experience of the constitutional monarchies of north-western Europe, especially those of Scandinavia, casts a good deal of light on what might happen; while West Germany's experience shows what changes are needed in governmental relationships to make stable coalition possible.

This book is the third which I have written attempting to trace the inter-connections between constitutional ideas and political reality. Being unwritten and relying so much upon precedent, the British Constitution is peculiarly dependent upon the changing perceptions of party advantage held by political leaders. The British Constitution is, in the words of Professor J. G. Griffith, a 'political constitution'[2] (although Professor Griffith's interpretation of this term is different from mine). It cannot be understood without an understanding of the political context within which past precedents have been set.

[1] Walter Bagehot, Introduction to the second edition of *The English Constitution* (1872), *The Collected Works of Walter Bagehot* (The Economist, 1974), vol. 5, p. 167.
[2] J.G. Griffith, 'The political constitution', *Modern Law Review*, 42 (1979).

Introduction

In *Devolution* (Oxford University Press, 1979) I sought to analyse the attempts made by British politicians over the last hundred years to deal with the problems raised by nationalist parties in the non-English parts of the United Kingdom. It became clear that one factor preventing political leaders from resolving these problems successfully was a doctrinaire if undisclosed commitment to a rigid and narrow conception of parliamentary supremacy which precluded the sharing of power either between Westminster and Dublin in the nineteenth century, or between Westminster and Edinburgh in the twentieth.

In the second book, *The People and the Party System*, an investigation into the debate on the referendum and electoral reform in British politics, I attempted to show that the notion of parliamentary supremacy had allowed the political parties to acquire a degree of unregulated power unmatched in any other democracy. Looked at in their historical context, the referendum and the single transferable vote method of proportional representation, far from being incompatible with the Constitution, were seen to be the means of making effective the central principle of constitutional democracy, that government should be responsible to the will of the electorate rather than the needs of the parties.

Multi-Party Politics and the Constitution fulfils a complementary purpose. It is hoped that it may cast light on current constitutional conventions and upon the reasons why the two-party system finds itself under such strong challenge. But it does not seek to predict the future, something for which the political scientist is no better equipped than the educated layman. It seeks only to clarify the conventions of the Constitution by charting alternative possibilities. But, if multi-party politics turns out to become an enduring feature of British life, then what follows may prove a useful guide to the constitutional changes that will result.

Part I

Multi-party politics

The two-party system and its challengers

I

Britain has a good claim to be regarded as the political home of the two-party system. For at least the last hundred years representative government in Britain has been conceived of as essentially a contest between two opposed points of view, each competing for the support of the electorate and the right to govern. It is this which constitutes the essence of the Westminster Model of government as it has been developed in Britain, and exported with varying degrees of success, to countries abroad. So much indeed has this model taken hold, that British political writers have found it difficult to understand how representative government can work when the basic assumption of a two-party system is removed; and difficult also to appreciate how the advent of multi-party politics might affect the British Constitution, many of whose provisions and conventions presuppose a two-party system. Indeed, the two-party system is one of those 'tacit understandings' which, according to Sidney Low, dominate our constitutional thinking, even if the understandings themselves 'are not always understood'.[1]

Since Britain has been regarded, at least until recent years, as the prototype of a flourishing democracy, it became natural to believe that the two-party system was a norm to which other nations should aspire. Macaulay seems to have been the first to identify the two-party system not only with good government, but even with natural tendencies of the human mind for he claimed that the day on which the Long Parliament reassembled in 1641 was 'one of the most remarkable epochs in our history', because 'From that day dates the corporate existence of the two great parties which have ever since alternately governed the country. In one sense, indeed, the distinction which then became obvious had always existed, and always must exist. For it has its origin in diversities of temper, of understanding and of interest, which are found in all societies,

---

[1] Sidney Low, *The Governance of England* (T. Fisher Unwin, 1904), p. 12.

and which will be found till the human mind ceases to be drawn in opposite directions by the charm of habit and the charm of novelty.'[2]

Later writers have been unwilling to go as far as Macaulay, but have merely contented themselves with the assertion that a two-party system was an essential precondition of a well-ordered system of government. 'A division into two parties', declared Lowell, 'is not only the normal result of the parliamentary system, but also an essential condition of its success';[3] while, for Duverger, '... the two-party system seems to correspond to the nature of things, that is to say that political choice usually takes the form of a choice between two alternatives'.[4]

The two-party system, then, was held not only to be a central characteristic of the British system of democracy, but essential to the smooth working of parliamentary government. For it was only under such a system that it was possible to secure stability, genuine accountability and a democratic alternation of power. With a two-party system, one of the two parties would gain an overall majority in a general election. There would be no need for coalition government or minority rule. The party which won the election could rule on its own, unchallenged, until the time came for the next general election when its record would be clearly on display before the electorate. There would be no danger of the government being unable to carry out its programme, except on the rare occasions when it failed to retain the adherence of its back-bench supporters, or when there was a party split. The rapid turnover of governments so characteristic of Continental multi-party systems would therefore be avoided.

With a two-party system, the electors would have a reasonable assurance that the programme for which they had voted would in fact be carried out. Accountability would thus be more direct when power was clearly concentrated in the executive rather than shared between different parties in a coalition government, or between a minority government and the legislature. The legitimacy of the democratic system would be assured, and the electorate would reap the benefits of a strong and stable government.

In such a system, moreover, the Opposition would have a major incentive to display responsibility and moderation if it wished to be returned to power. With only two parties, the floating voter – the voter in the middle of the political spectrum – would decide elections. The opposition, therefore, would have to justify itself as an alternative government

---

[2] T.B. Macaulay, *The History of England* (Chatto and Windus edition, 1905), vol. 1, p. 88.
[3] A.L. Lowell, *Government and Parties in Continental Europe* (Longmans Green, 1897), vol. 1, p. 72.
[4] Maurice Duverger, *Political Parties* (2nd English edition, Methuen, 1959), p. 215.

– it could not enjoy the luxury of unconstructive criticism – while extremism would serve merely to alienate the floating voter, and therefore render its opposition status permanent. In this way, the two-party system was thought not only to constitute the general practice of British democracy, but also to represent the ideal for successful government everywhere.

II

This model, over-simplified as it inevitably was, has never wholly corresponded with reality even in Britain. For, since the emergence of mass politics in the nineteenth century, there have always been more than two parties represented in the legislature. The nearest Britain has come to being a two-party system in the last hundred years was in 1951 when all but 3.2% of the electorate voted for Labour or the Conservatives; while in parliamentary terms, 1959 constituted the highwater mark of the two-party system, when only 7 MPs – 6 Liberals and an Independent Conservative, Sir David Robertson – disturbed the hegemony of the two major parties.

For most of this period, other parties have secured significant representation at Westminster. Until 1918, the Irish Nationalists enjoyed a virtual monopoly of seats in Ireland outside north-east Ulster; while the Liberal Unionists and, from 1900 the Labour Party, undermined the dominance of the Liberals and Conservatives. After the First World War, the situation became even more complicated since, between 1918 and 1923 the Liberal Party was split between supporters of Asquith and Lloyd George, with Labour gradually replacing the Liberals as the main party of the Left. This transformed the 1920s into a period of three-party politics, with 'hung' Parliaments in which no party won an overall majority occurring in 1923 and 1929. In 1931, the formation of the National Government led to a further upheaval. The Labour Party split, at parliamentary if not at constituency level, between a small number of supporters of the National Government – the National Labour Party – and the vast majority of Labour MPs who came out in opposition to the Government. The Liberals in turn divided three ways, one group, the Liberal Nationals led by Sir John Simon, coming to identify themselves wholly with the Conservative Party; a second, led by Sir Herbert Samuel, serving in the National Government until 1932, but from a more independent position; while a third small family group led by Lloyd George came out in total opposition to the National Government.

In the years after 1945, the position was simplified. Until the 1970s, only the Liberal Party managed to retain a permanent foothold in Parliament against the massed battalions of Labour and the Conservatives. Britain experienced 'the longest period of unambiguous single-party responsibility – since the Whig supremacy'.[5] Not until the 1970s were the Liberals joined by Nationalists from Scotland and Wales able to win seats in a general election, and by separate Ulster parties, the Ulster Unionists having, by the time of the dramatic February 1974 general election, severed their links with the Conservative Party. The two general elections of 1974, with their massive surge in Liberal and Scottish Nationalist support, seemed indeed to herald the end of two-party dominance; while in 1981 a new party – the Social Democratic Party – was formed, making it even less likely that a two-party system would be restored.

Yet although in formal terms Britain could not be described as a two-party system, the mechanics of her political system have been, at least until the 1970s, of the two-party type. At only three general elections since 1918 – those of 1923, 1929 and February 1974 – has a single party failed to win an overall majority; while the habits of politicians and electors alike have been influenced by the alternation of power between two main parties, or at least the expectation of it.

Third parties, with the exception of the Labour Party at the beginning of the century, have been either parties representing the non-English parts of the United Kingdom, such as the Irish or Scottish Nationalists; or splinters from one of the major parties, such as the Liberal Unionists or the National Labour Party. These parties have not fundamentally disturbed the two-party system because their allegiance to one of the two major parties has rarely been in doubt. From 1886, the Irish Nationalists would sustain only a Liberal Government, while the Liberal Unionists would support only Conservative Governments, finally merging with the Conservatives in 1912. Likewise, the National Labour Party was formed in 1931 to support the National Government, and differences with the Conservatives had to be subordinated to that single overriding aim. For each of these groups, one overriding issue – Home Rule for the Irish Nationalists and Liberal Unionists, the need to pursue the National Government's economy programme for the National Labour Party –determined their parliamentary allegiance. They were, therefore, unable to use their position in Parliament to bargain effectively for policies or office, because they could not switch allies if their demands were not met.

Labour, which did not become an independent national party until 1918, *was* willing to make its support for pre-First World War Liberal governments conditional, and indeed it secured important legislative

[5] David Butler, '1945–1977', in David Butler (ed.), *Coalitions in British Politics* (Macmillan, 1978), p. 95.

gains during this period. But Labour's bargaining power was limited by the fact that it could never support the Conservatives, and it would have been too dangerous before 1914 to break the electoral pact with the Liberals and fight them in the constituencies. So politics before the First World War did not diverge very markedly from the two-party model. There was a Conservative Party with its by now virtually indistinguishable Liberal Unionist allies, faced by a Liberal Party which could invariably count upon the support of Labour and the Irish Nationalists. There were, if not two parties, two blocs and the battle lines between them were perfectly clear. This has been the situation in British politics through most of the twentieth century; and it is this two-party norm which the events of the 1970s and the formation of the Social Democratic Party have undermined.

III

The 1970s, then, saw the development of a challenge to the two-party system. The increase in support for minor parties can be charted as in table 1.

Table 1. *Electoral support for minor parties*

General election	% vote for Labour and Conservative Parties	% vote for Liberals	% vote for parties other than Conservatives Labour or Liberals	No. of Liberal MPs	No. of MPs belonging to parties other than the Conservatives or Labour
1945	87.6	9.0	3.4	12	22
1950	89.6	9.1	1.3	9	3
1951	96.8	2.5	0.7	6	3
1955	96.1	2.7	1.2	6	3
1959	93.2	5.9	0.9	6	1
1964	87.5	11.2	1.3	9	0
1966	90.0	8.5	1.5	12	2
1970 Feb	89.5	7.5	3.0	6	7
1974 Oct	75.1	19.3	5.6	14	23
1974	75.0	18.3	6.7	13	26
1979	80.8	13.8	5.4	11	16

By July 1982, the number of MPs not belonging to the two major parties amounted to 58, the largest minor party representation in the Commons since 1931. This had occurred through the formation of the SDP, with 30 MPs (all but one former Labour MPs), and a Liberal by-election victor. The total of 58 minor party MPs comprised 30 Social Democrats, 12 Liberals, 12 members from Northern Ireland constituencies, 2 Scottish Nationalists and 2 Welsh Nationalists.

The challenge to the two-party system, as the table shows, is far more striking at the electoral than at the parliamentary level. In February 1974, for example, nearly a fifth of those voting supported Liberal candidates, yet the Liberals secured only 14 or 2.2% of the 635 seats at Westminster: while in October 1974, the Scottish Nationalists secured nearly one-third of the Scottish vote – 30.4%, yet gained only 11 or 15.5% of the 71 Scottish seats, about half the number to which they would have been entitled under a strictly proportional system operating in Scotland. Conversely, the Labour and Conservative Parties, which in 1951 secured 96.8% of the vote and 616 out of the 625 seats in the Commons, in 1979 secured only 80.8% of the vote and yet still retained 608 out of the 635 seats in the Commons. Although, therefore, the minor parties have in recent years enjoyed a large increase in support, they have not been able to secure a parliamentary breakthrough by overcoming the high threshold which the 'first past the post' electoral system imposes upon them.

There are two kinds of challengers to the two-party system. First, there are the nationalist parties in Wales and Scotland, and the parliamentary representatives of Northern Ireland. The formerly dominant party in Northern Ireland, the Ulster Unionists, used to be for all practical purposes an adjunct of the Conservative Party in the House of Commons, and they always won at least 8 of the 12 parliamentary seats in the province. Since February 1974, however, the link between the Ulster Unionists and the Conservatives has been broken. Today Northern Ireland MPs owe no allegiance to any political party on the mainland, and none of the British parties fight elections in the province. Thus, a part of the increase in the number of MPs from 'other' parties in column 6 of the table can be explained simply by the fact that at least 8 MPs who, before 1974, would be counted as part of the Conservative Party's strength, are now to be counted with MPs from 'other' parties. Since the number of MPs representing Northern Ireland constituencies in the Commons is to be increased at the next general election from 12 to 17, it can be expected that the number of MPs from other parties in the Parliament elected in 1983 or 1984 will automatically rise to reflect this development.

Of the parties from Scotland and Wales, it is the Scottish Nationalists who made the most spectacular advance in the 1970s, only to fall back equally dramatically in the general election of 1979. Yet this decline was exaggerated by the electoral system, for the SNP still commanded the support of one-sixth of the Scottish electorate in 1979, even though it obtained only two seats.

General Election	% of Scottish vote	Seats
1970	11.4	1
February 1974	21.9	7
October 1974	30.4	11
1979	17.3	2

Plaid Cymru, on the other hand, has been unable to make any electoral progress at all.

General Election	% of Welsh vote	Seats
1970	11.5	0
February 1974	10.7	2
October 1974	10.8	3
1979	8.1	2

Plaid Cymru's strength seems largely confined to the Welsh-speaking areas of north-west Wales, and, whereas the SNP can be seen by the Scottish voter as the party of Scotland, Plaid Cymru is increasingly regarded as the party only of Welsh Wales. To this extent, its chances of further electoral advance are severely limited.

The second type of party seeking to challenge the two major parties is embodied in the new formation – the Liberal–SDP Alliance. This Alliance will hope to build upon the support of the Liberals, who have made striking if discontinuous electoral advances since the 1950s. The Liberals reached their electoral nadir in 1951 when they gained only 2.5% of the vote, since when they have gained support after periods of Conservative rule in 1964 and February 1974, only to fall back after periods of Labour government in 1951, 1970 and 1979. Yet each peak has been higher than the last. The peak of February 1974 was higher than that of 1964; and when the Liberal vote fell back in 1979, it fell to a higher plateau than in 1970 or 1951.

The SDP, by contrast, had not, by the autumn of 1982, faced any similar electoral test. It had not fought in a general election: only one of its MPs – Bruce Douglas-Mann – had resigned his seat to stand for re-election under the SDP label, and he was defeated at a by-election in his Mitcham and Morden constituency in May 1982. By July 1982, only 2 of the SDP MPs – its leader Roy Jenkins, and its President, Shirley Williams

– had been elected under the SDP banner in by-elections. Electorally, therefore, the SDP remains very much of an unknown quantity.

IV

The new challengers unlike their predecessors owe no clear allegiance to either of the two major parties. Many previous minor parties, such as the Liberal Unionists or Liberal Nationals, have been splinters from a major party and have been reabsorbed by the other major party. The SDP, although a splinter from Labour, is unlikely to follow this path. The Liberals, also, will certainly preserve their independence which they guarded tenaciously even in the Party's darkest days. Nor are the parties of the non-English parts of the United Kingdom, with the possible exception of the Welsh Nationalists, likely to prove firm allies of either major party. The Protestant parties in Ulster are now thoroughly suspicious of the Conservatives, doubting the wholeheartedness of the Conservative commitment to the province; while the allegiance of the Catholic parties to Labour can no longer be taken for granted either. It should be remembered, for example, that Gerry Fitt, the then leader of Northern Ireland's Social Democratic and Labour Party, cast his vote against the Labour government in the no-confidence motion of March 1979 in disgust at that government's Ulster policy. Had he not done so, the Callaghan government would have survived.

During the mid-1970s, the SNP appeared to become relatively sympathetic to the Labour-Party in the belief that Labour would establish a Scottish Assembly. When the prospect of devolution collapsed, however, partly due to the hostility of Labour back-benchers to devolution, the SNP had no hesitation in voting against Labour – in March 1977 after the failure of the first devolution bill in a no-confidence motion, and then again in the final no-confidence vote of March 1979 which brought down the government. Since 1979, the SNP has turned its back on devolution while Labour, although still officially committed to a Scottish Assembly, may well be expected to show scant enthusiasm for it in office. There is no reason, therefore, to believe that the SNP will ally itself for long to the Labour Party.

There is a further and perhaps more important difference between contemporary challengers to the two-party system and their predecessors. For the challengers today seek not only political influence, but also an alteration in the rules of the game under which political influence is secured. The nationalist parties and the Liberals and Social Democrats are all parties of constitutional reform. The Scottish and Welsh Nationalists, of course, seek self-government for their countries. This is usually understood as full independence with representation at the United

Nations; but the nationalist parties might well be prepared to settle instead for a substantial measure of Home Rule. The Ulster parties seek to alter the constitutional relationship between the mainland of Britain and Northern Ireland. The Protestant parties reject power-sharing with Catholics and seek either a restoration of Stormont, or – if that is not possible – integration with the rest of the United Kingdom and an end to recognition of the Irish dimension to the government of Northern Ireland. The Catholic parties, by contrast, seek the institutional recognition of Irish unity, something which is repugnant to the Protestants of the North, and on the whole unacceptable to governments in London.

The challenge offered by the Liberals and the SDP is different in kind, but could prove even more formidable in its effects. For these two parties seek, in alliance, to alter the British electoral system to one of proportional representation – the single transferable vote was the favoured variant recommended in the two parties' joint report on electoral reform published in July 1982,[5a] but the additional member system as used, for example, in West Germany, would also be perfectly acceptable. Reform of the electoral system would have the effect of entrenching multi-party politics in Britain, since it would make the representation of the parties in Parliament correspond much more closely with their strength in the electorate. The plurality system – generally known as the first past the post system – manufactures parliamentary majorities in Britain, as it does in other countries employing it. The system gives an absolute majority of parliamentary seats to a party winning a good deal less than half of the popular vote. Indeed no party in Britain since the war has succeeded in securing 50% of the vote – the Conservatives came nearest in 1955 and 1959 when they secured 49.7% and 49.4% of the vote respectively, while the greatest landslide in terms of seats was secured by Labour in 1945 when it won 393 seats out of 640 in the House of Commons and an overall majority of 146, on only 47.8% of the vote. Since 1970, moreover, no party has succeeded in gaining even 45% of the vote. Proportional representation, then, would confirm the position of the challengers to the two-party system; and indeed its very concession by one of the two major parties would be a signal that they were unable any longer to retain their hegemony.

The challenge to the two-party system today, therefore, is rather different from what it was in the 1920s when the Labour Party supplanted the Liberals. For Labour sought wide-ranging social and economic reforms rather than constitutional change. It accepted in practice the central features of the Westminster Model – the supremacy of Parlia-

---

[5a] *Electoral Reform: First Report of the Joint Liberal/SDP Commission on Constitutional Reform.*

ment, the unitary state and the majoritarian electoral system, seeking merely to replace the Liberals as one of the major parties able to benefit from the plenitude of power which the British Constitution offers to a majority government. Labour sought fundamentally to control the state not to reform it.

Contemporary challengers to the two-party system, by contrast, seek profound and lasting constitutional changes, which it would be difficult for any future government to reverse. If they were to be successful in achieving their aims, the consequences for the future government of Britain would be wide-ranging indeed.

V

The new forces in British politics owe their existence to a number of different factors. Yet they have in common that they each reflect genuine discontents without which they would have been, like the National Front and the Communist Party, unable to maintain even a narrow foothold on the British political system. The discontents reflected by the challengers to the two-party system can be divided into two types; the failure of successive British governments to comprehend the nature of the politics of territoriality; and their failure to reverse Britain's economic decline or accommodate themselves to the exigencies of social change.

In Northern Ireland, the increase in political violence after 1968 brought the politics of the province back to Westminster from where it had been absent for so long. This was bound to strain the alliance between the Conservatives and the Ulster Unionists. For the Conservatives could not remain indifferent to the consequences of discrimination against the Catholic minority nor to the international repercussions of civil disturbance in the province. The imposition of direct rule in 1972 was but a consequence of this divergence of view; for what precipitated it was the demand made by the Heath government that Westminster be given responsibility for internal security in Northern Ireland, something which the Northern Ireland government was unwilling to concede.

With regard to Scotland and Wales, it would not be difficult for the perceptive observer to find examples of neglect and condescension on the part of the British government, resented although, or perhaps because, the economic position of Scotland and Wales *vis-à-vis* the rest of the United Kingdom has steadily improved during the post-war period. In Wales, feelings of neglect have focussed largely upon the fear that the language may be dying; while in Scotland the feelings of resentment directed at London were given force and strength by the discovery of oil in the North Sea, which in the view of Scottish Nationalists, would enable Scotland to enjoy self-government without her standard of living being lowered.

The problem of how the non-English parts of the United Kingdom should be governed has been a source of great unease to successive British governments. Administrations of both Right and Left have found it difficult to deal with the politics of territoriality. For the issues which it raises lie far from the familiar agenda of British politics. They challenge the methods by which governments seek to resolve conflict; for, unlike socio-economic issues, they are generally not susceptible to solution by the processes of bargaining and compromise between different social groups. Such bargaining procedures presuppose a framework of stable consensus, a common set of rules accepted by both parties to a dispute. Yet what is characteristic about issues of territoriality is precisely that they offer a challenge to this kind of consensual framework.

Furthermore, issues of territoriality also challenge the two major parties' understanding of the British Constitution. For any serious attempt to confront the problems posed by territorial conflict must involve the acceptance of such notions as devolution and power-sharing which are profoundly alien to the ideologies of the Labour and Conservative Parties. For the Conservatives, of course, devolution, like Irish Home Rule before 1914, involves a direct challenge to the integrity of the country and to national identity which is based firmly upon the sovereignty of Parliament and the unitary state. To ask that power be shared, therefore, 'is a demand for the Grail, or at least a bit of it',[6] for a portion of that sovereignty which is both precious and indivisible.

For the Left, also, the politics of territoriality involves a challenge which it is unable to meet. The central aim of the Left wing of the Labour Party is to gain control over the commanding heights of the British economy through public ownership and other methods of public control. This objective requires centralised government and the concentration of political power in London. For the Labour Right, the achievement of equality entails the equal allocation of resources between regions and this can only be achieved through the agency of a strong central government. The central government is the only body able to secure the equitable distribution of public resources on the basis of need and so the philosophy of equality entails central determination of the allocation of public expenditure. The economic difficulties faced by particular nations or regions of the United Kingdom require, therefore, not the devolution of power, but, on the contrary, stronger central control over the regional allocation of resources. This is also necessary if other aspirations of the Labour Party, such as comprehensive education, are to be achieved. As

[6] Tom Nairn, *The Break-Up of Britain* (2nd edition, Verso, 1981), p. 61.

Mr Colin Phipps, then a Labour MP, put it during the parliamentary debates on the Scotland and Wales Bill, 'Any Labour Government who gave up central power to decide on matters such as comprehensive education and the moving of money around the United Kingdom would be foolish. The under-privileged child in Eastbourne is as important as the under-privileged child in Glasgow. If comprehensive education is right in Glasgow, it is right in the South of England ...' (14 December 1976, col. 1369). The recognition of territoriality, therefore, threatens one of the central foundations of the post-war consensus, the notion that the allocation of resources should depend not upon geography but upon need.

The Labour Party conceives of political conflict as being fundamentally socio-economic in nature, and territorial disputes must be resolved within this framework. On this view, the grievances of Scotland flow from working-class deprivation no different in kind from the problems of Liverpool or Birmingham, and susceptible to similar treatment. 'There is,' Mr W. Marshall, the then Scottish Secretary to the Labour Party, told the Royal Commission on the Constitution, 'no such thing as a separate political will for Scotland.'[7] So the natural response of Labour governments to discontent in the 'periphery' was to treat it as something fundamentally economic in nature to be bought off with economic benefits. That was the approach adopted between 1964 and 1970, and between February and October 1974. It was only when the Scottish Nationalists threatened Labour's electoral hegemony in Scotland that the policy of devolution came to be adopted, hesitantly and half-heartedly, in a manner which almost ensured that it would be unsuccessful in quenching Scottish grievances.

For the two major parties, therefore, territorial issues 'fell outside the characteristic contours of English constitutionalism. They are not the kind of problems it was slowly formed to deal with, and they will resist or destroy the typical remedies which it inspires'.[8] With the election of the Conservative government in 1979, Whitehall became imbued with scepticism as to the benefits of government intervention in the economies of Scotland and Wales. The new government's attitude towards Scotland and Wales could be described as one of not very benign neglect stemming from the belief that their problems were no different in kind from those affecting England, and could be resolved by a rigorous application of the free market philosophy. Such an approach, however, seemed hardly likely to eradicate growing differences in political behaviour between the

---

[7] Royal Commission on the Constitution: Minutes of Evidence (HMSO, 1969), vol. 2, para. 126.
[8] Nairn, *Break-Up of Britain*, p. 61.

nations and regions of the United Kingdom. It is unlikely, therefore, that the challenges of the parties of the non-English parts of the United Kingdom will diminish in the years to come, unless governments display a far greater degree of sensitivity to their distinctive needs than they have shown in the past.

VI

If, in the non-English parts of the United Kingdom, the challenges to the two-party system have been a response to the absence of an understanding of territorial politics on the part of the major parties, the formation of the SDP is a result of the break-up of the consensus which has dominated British politics since 1940. This consensus, whose intellectual progenitors were Keynes and Beveridge, held that both economic stability and social security could be obtained by intelligent government intervention within the framework of the mixed economy. It thus made the arguments for both the free market economy and for a wholly publicly-owned economy appear equally obsolete.

During the 1960s and 1970s, British governments found it increasingly difficult to maintain this consensus in a period of economic decline and growing social discontent. The Heath government elected in 1970 sought to maintain it by a vigorous modernisation programme which involved Britain's entry into the EEC, the floating of the pound, and, after 1972, a considerable degree of industrial intervention together with a statutory prices and incomes policy. This experiment, however, was brought to a rapid end by the economic recession which followed the Yom Kippur War of 1973, and the conflict with the miners which led to the demise of the Heath administration in February 1974. The Wilson and Callaghan governments which succeeded it sought to preserve the fundamentals of the post-war consensus through a 'Social Contract' agreed with the TUC. This involved an unprecedented degree of consultation between the government and the trade unions with the aim of ensuring the voluntary control of wages so that the rise in prices could be controlled without deflating the economy.

With the 'winter of discontent' of 1978–79, and the collapse of Labour's hopes, it seemed that both parties had abandoned the middle ground of politics for which they had been competing in earlier years. Labour began to repudiate the mixed economy which previous Labour governments had devoted themselves to managing. The Party's reaction to its electoral defeat in 1979 was to claim that it had failed in its aims because it had lacked sufficient control over the economy. The alternative economic strategy which the Party adopted in Opposition committed it to a wide extension of public control, as well as withdrawal from the Common Market and controls on imports and the export of capital. The Party sought to free itself from the toils of international capitalism which, through the International Monetary Fund's 1976 demands for cuts in public expenditure in return for financial support, had ended Labour's hopes of economic expansion. The Left wing of the Party therefore launched a campaign for a return to socialist policies, to be secured by making future Labour governments accountable to the Labour move- ment as a whole. Their attempt to achieve this goal led directly to the defection of the Social Democrats.

At the 1980 Labour Party Conference, the Labour Left gained two important victories securing the mandatory re-selection of Labour MPs and the election of the Party leader by an electoral college rather than, as hitherto, by the parliamentary party. At a special party conference held in January 1981, the composition of the electoral college was decided. 40% of the votes for the leader were to be cast by the trade unions, 30% by the Parliamentary Party and 30% by the constituency associations. The effect of this change was seen in the first election held under the new system, a contest for the deputy leadership held at the 1981 Party Conference in Brighton. This showed that, on the second ballot, while Denis Healey, the candidate of the Right, won 51% of the vote, Tony Benn, his left-wing opponent, had 49% even though enjoying the support of barely one-third of the Parliamentary Party. The new method of electing the leader was the precipitating factor in the defection of the Social Democrats from the Labour Party. Immediately after the special conference of January 1981, Roy Jenkins, David Owen, Shirley Williams and William Rodgers issued the so-called Limehouse Declaration and formed a Council for Social Democracy. Two months later, in March 1981, the new Social Democratic Party was born.

The Conservatives too were widely thought to be vacating the centre ground of politics. The post-war Conservative Party had faced the dilemma of how it was to survive in an era in which its most potent symbols – Empire, patriotism and religion – seemed increasingly to be electoral liabilities rather than advantages. The Party of Empire had to accommodate itself to the reality of Commonwealth; while the Party of Church and State had to accommodate itself to the scepticism of the post-war era and the adversary culture which gained such great influence in the 1960s. The Conservative response to this dilemma was to empha- sise its governing skills; the claim of Macmillan and Heath alike was that the Conservatives could manage the mixed economy and the Welfare State better than their opponents. Unfortunately, the managerial skills of the Conservatives could do little to reverse the long process of economic decline, while the pursuit of economic growth raised expectations which could not be met; further, the conflict with the miners in 1973–74 undermined the Conservative claim that they were defenders of consensus and social order. Far from appearing as experienced guardians of the state, the Conservatives seemed in 1974 to have led the country to a position which tempted many to ask whether Britain was governable at all by an administration which did not enjoy close links with the trade unions.

These discontents were focussed in the opposition to Edward Heath and his defeat in the first ballot of the leadership election in January 1975. Margaret Thatcher's election to the Conservative leadership owed as much to a general feeling that Heath was an electoral liability as to specific ideological factors. But once she had obtained the leadership, she steered the Party slowly but surely towards her own brand of Conservatism, which had little in common with the more consensual approach of Churchill and Macmillan in the 1950s, or with the *dirigisme* of the Heath administration.

The Conservative Party was becoming profoundly sceptical of government intervention in economic affairs. Government, Conservatives were coming to believe, could not directly influence the growth-rate of industry or the level of employment. All that it could do was to create a congenial climate for business enterprise by providing stability in the value of money. Any attempt to do more than this would be self-defeating since it would stimulate inflation, the greatest single deterrent to industrial recovery. Further, Conservatives came to believe that the wide range of benefits offered by the Welfare State also hindered economic progress, both because they undermined private initiative, and because they required a large public sector and bureaucracy to administer them. Thus, the two pillars of the post-war consensus – the mixed economy and the Welfare State – were seen by Conservatives, not as an essential framework within which government should operate, but as themselves part of the explanation for Britain's economic decline.

Mrs Thatcher proposed to reverse this decline by ignoring the constraints imposed by the post-war consensus. She was unwilling to accept the boundaries of the mixed economy established by post-war governments as final, and sought to reduce drastically the size of the public sector. She was unwilling, also, to accept the unions as corporate partners with government, and sought to weaken their bargaining strength, less perhaps through legislation than through the adoption of economic measures which, unlike an incomes policy, did not depend upon union consent; and by a willingness to tolerate higher levels of unemployment than had been admissible under the post-war consensus. Finally, Mrs

Thatcher proposed to lower expectations of what the state could do. The withdrawal of government from detailed intervention in the affairs of industry would of itself strengthen the state by confining its activities to areas such as the control of inflation, defence and the maintenance of law and order where it had a chance of achieving the limited objectives which it set itself. But the withdrawal of government would also contribute towards changes in popular attitudes, leading, it was hoped, to a restoration of individual responsibility and a return to those values of thrift and self-discipline which the Conservatives saw as essential to economic success.

It is, no doubt, far too soon to determine whether such policies can succeed in regenerating the British economy. Certainly their short-term costs in terms of higher unemployment and industrial bankruptcies have been considerable. Further, the radicalism of Mrs Thatcher's political ethos – a radicalism reflected, perhaps, more in the theory than in the practice of her administration – was bound to prove disconcerting to many Conservatives. For the Conservative Party has relied for its success largely upon the strength of the conservative interest in the country, an interest which seeks not radical change but stability and social peace. It was this interest which politicians such as Stanley Baldwin and Harold Macmillan had succeeded in identifying with the modern Conservative Party. Mrs Thatcher's Conservatism, by contrast, was characterised by a rather restless and radical quest for efficiency and self-reliance. The conflict between those social forces making for stability and the ethos of Mrs Thatcher's Conservative Party is one which could have profound import for the future of the Party; and it would not be surprising, perhaps, if an element of the Conservative Party's natural political constituency was to come to believe that conservative values might better be served by another political party.

VII

Both political parties, therefore, have chosen to break with the politics of the post-war consensus. They have done so, despite the fact that many electors and a considerable number of MPs – perhaps even a majority – are by no means confident that either the alternative economic policy or the policies associated with the free market can secure economic salvation. In theory, the flight from the centre ought to have led to electoral disaster, for the conventional wisdom of British politics declared that the logic of a two-party system pushed the parties to the centre of the political spectrum where the floating voter was to be found. Yet since 1970, although after each election defeat the major opposition party has moved away from the centre rather than towards it, it was the party which had vacated the centre ground which won the succeeding election. In 1970, February 1974 and 1979, the party offering radical change won the election, while the party occupying the middle ground lost it.

One of the factors which the consensus model of British politics ignored was that parties are not merely economic entities seeking to maximise their vote. They are, after all, organisations composed of partisans with strongly-held views as to how the ideal society should be constructed, and anxious to implement policies which will make the advent of such a society more likely. Therefore they seek to alter the attitudes of the electorate, rather than merely accommodating themselves to these attitudes. Moreover, the economic model neglects the belief of some party leaders that they must rely upon the support of dedicated activists if essential tasks are to be carried out. These activists will generally tend to be those most devoted to the ideology of the party. The economic model assumes that they are less powerful than the floating voters since they cannot desert to the other side, but must stick to their party. This, however, is to assume that 'exit', to adopt Albert Hirschman's terminology, is the only possible response to an organisation which fails to offer satisfaction. But there is also, following Hirschman, the possibility of 'voice' for those who cannot leave the party because they feel such strong allegiance to its central tenets. Such individuals, if dissatisfied with the compromises which their party is making, can devote their energies to maintaining the purity of party doctrine; and, since they are likely to possess more zeal than their centrist counterparts, they will probably devote more time and energy to the task. For this reason, a party in a two-party system will not necessarily behave as an economic vote-maximiser, 'because "those who have nowhere else to go" are not powerless but influential'.[9] Developments in the Labour Party since 1970, of course, offer a near perfect illustration of this thesis.

It is for this reason that the response of a party to electoral defeat may be to cling to its basic tenets with even greater zeal, rather than moderate them so as to accommodate the party to the wishes of the voters. That such a process has not been electorally disastrous is due to two features of Britain's political system. The first is the electoral system which enables a party to win office on much less than 50% of the vote. In February and October 1974, the Labour Party was able to form governments although its vote was 37.1% and 39.2% respectively, far lower than the 43.0% which Labour had secured in 1970 when it had been defeated by the Conservatives. Indeed Labour's loss of support between

[9] Albert O. Hirschman, *Exit, Voice and Loyalty* (Harvard University Press, 1967), p. 72.

1970 and February 1974 was the greatest suffered by any opposition party in the post-war period. The Conservatives, by contrast, gained a higher percentage of the vote in 1979 than in either of the elections of 1974. Yet their electoral success obscured the fact that their share of the vote – 43.9% – was the smallest enjoyed by a single-party government with a secure overall majority since 1922.

The second factor enabling politicians to desert the centre ground and embrace views which may not be supported by a majority of the electorate is the absence of any formal check upon the omni-competence of government in Britain. For British governments do not have to overcome the checks – such as a strong second chamber, a written constitution, a Bill of Rights, or a federal system of government – which constrain governments in other countries. The consequence is that governments, even though representing a minority of the voters, can, in general, ensure that their programme meets with no hostility from Parliament or the judiciary. It is this combination of a plurality system of election enabling parties to form single-party governments on a minority of the vote, together with the supremacy of the Commons, which makes British government approach the condition which Lord Hailsham in his book *The Dilemma of Democracy* (1976) called 'elective dictatorship'. Britain and New Zealand are, in fact, the only modern democracies which continue to employ the plurality system and impose no formal restrictions on the power of a government elected under this system. But, whereas New Zealand is a homogeneous country of 3 million people without important responsibilities in foreign affairs, the United Kingdom is a country of 55 million people with many social antagonisms and conflicts, playing a leading part in the EEC and in the Western defensive alliance.

The provisions of the British Constitution together with the electoral system enable organised minorities to control political parties and then to use the supremacy of Parliament to ensure that their notions become translated into legislation. Because political parties need dedicated supporters, and because the British Constitution grants government almost complete freedom from interference by Parliament and the courts, a group representing only a minority in its party and a minority in the country may be able to secure the implementation of its legislative ideas. Majority rule can easily become transformed into rule by a minority of a minority.

Given the eagerness of the two main parties to vacate the centre ground of politics together with Britain's continuing economic decline under different governments in the 1970s, it is hardly surprising that a political space has been created which a new party now seeks to occupy. It is to an analysis of this new party – the SDP – and its Alliance with the Liberals that we must now turn.

2

The Social Democratic Party
and the Alliance

I

The SDP was founded in 1981 as a break-away from the Labour Party. The immediate factor precipitating its formation was, as we have seen, the Labour Party's commitment to an electoral college giving the trade unions a preponderant voice in the election of the Party leader. Yet this was but the culminating point in the long quarrel between the Social Democrats and the Left wing of the Party, a quarrel based on deep-seated policy differences. For the Social Democrats remained committed to the mixed economy, the NATO alliance, and therefore a strategy involving the retention of nuclear weapons, and membership of the Common Market. The Labour Party, on the other hand, was becoming more hostile to private industry, and at its 1980 Conference accepted unilateral nuclear disarmament (although also passing a contradictory motion affirming support for NATO) and committed the Party to withdrawal from the Common Market without a referendum.

The struggle between Right and Left is, of course, no new feature of the Labour Party's history. But during the 1970s it took on a new and more menacing character. For during earlier periods, the conflict had taken the form of a disagreement about means amongst politicians whose basic aims were fundamentally similar. In the 1970s, by contrast, the Labour Party began to appear as an incompatible coalition of reformists and socialists. The latter, moreover, were buttressed by extra-parliamentary activists, many of whom favoured a more revolutionary approach to politics than the Labour Party had ever previously been willing to consider. These activists came to enjoy the support of a section of the Left wing of the Parliamentary Party who were not themselves revolutionaries but who sought the backing of the extra-parliamentary party in the battle between Left and Right. In addition, the abolition in 1973 of the proscribed list of organisations debarring Trotskyite and fellow-travelling groups, from membership of the Party, meant that the anti-democratic Left was, by contrast with previous periods of the Party's history, increasingly to be found inside rather than outside the Party.

The Right was further weakened by developments in the trade unions which had, since the 1950s, become more militant and less willing to defer to the parliamentary leadership. This meant that the block vote could no longer be used, as it had been until the 1950s, to maintain the Labour Party on a Right-wing course. No doubt the block vote was always indefensible in principle but, until the 1970s, it could perhaps be defended pragmatically as allowing the Labour Party to produce policies which the majority of its supporters and voters, if not its activists, actually favoured. During the 1970s, however, the block vote was no longer available as an automatic barrier against the Left of the Party. The disintegration of assured trade union support for the Party leadership revealed that the constitutional structure of the Labour Party lay wide open to infiltration by elements whose conception of socialism had little if anything in common with that held by leaders such as Attlee, Gaitskell, Wilson and Callaghan. Indeed, as Sidney Webb had noticed in 1930, 'the constituency parties were frequently unrepresentative groups of nonentities dominated by fanatics and cranks, and extremists, and ... if the block vote of the Trade Unions were eliminated it would be impracticable to continue to vest the control of policies in Labour Party Conferences'.[1]

After the 1979 election defeat, the battle between Left and Right centred on organisational questions – how should the Party leader be chosen, should Labour MPs have to face mandatory re-selection before each general election, and should the election manifesto be drawn up by the National Executive rather than, as hitherto, jointly by the National Executive and the parliamentary leadership. But, as always in politics, these disputes about organisation were in reality disputes about political power. The Left, during the 1950s, had found themselves in a permanent minority of around one-third in the Parliamentary Party. Their successors were, therefore, determined to shift the arena of battle away from the Parliamentary Party to the Party Conference and the extra-parliamentary party. Their victory in 1980 signalled a definite shift to the Left in the Party.

It was not the Right as a whole, but only a section of it, which broke off from Labour to form the new party. That section which led the SDP comprised the social reforming and modernising part of the Right, as opposed to the pragmatists who believed that the Labour coalition could still be maintained. This difference in attitude between the two elements

[1] The Diary of Beatrice Webb, quoted in R.T. Mackenzie, *British Political Parties* (2nd revised edition, Heinemann, 1964), p. 505.

in the Labour Right embodies itself most clearly in different attitudes towards the EEC. For the principal leaders of the SDP, membership of the Common Market had a particular emotional resonance. Roy Jenkins had been, until 1981, President of the European Commission, and support for the EEC had been one of the cornerstones of his political career. He had continued to press for British membership even when the Party leader, his friend Hugh Gaitskell, had come out against the Community in 1962. In 1972, Jenkins had resigned from Labour's Shadow Cabinet, sacrificing his position as Deputy Leader of the Party because he was unable to accept Labour's commitment to the referendum. David Owen had resigned as a junior opposition spokesman at the same time, while Shirley Williams had made it clear in 1974 that if Britain withdrew from the Common Market, she would retire from politics. All three had contravened a three-line whip, to lead 66 other Labour MPs into voting with the Conservatives in supporting the second reading of the European Communities Bill in 1971.

It had seemed in the early 1970s as if it would be the EEC which would split the Labour Party. The issue was posed by Dick Taverne. When his constituency association in Lincoln refused to re-adopt him because of his support for the EEC, he resigned his seat and in 1973 won a by-election fighting as a Democratic Labour candidate; he argued in words which many at the time thought excessive but which now seem prophetic, that 'we may be approaching one of those periods in British politics when existing party alignments break up and re-form ... It is not impossible that Britain's role in Europe will prove to be an issue with the same catalystic effect on the Labour Party as the Corn Laws had on the Tories in the last century.... In time the pro-Europeans may be forced to realise that an anti-European Labour Party is incompatible with the ideals of social democracy.' Taverne then posed with some prescience the question 'Suppose that the majority, or even at first a minority, of the social democratic group in Parliament, grow weary of the long struggle to make a coalition of incompatibles work ... Politics in Britain would be transformed overnight. What might then start as a Lib-Lab alliance would soon emerge as a new radical or social democratic party.'[2]

Survey evidence, as opposed to the prevailing political wisdom of the time, seemed to show that a realignment of the type favoured by Taverne could secure the support of a large proportion of the electorate. In September 1972, *The Times* published the results of an opinion poll showing that 35% of the electorate, a larger proportion than would be willing to vote for a single-party Conservative or Labour government,

[2] Dick Taverne, *The Future of the Left: Lincoln and After* (Cape, 1974), pp. 98, 108, 117, 159.

would support an alliance between the Right wing of the Labour Party and the Liberals. Admittedly, an even higher proportion of the electorate – 40% – claimed that they would vote for a coalition of Liberals and Conservative moderates, yet *The Times* concentrated upon the realignment on the Left, rather than on the Right. There were, it claimed, 12 million Jenkinsites in Britain and 'The Liberal–Labour coalition . . . could produce an explosion of support from frustrated voters' (30 September 1972).

Nevertheless, Taverne was premature in his belief that the Labour Party was on the verge of a split. That the Party did not split was due to the referendum device which enabled both pro- and anti-marketeers to fight under the same banner. The referendum was, in James Callaghan's words, 'a rubber dinghy into which we may well all have to climb'.[3] Without it, Taverne's prediction might well have come true; the Labour Party might have split, and a Social Democratic break-away have been formed during the mid-1970s.

Most of the leaders of the SDP belong to that section of the Right which regards Britain's membership of the EEC as being an issue of supreme importance. They would accept David Marquand's character-isation of the EEC as 'the most hopeful political experiment of our time'.[4] Yet the real basis of the division in the Labour Right was between those who did or did not believe that the Labour Party could be saved for those causes in which the Right genuinely believed. The Europeans were more likely to despair precisely because they cared so deeply about the EEC, but it was not the European issue *per se* which drove them out.

Were the Labour Party to return to the kinds of policies which it adopted in the 1950s and 1960s, the leaders of the SDP might be seen to have made a misjudgment, and the SDP could become merely a pro-European rump. If, on the other hand, the judgment of the defectors proves correct, and the swing to the Left in the Labour Party continues, the Labour Right will come under further pressure, and another Labour split is by no means impossible.

The formation of the SDP, therefore, has not ended the division in the Labour Party. Instead it has split the Labour Right in two.

II

In calling itself Social Democratic, the new party explicitly linked itself to a political stance associated in Britain with names such as Hugh Gaitskell and Anthony Crosland. In addition, of course, the main parties of the Left in West Germany, Denmark, Sweden and Finland – fellow-members

---

[3] Quoted in Mark Hatfield, *The House the Left Built* (Gollancz, 1978), p. 70.
[4] David Marquand, *A Parliament for Europe* (Cape, 1979), p. vii.

with the Labour Party of the Socialist International – call themselves Social Democrat. The SDP, therefore, has identified itself with a specific political tradition. What is the content of this tradition?

The essence of the Gaitskellite brand of socialism was the view that the socialist aim of equality could be achieved without wholesale public ownership. Public ownership was but a means, no doubt very important, but still only a means towards the achievement of socialism. It should not be identified with the end itself. The Labour Party Constitution, drawn up in 1918, had become an anachronism, since the only domestic policy aim which it mentioned was public ownership. Yet experience of the working of the British economy seemed to have shown that a high level of employment as well as of social welfare could be achieved without wholesale public ownership; while the process of nationalisation itself had cast doubt on many of the advantages claimed for public ownership, and it had not led to any significant advances in social equality.

Such a conclusion has become a commonplace for most European parties of the democratic Left, which have adopted the Revisionist view of how socialism should be achieved. The Social Democratic parties in West Germany and Scandinavia certainly do not regard public ownership or the extension of state control as their most important policy aim. Indeed, after 44 years of Social Democratic government in Sweden, 95% of the country's industry still remained in private hands. In Britain, however, when Hugh Gaitskell attempted to alter the Labour Party's Constitution by deleting Clause 4, he was compelled to withdraw, because he faced, as he himself admitted, 'the reaction, not only ... of people who would ordinarily be regarded as left-wing ... but of many other people in the Movement who ... would probably describe themselves as right-wing'.[5]

The SDP, like the Revisionists, reject Clause 4-type socialism. Indeed, in broadly accepting the current line of demarcation between the public and private sectors, the new party goes further than Gaitskell and Crosland ever did. For Gaitskell and Crosland, even though they did not regard public ownership as defining the content of socialism, were far from content with the existing structure of private industry. Gaitskell was a strong supporter of the state purchasing large share-holdings in private companies, an approach laid out, for example, in the Labour Party's policy document *Industry and Society* (1957); while he strongly advocated the nationalisation of all development land, 'a hobby of mine for a number of years',[6] and an aim reiterated by Crosland in *Socialism*

[5] Labour Party Conference Report, 1960, pp. 218–19.
[6] Philip Williams, *Hugh Gaitskell* (Cape, 1979), p. 659. The comment was made in April 1962.

Now (1974). Indeed in the view of Gaitskell's friend, the economic historian M. M. Postan, his shopping list of industries to be nationalised 'would have been far wider than that of many defenders of Clause 4'.[7]

The SDP also goes beyond Revisionism in abjuring the class basis of politics. The new party rejects affiliation from the trade unions (or any other corporate body), and membership is possible only on an individual basis. Whereas the Labour Party has been described as a 'collective expression of democratic sentiment based on the working-class movement and on the constituency organisations of the workers by hand and brain',[8] the SDP is a party of individual membership which claims to represent all classes; or rather, it denies that economic relationships alone shape society. Political authority derives not from social groups possessing corporate unity, but from individuals who combine together united by a common interest. This conception, of course, has little in common with that held by socialists.

Yet even this does not exhaust the divergencies between the SDP and the Labour Revisionists. For the socialist, whether Right or Left, the most important issues on the political agenda are socio-economic in nature. His central concerns are with the level of employment, with social and educational reform, and with the expansion of public services. For the SDP, of course, the regeneration of the British economy is of central importance; but so also is constitutional reform. Indeed, David Marquand, a member of the new party's Council, has declared that the most urgent task for Social Democrats 'is to devise a constitutional structure'[9] which will allow the Party's ideals of power-sharing and power-diffusion to be realised.

The Labour Right assumed, understandably perhaps in the light of the reforms of the 1940s establishing the Welfare State, that the state would remain an efficient and essentially benign agency of social change. The expansion of the state, necessary to secure the further advance of democratic socialism, would not alter its character. Public services would remain both effective and accountable to those whom they were to serve. 'Crosland', according to Marquand, 'took the traditional structure of the British state for granted, and failed to see that the centralist, elitist logic underlying it was incompatible with his own libertarian and egalitarian values'.[10]

---

7 M. Postan in W.T. Rodgers (ed.), *Hugh Gaitskell 1906–1963* (Thames and Hudson, 1964), p. 64.
8 A.H. Birch, *Representative and Responsible Government* (Allen and Unwin, 1964), p. 123.
9 David Marquand, *Russet-Coated Captains: The Challenge of Social Democracy* (SDP Open Forum 5, 1981), p. 17.
10 David Marquand, 'What the Social Democrats should try to achieve', in *London Review of Books*, 7–20 May 1981, p. 9.

There was, moreover, an undeniable element of paternalism in the approach of Gaitskell and Crosland, which again was understandable in the conditions of the 1940s and 1950s, but is less acceptable in the 1980s. The Revisionists were unable entirely to rid themselves of the Fabian assumption that social improvement could be secured solely through the agency of government. Society seemed to be divided between those who held the levers of power, and those to whom good was done. 'We, as middle-class socialists', said Gaitskell to Richard Crossman, 'have got to have a profound humility. Though it's a funny way of putting it, we've got to know that we lead them because they can't do it without us, with our abilities, and yet we must feel humble to working people.'[11]

The Revisionism of Gaitskell and Crosland was, in essence, a philosophy of economic management. Its central aim was to redistribute income and equalise economic power. Its conception of reform was 'mechanical' and it assumed that change could be imposed from above. The 'moral reformer', by contrast, believes that the transformation of society depends upon changes in attitudes as well as action by government.[12] The approach of the SDP can be seen as an attempt to repair the defects of 'mechanical' reform and to humanise the state. In its rejection of mechanistic or economic analyses of society, its concern with constitutional issues and with the mobilising of consent, the SDP tacitly dissociates itself both from traditional social democratic philosophies as understood either by the Gaitskellite Revisionists in Britain or the Social Democratic parties in West Germany and Scandinavia.

There are two further differences between the SDP and the Continental Social Democratic parties. The first is that the Continental parties are parties of government, rather than break-aways from pre-existing democratic socialist parties; while the second is that the SDP, unlike its Continental namesakes, has entered into an electoral pact with the Liberal Party, a party of the centre (or centre-left). The Social Democrats in West Germany did, it is true, enter into a governmental coalition with the FDP, the West German equivalent of the Liberal Party, but co-operation in Germany was confined to governmental level. The coalition was not buttressed by an electoral pact.

The Alliance with the Liberals is bound to shape the future of the SDP for a considerable period of time. Since both parties have the same immediate aim in view – the achievement of proportional representation

---

[11] Janet Morgan (ed.), *The Backbench Diaries of Richard Crossman* (Hamish Hamilton and Jonathan Cape, 1981), pp. 769–70.
[12] The distinction between 'mechanical' and 'moral' reformers is made by Peter Clarke in *Liberals and Social Democrats* (Cambridge University Press, 1978).

– it would be foolish for them to oppose each other at the polls. Yet the Alliance is more than a marriage of convenience, for there is a considerable degree of ideological convergence between the policies of the two parties. Both parties support not only proportional representation, but also other constitutional reforms such as devolution and the introduction of a Bill of Rights. Both parties are strong advocates of Britain's continued membership of the Common Market. Both parties support the mixed economy, and favour some kind of incomes policy. Both parties are sympathetic to worker participation on company boards. The policies of the SDP have far more in common with Liberal ideas than they do with the policies of the Labour Party. In fact the Alliance between the Liberals and the SDP also signifies the coming together of two political traditions which, until 1914, co-operated together, but whose paths diverged in the inter-war period.

III

In the late nineteenth century, social democracy was used in Britain as a synonym for socialism, or even for Marxism, as with H. M. Hyndman's Social Democratic Federation, known as the Social Democratic Party between 1908 and 1911; and, of course, the German Social Democrat Party was explicitly Marxist during this period. Yet the term social democracy was also used by the 'New Liberals', who were orientated towards the politics of social reform, in a sense somewhat similar to its contemporary meaning. 'Political democracy achieved', argued Beatrice Potter in 1890, 'what more is there to do, unless you are prepared for Social or Industrial Democracy.'[13] 'The old Liberalism', wrote Hobhouse in 1904, 'had done its work. It had been all very well in its time, but political democracy and the rest were now well-established facts. What was needed was to build a social democracy on the basis so prepared, and for that we needed new formulas, new inspirations.'[14] Hobhouse identified the central task facing the 'New Liberals' as the achievement of social democracy. Social reform ought to constitute the basic agenda of the politics of the future, and it could unite the Liberals and the nascent Labour Party in a Progressive Alliance, which Ramsay MacDonald hoped might eventually become a 'united democratic party appealing to the people on behalf of a simple, comprehensive belief in social reconstruction'. The new politics of social reform could serve 'to

[13] The Diary of Beatrice Webb, 31 December 1890, quoted in Clarke, *Liberals and Social Democrats*, p. 42.
[14] L.T. Hobhouse, *Democracy and Reaction* (1904), pp. 209–10, quoted in Peter Clarke, *Lancashire and the New Liberalism* (Cambridge University Press, 1971), p. 173.

resist Tory reaction and Socialism and drive a wedge between the practical and impractical Labour politicians'.[15]

From 1903, until after the second election of 1910, the Liberals and Labour co-operated through an electoral pact – the Gladstone–MacDonald pact, named after the Liberal Chief Whip, Herbert Gladstone, and the Labour leader, Ramsay MacDonald – by which seats were allocated in England and Wales – the pact did not operate in Scotland – so as to avoid a split vote between the two left-wing parties. The pact was a secret one, but, inevitably, politicians suspected that the two parties were co-operating in the constituencies, and suspicions were aroused amongst the ideologues of both parties. The purer socialists saw it as a weak-kneed compromise, while many on the Right of the Liberal Party were fearful of the taint of socialism, and in 1906 the Master of Elibank, the Liberal Chief Whip, went so far as to call for a 'crusade' against socialism. Yet as the chief Liberal organiser, Jesse Herbert, commented to Herbert Gladstone after the 1906 general election: 'Was there ever such a justification of a policy by results?' In 1917, the Master of Elibank, who had been sceptical of co-operation, could look back and say, 'Theirs has been the most formidable political combination that this country has ever known. Look what has been achieved within the last ten years.'[16]

The Progressive Alliance was an alliance of the centre-left against the ideological extremes; it conceived of politics as a struggle between Progressives and Conservatives; and, until the First World War it was able to hold at bay both the Conservatives and the socialist Left. Its dominance seemed unchallengeable. Yet by 1918, the Alliance was irreparably broken. This was the result of a number of different factors conspiring together to alter the basic alignments of politics.

The war itself had split the Liberal Party, and the Party's most prominent social reformer, Lloyd George, led a Conservative-dominated government from 1916; the expansion of the franchise gave Labour a new electoral clientele to which it could appeal; while the social hostility between the working-class representatives of Labour and the more self-assured Liberals proved a serious barrier to continued co-operation. Most important of all, perhaps, the Gladstone–MacDonald pact had broken down even before 1914, since Labour, as a national party, insisted upon running candidates over the country as a whole, and was no longer prepared to be confined by the Liberals to fighting a small

[15] J.A. Pease, Liberal Chief Whip, 19 October 1908, quoted in Martin Petter, 'The Progressive Alliance', in *History* (February 1973), p. 48.

[16] Jesse Herbert, Herbert Gladstone's assistant, to Herbert Gladstone, February 1906, quoted in Philip P. Poirier, *The Advent of the Labour Party* (Allen and Unwin, 1958), p. 264. The Master of Elibank, quoted in Clarke, *Lancashire and the New Liberalism*, p. 394.

number of seats. This meant that electoral reform was essential if the Progressive Alliance was to be maintained, so that two candidates of the Left could run in the same constituency without splitting the vote. The failure of the Lloyd George government and of the Liberal Party to support proportional representation in 1917–18, therefore, not only doomed the Liberals. It also destroyed the hopes of the Progressive Alliance.

During the inter-war years, therefore, 'the legacy of historical development and the traditional loyalties of class and occupation'[17] reasserted themselves over the self-interest of the two parties and the very real ideological similarities which had bound them together. Instead of seeing the Liberals as partners in a Progressive Alliance, Labour came to regard them as a 'capitalist' party and therefore a party on the Right of the political spectrum. Between the wars, the political cleavage was between the 'socialist' and 'capitalist' parties, rather than between 'Progressives' and Conservatives. But because the parties of the Left were split, the Conservatives were able to dominate the politics of the period: the two Labour minority governments were unwilling to co-operate whole-heartedly with the Liberals, and both ended in failure, the second collapsing amidst the financial crisis of 1931.

It can be argued, then, that before the First World War two complementary political traditions – liberalism and social democracy – were able to co-operate together to the benefit of the reforming elements in British politics; while after 1918 the Progressive Alliance was torn asunder. The conventional view of most on the Left was that socialism and liberalism were conflicting ideologies and that liberalism had been superseded by socialism as the dominant ideology of social reform. The difficulties of the Labour Party and the formation of the SDP have, however, forced a reappraisal of this conventional view, so that the ideals which Liberals and social democrats hold in common come to be seen as more important than the factors which in the past divided them.

It can certainly be argued that there is an ideological affinity between the two parties comprising the Liberal–SDP Alliance. In a pamphlet published before the SDP was founded, David Steel, the Liberal leader, claimed that the Labour Party had taken four wrong turnings after the First World War. Its Constitution had given a dominant role in the Party to the trade unions; it had continued to base its appeal upon class despite the evidence that social change was eroding class barriers; it had identified socialism with centralisation; and it had shared the Fabian 'preference for paternal authority over fraternal democracy'. These wrong turnings had prevented co-operation between the two parties. 'If

17 Petter, 'The Progressive Alliance', p. 58.

these wrong directions had not been taken', continued Steel, 'I believe the elements which radical liberals and socialists have in common would have found common political expression earlier.'[18]

The Progressive Alliance before the First World War had ensured the dominance of the radical Left in British politics. Its break-up during the inter-war years led to Conservative hegemony. It is too soon to tell whether a new Alliance bringing together the two political traditions which were torn apart in the years of the First World War, can recreate the dominant position in British politics which the Liberals enjoyed before the First World War.

IV

The Alliance claims to be seeking a political realignment. What this means is, however, not very clear. For the SDP could either co-operate with the Liberals in an attempt to replace Labour, as Labour replaced the Liberals in the 1920s; or it could choose to act independently of the Liberals to replace Labour; or alternatively to maintain the Alliance as a third force in a tripolar political system enabling the British electorate for the first time since the 1920s to choose between three genuine alternative candidates for government. The notion of realignment is thus a highly ambiguous one – it could imply the restoration of a two-party system with the SDP replacing Labour; or that a permanent three-party system would be instituted so enabling a wider spectrum of electoral opinion to be effectively represented.

The idea of a realignment of the Left in British politics is closely associated with Jo Grimond's period as leader of the Liberal Party between 1956 and 1967. Grimond believed that much of the malaise which he detected in post-war politics could be explained by the fact that the parties whose function it was to channel new ideas into politics, had become little more than representatives of large social interests – primarily employers and trade unions. Yet, in Grimond's view, the process of social change was beginning to loosen class alignments and thus weaken party identification since that was largely determined by class. There was a political space, therefore, for a party based not on the representation of social interests, but upon the representation of opinion, after the fashion of the Liberals in their great days before the First World War, when they had been a party whose supporters were united not by membership of any particular social group but through common adherence to a set of political ideals and principles.

---

[18] David Steel, *Labour at 80: Time to Retire* (Liberal Publications Department, 1980), p. 3.

Grimond believed that there was a radical constituency which could form the basis of a new non-socialist and undoctrinaire party of the Left capable of challenging the hegemony of the Conservatives in British politics. This constituency was impatient with class distinctions and outworn political creeds; it was eager to press forward with the modernisation of the British economy and passionately committed to British membership of the Common Market. Unfortunately, however, its adherents were scattered by the party system. Many of them, of course, belonged to the Liberal Party; but many others were Labour supporters engaged in what Grimond saw as a hopeless attempt to wean the Labour Party away from its doctrinaire commitment to nationalisation and its dependence upon the trade unions, themselves a serious barrier to the economic modernisation which radicals sought. There were even some members of this radical constituency in the Conservative Party who saw their task as one of liberalising that Party's approach to decolonisation, race relations and civil liberties.

Because they were scattered, the radicals were powerless. They were divided by a party system within which old loyalties and organisational ties cut across those fundamental differences of political opinion which a well-ordered party system ought to reflect. And because radicals were powerless, Britain was faced with the alternation of two conservative parties. For the conservatives dominated both of the major political parties – in the Conservative Party they slowed down the process of modernisation; while in the Labour Party they resisted any tampering with Clause 4 or the privileges of the trade unions. Grimond believed that radicals needed to be united in one party if they were to be effective; and that party should be an amalgam of the Liberal Party and the Right wing of the Labour Party. What he was arguing for, of course, was a recreation of the Progressive Alliance of the years before the First World War.

The premiss upon which this view of realignment was based was that the problems faced by the Labour Party after its third electoral defeat in 1959 were terminal. The Party would never be able to reconcile its Right and Left wings, and would prove quite unable to defeat the Conservatives. As Mark Bonham-Carter, one of Grimond's leading lieutenants, put it, 'Since 1931, with a single interval of six years, this country has been governed by a Conservative, or a Conservative dominated, administration ... this is how the "two-party" system, of which we hear so much, has worked. It has led to what is virtually one-party government.'[19]

[19] Mark Bonham-Carter, 'Liberals and the political future', in George Watson (ed.), *Radical Alternative* (Eyre and Spottiswoode, 1962).

However, the Labour Party's two electoral victories in 1964 and 1966 undermined the credibility of Grimond's strategy, and it is no coincidence that he resigned the leadership of the Liberal Party less than a year after the 1966 election. It is clear in retrospect that Grimond was highly prescient in detecting that the problems of the Labour Party might prove insoluble, and that there would be a break-away of a section of the Right wing, but he telescoped the time-scale within which these events would occur.

Unfortunately the Liberal Party, was rather poorly suited to follow Grimond's realignment strategy. Its vote was derived roughly equally from the two major parties, but its electoral strength was concentrated primarily in Conservative-held seats, and its by-election successes such as those at Torrington in 1958 and Orpington in 1962 were the result of mid-term discontent with Conservative governments. Realignment on Grimondite lines, however, would have required the Liberal Party to attack Labour's base in the industrial conurbations and this it seemed unable to do. For this reason, Liberal successes, even when they came with the aid of Labour votes, threatened Conservative and not Labour seats, and so actually assisted the Labour Party. Indeed, it was the Liberal upsurge in February 1974 which allowed the Labour Party to become the largest party in the Commons, and form a minority government even though Labour secured less votes than Conservatives and a far smaller percentage share of the poll than it had gained in 1970.

It might be suggested that the formation of the SDP will serve to remedy this weakness. For the SDP, unlike the Liberals, already enjoys an organisational base in the conurbations, especially in Tyneside and Teeside, where the constituencies of a number of its MPs lie. Thus the SDP, in contrast to the Liberals, may be able to threaten Labour in its own heartland. Perhaps, then, the Alliance may prove more successful in implementing the Grimond strategy than the Liberal Party alone has been. If that is the case, then the Alliance can replace the Labour Party as the main party of the Left in Britain and take its place in a re-formed two-party system. That would be the first strategy of realignment and one which we might call Grimondite.

Alternatively, the SDP might take the view that Labour supporters in the industrial conurbations will not support a party which allies itself with a party of the centre such as the Liberals. On this view, which we might christen Owenite, since it is the strategy associated with the Left wing of the SDP whose most prominent spokesmen are David Owen and Shirley Williams, a permanent Alliance would, by merging its identity with that of the Liberals, alienate the SDP's electoral constituency. If such a view prevails, the Alliance with the Liberals will prove to be only a temporary one, to be maintained until electoral reform has been won. The SDP would then hope to erode Labour's support and eventually replace it as the main party of the Left. The major party of the Left would be a Revisionist Social Democratic Party not wholly dissimilar from that which Hugh Gaitskell had tried to create; but this aim would be achieved through the destruction, rather than the reform of the Labour Party as Gaitskell had hoped.

This strategy would entail the creation of a new three-party system – with the SDP being the party of the Left, opposing the Liberal and Conservative Parties. Or, if a small Labour Party survived as a splinter to the Left of the SDP, there would be a four-party system, with perhaps the SDP and the Conservatives as the two major parties, the Liberals as a small centre party, and Labour as a small party on the Left. Of course, the achievement of electoral reform would mean that single-party government would be unlikely, and so the SDP might have to be able to govern in coalition with the Liberals as the SPD has done in West Germany. The analogy indeed would be a very close one; for the SDP would then have become a modernised social democratic party like the West German Social Democrats who at their Bad Godesberg Conference in 1959 jettisoned the commitment to a wide extension of public ownership. But the two parties would retain their separate identity.

This strategy presupposes that the Labour Party is in a terminal state and that it will rapidly disintegrate. If this view proves to have underestimated the recuperative possibilities of the Labour Party, and, like Grimond, to have telescoped a long process of development into a short period of time, then the British party system could consist of a Conservative Party, a Liberal Party and two left-wing parties of roughly equal size – Labour and the SDP – competing for very much the same electoral constituency. The consequence, as in the 1920s, may be that disunity on the Left makes for long periods of Conservative rule, interrupted only by short-lived governments of the Left. Furthermore, the SDP would lose the chance of attracting Conservative voters disillusioned with the performance of Conservative governments, yet believing that the Liberal Party on its own lacks sufficient credibility to pose as a convincing candidate for government.

The third strategy for the Alliance is closely associated with Roy Jenkins who became the SDP leader in the summer of 1982. It is that the SDP and the Liberals should retain their Alliance even after proportional representation has been achieved, and take their place as a party of the centre, or perhaps of the centre-left, in what will become a three-party system, one offering the electors permanently what they were offered temporarily in the 1920s: the possibility of choosing from three alternative candidates for government. This strategy, unlike that which sees the SDP as a party of the Left whose aim it is to supplant Labour, is not afraid of envisaging the possibility of a coalition government with the Conservatives either to secure proportional representation, or even after proportional representation has been secured, should circumstances warrant. Such a view, therefore, stands a stronger chance of attracting the permanent allegiance of ex-Conservative voters to the Alliance, while, arguably, making the SDP a less attractive option for the Labour voter in the industrial conurbations. The strategy points eventually, perhaps, to a merger between the Liberals and the SDP, but that would not be strictly necessary provided that the electoral pact can be maintained. The aim would be to create, through a movement of the political centre, a new configuration of the party spectrum permanently breaking up the traditional pattern of bipartite parliamentary politics. But the danger of this strategy is the same as that proposed by Grimond, in that it may succeed only in Conservative-held seats, so allowing Labour to form a single-party government on less than 40% of the popular vote. In the 1979 general election, the Liberals were second in 79 of the 339 seats won by the Conservatives, but in only 2 of the 269 seats won by Labour. Conceptually, therefore, the Alliance may see itself as a formation of the centre, and an alternative to either Labour or the Conservatives, but, under the first-past-the-post electoral system, it is the geographical distribution of party support which determines the nature of the challenge which a party offers; and geographically, the centre seems to be an alternative to the Conservatives, and not to Labour. The consequence, therefore, could be that an increase in support for the Alliance, unless this support comes very disproportionately from Labour voters – and this seems highly unlikely – would aid Labour to become the largest single party in the Commons, since Conservative seats are more vulnerable than Labour to an increase in support for the Alliance. The paradoxical effect would be to enable the Labour Party, which the SDP regards as too extreme to be entrusted with power, to gain office on less than two-fifths of the popular vote. The SDP would have achieved the precise opposite of what it set out to do.

Realignment, then, can occur in one of three different ways which, for the purpose of convenience, may be labelled the Grimondite, Owenite and Jenkinsite. It may help to illustrate these three variants in diagrammatic form.

1. *Grimondite*	Small left-wing Labour Party	Realigned radical party comprising Liberals and right-wing Labour	Conservatives

2. *Owenite*	Small left-wing Labour Party	SDP	Liberals	Conservatives
3. *Jenkinsite*	Labour Party		Liberal–SDP Alliance	Conservatives

Which of these scenarios comes to predominate will, of course, depend not only upon the attitudes taken by the leaders of the SDP and the Alliance, but also upon the attitudes of those voters who support them. To what extent do the perceptions of the electorate correspond with the views of the SDP taken by its leaders?

V

Survey findings purporting to describe the attitudes of the electorate towards a new political party must be treated with even more than the normal degree of caution. For the SDP has not been in existence long enough to find an assured place within the political spectrum, and it has yet to fight a general election. Many of those questioned by opinion-poll researchers need prompting by the interviewer to remind them of the very existence of the SDP and the Alliance; and the answers to such prompted questions invariably show the Alliance to enjoy rather more support than the answers to unprompted questions would appear to indicate. Furthermore, the evidence of surveys is, perhaps, particularly unreliable when it comes to analysing the electorate's perception of the political parties along a Left–Right continuum. For a significant minority of the electorate does not understand the use of the terms 'Left' and 'Right' while a further, albeit smaller, minority, believe that they understand the terms but in fact misconceive their use. Indeed, in a series of unpublished polls conducted by Gallup between June 1981 and March 1982, 40% of a sample had to be excluded because they felt unable to place the SDP on a Left–Right spectrum at all.

Nevertheless, such evidence as is available makes it clear that the new party is seen by the electorate as being closer to the Liberals than to the Labour Party. The available evidence has been summed up by Ivor Crewe in the following way: 'the SDP is seen, both by its own supporters and the electorate as a whole, as a centre party, not a left-of-centre party ... the SDP is placed very close to the Liberal Party, always fractionally to its left. No group of respondents places it closer to the Labour Party than to the Liberal Party. Indeed, the electors who position it closest to the Liberal Party are SDP supporters themselves'. Furthermore, 'SDP supporters place not only their party but themselves in the centre; they are, in fact, fractionally to its right. Typical SDP supporters do not see themselves as moderate but left-of-centre voters abandoned by a left-wards-drifting Labour Party. They see themselves as "middle-of-the roaders".[20]

Further, the social-class profile of the SDP voter resembles that of the Liberal voter, far more than the Labour voter. For, instead of its support being concentrated amongst the working class, as is the case with the Labour Party, SDP support is, like Liberal support, fairly evenly distributed in class terms amongst the electorate. This can be seen from the figures derived from Gallup (see table 2). It can be seen that the social-class profile for the SDP differs sharply from that for the Labour Party, and that the social profile of the Liberal/SDP Alliance vote is very nearly a microcosm of that of the population as a whole. The SDP is not, sociologically, a modernised version of the Labour Party, but rather complements the Liberals. We have already seen that the two parties are *ideologically* compatible, since the ideals of both flow from streams of thought which seemed about to merge in the years before 1914. It now seems that the SDP and the Liberals are also looked upon by the electorate as being, on the whole, similar.

Table 2. *The social-class profile of the parties*

Social Class	All	Con	Lab	Lib	SDP	Lib/SDP Alliance
AB	16	26	7	15	19	17
C1	22	28	15	21	26	24
C2	32	26	37	33	31	32
DE	30	19	42	32	25	28

Source: Gallup Report, *Political Tracking Study*, October 1981, adapted by Ivor Crewe in 'Is Britain's two-party system really about to crumble? The Social Democratic–Liberal Alliance and the prospects for realignment', *Electoral Studies*, 1, no. 3 (Dec. 1982), p. 292.

VI

Analysis both of the ideological and the electoral basis of the SDP seems, therefore, to lead to the same conclusion. The SDP is not to be understood as a modernised Labour Party similar in nature to the Social Democratic parties of the Continent. Rather, it is a party of the centre, or

---

[20] Ivor Crewe, 'Is Britain's two-party system really about to crumble? The Social Democratic–Liberal Alliance and the prospects for realignment', *Electoral Studies*, 1 (1982), pp. 301–2.

possibly of the centre-left, and the Alliance with the Liberals heralds a new centre formation in British politics which, unless the Labour Party disintegrates rapidly, will take its place in a tripolar political system. The SDP, then, will add strength to the centre, rather than realigning the Left.

The dominant themes of this new centre formation are likely to be constitutional reform and economic reconstruction. They are strongly inter-linked. Pre-eminent amongst the constitutional reforms demanded by the Alliance, is, of course, proportional representation which would serve to counter the centrifugal tendencies of the political system, and, in Roy Jenkins' words, lead to a 'strengthening of the political centre'.[21] It would also, in the view of the Alliance, make possible the re-introduction of consensus policies in the economic field – incomes policy, the development of tripartite co-operation between government, employers and employees, and the establishment of an institutional framework within which common objectives can be pursued. These policies would, the Alliance believes, enjoy a better prospect of success if they can be pursued in the more favourable political climate which proportional representation would create. For if they have failed in the past, it is precisely because governments have proved unable to mobilise the consent of the electorate to support them. It is not the policies themselves which are at fault, therefore, but the political culture within which they have been implemented. With electoral reform, on the other hand, greater predictability and confidence would be assured. Changes of government would more often take the form of changes in coalition partner rather than the ejection of one party from office and its replacement by another dedicated to diametrically opposite policies. There would be an assurance of stability in such policy areas as the line of demarcation between public and private industry, pay policy and the structure of taxation, and this might encourage industrial progress.

But proportional representation will also assist in the creation of the kind of society desired by Liberals and Social Democrats, since it will enable a wider range of opinion to secure representation. Far from sharing the conventional distaste for Continental-style, multi-party politics, the Alliance seems positively to welcome it as being more capable of reflecting the diversity of opinion in a modern society. In the words of a Liberal Party document:

... the party system should reflect the realities of public opinion. The present one clearly works badly, forcing some issues into an artificial mould, obscuring others, and generally making government less representative. It should be

---

21 Roy Jenkins, *Home Thoughts from Abroad* (BBC Dimbleby Lecture 1979), p. 10.

replaced, and necessarily at this stage, by a multi-party one. The institutions, and particularly the method, of election, should be natural channels allowing the system to develop in tune with popular feeling.[22]

In a sophisticated industrial society, multi-party politics is more 'natural' than a two-party system because there is a far wider diversity of interests seeking representation than can be accommodated by two major parties whose *raison d'être* is a socio-economic cleavage based upon class. For if society contains a large number of different interests, social stability will not be gained through the victory of one group of interests over another. Instead, these interests should be represented both in government and in industry in proportion to their strength amongst the electorate; and a spirit of compromise and mutual accommodation should temper the process of majority decision-taking.

The Alliance, it can be seen, adheres to a philosophy of social harmony. The optimistic assumption is made that the wide representation of social interests will lead to compromise and agreement, rather than immobilism, since these interests will be concerned with the common good of the community as a whole. The model is essentially Scandinavian, 'orderly, efficient, peaceable, small scale ... As Britain moves further away from any nostalgia for an Imperial past, this Nordic pattern of social devolution may well become more attractive.'[23] But it may well be that such an approach under-estimates the very real degree of social conflict in Britain, which is not susceptible to the techniques of compromise and accommodation proposed by the Alliance. A model of government which proves workable in a small-scale homogeneous society such as Denmark or Sweden is not necessarily suited to the facts of life in contemporary Britain.

VII

The new centre formation in British politics is to be understood as a different *kind* of grouping from the Labour or Conservative Parties. For, as we have already seen, it seeks not only to alter the configuration of parties but also the political system itself. If it succeeds, the British party system will have become both multi-party and coalitional in nature. It is the West German model which many of the Alliance leaders have in mind when they argue for a political system of this kind, and some hints as to how the British system might work after proportional representation can

---

[22] *Power to the People: The Machinery of Government* (Liberal Publications Department, 1974), p. 7.
[23] William Rees-Mogg, 'Political Testament' (Review of Shirley Williams, *Politics is for People* (Allen Lane and Penguin, 1981)), *The Times*, 16 April 1981.

be obtained from considering West German experience. For West Germany has a three-party system which operates very differently from Britain's. This is because the proportional electoral system gives the centre party – the Free Democrats – a pivotal position in the system, so that it acts as a centripetal force upon the two major parties, the Social Democrats (SPD), and the Christian Democrats (CDU/CSU). The proportion of the vote secured by the three main parties in West German general elections since 1969 is shown in table 3. Between 1969 and 1982, West Germany was governed by an SPD/FDP coalition. To defeat it the CDU/CSU had to gain over 50% of the vote or win over the FDP which in October 1982, finally decided to change coalition partners to support the CDU/CSU under Helmut Kohl.

Table 3. *Percentage vote of the three main West German parties*

Year	% vote of SPD	% vote of FDP	% vote of CDU/CSU
1969	42.7	5.8	46.1
1972	45.8	8.4	44.9
1976	42.6	7.9	48.6
1980	42.9	10.6	44.5

Two conclusions stand out from the table. The first is that the inclusion of one of the major parties in government depends not only upon its own strength, but also upon how attractive it is as a coalition partner. The CDU/CSU, although it was supported by more of the electorate in 1969, 1976 and 1980 than the SPD (and in 1976 by more of the electorate than customarily supports a single-party government in the United Kingdom), was denied office because the FDP chose to remain in alliance with the SPD. Thus, the political system is, within certain limits, impervious to gains or losses by the major parties.

The second conclusion is that the FDP, which has failed to secure more than 10.6% of the vote since 1969 – a smaller percentage of the vote than the Liberal Party in Britain has gained in the last three elections – has determined whether the SPD or the CDU/CSU forms a government. The FDP does not, of course, have total freedom of choice of coalition partner, since its voters will expect it to form a coalition of a particular kind, and may desert it if its expectations are not fulfilled. But it does have some leeway in making its choice. Thus, the FDP with 10.6% of the vote in the 1980 elections, decided which of two major parties with over four times as many votes should be allowed to form a government; and it

44

has held this position since 1969 irrespective of the percentage of the vote which it has secured.

In place, then, of adversarial politics, the political centre becomes dominant, for any party which moves away from the centre makes its chances of forming a government more remote. This was illustrated in the 1980 elections when the choice of Strauss as CDU/CSU candidate for the Chancellorship encouraged some CDU/CSU voters to switch to the FDP and made it impossible for the FDP to support the CDU/CSU. Indeed, the retention of Helmut Kohl as CDU/CSU parliamentary leader had not a little to do with the CDU/CSU's perception that he was (as indeed proved to be the case), the leader most likely to be able to prise the FDP away from its alliance with the SDP, for he had himself been in coalition with the FDP in the provincial government of Rhineland-Pfalz.

The dynamics of such a system are clearly different from those in Britain, shaped by the plurality system of election where a party with the 44.5% of the vote secured by Strauss would be ensured of a reasonable majority of the seats in the Commons; while the 43.9% of the vote secured by Mrs Thatcher in 1979 would be insufficient to form a majority government under a system of proportional representation of the West German type unless she was able to secure a coalition with the Liberals – an unlikely prospect perhaps.

The advantage which this style of politics yields is greater continuity of government. The central disadvantage is that the system may become impervious to the signals of the electorate. It will be more difficult to reject the government of the day as long as that government retains the allegiance of its coalition partner. There is always a danger that such a political system may lead to immobilism with the governing coalition being effectively shielded from the electorate. Whether or not one views such a system favourably, therefore, depends essentially upon whether one's diagnosis of the British political system is that it has suffered too much from 'adversary politics' and that a degree of continuity would be desirable; or whether, on the contrary, one believes that the alternation between a single-party government and single-party opposition each with opposing views as to the nature of the good society, constitutes the very essence of democracy.

Within a multi-party political system entrenched by proportional representation, the Alliance would seek to take its place as a pivot or hinge grouping, willing to take part in a coalition government with either the Labour or Conservative Parties. Like the Free Democrats in West Germany, it would be seen as a corrective to the ideologies of the major parties – socialism and the free market. The Alliance would be a grouping whose central aim it was to urge balance and compromise upon the major parties.

Yet this role is not without its dangers for the Alliance, which could face difficulties in preserving its identity. Both liberalism and social democracy are, as we have seen, distinctive standpoints whose political traditions have deep roots in Britain's political culture. The leaders of the Alliance see it as a radical force. The Liberals have shown a particular concern for issues such as civil liberties, race relations and personal freedoms; while Roy Jenkins, the leader of the SDP, called in his Dimbleby Lecture of 1979 for a new 'radical centre'[24] in British politics. As Home Secretary he was associated with legislation on race relations, and with reform of the laws on homosexuality and abortion. So, although the Alliance places itself on the centre of the political spectrum insofar as economic policy is concerned, on what might be called 'Home Office' issues it lies on the Left of the Political spectrum, some distance away, one suspects, from the position of the majority of the electorate. The leaders of the Alliance, therefore, do not regard their parties as merely coalition partners, complementing and moderating the policies of the Labour and Conservative Parties. They also have distinctive policies of their own which they would like to see implemented. But a party whose central function is that of a corrective is not necessarily in the best position for gaining and retaining votes in its own right, as the German Free Democrats have discovered.

There is, then, a conflict between the moderating role which a pivot formation such as the Alliance seeks to play in government, and its role as an instrument for promoting liberal and social democratic ideals. The former role entails a conservative stance for the Alliance, preventing extremism and ensuring a greater degree of continuity in policy. In the latter role, however, it is the Alliance itself which can be considered 'extreme' and radical. The tension between the Alliance's position in the political spectrum and the radical nature of some of its policies is obviously something which will be difficult to resolve.

More fundamentally, it is worth asking whether the radicalism of the Alliance would not gradually come to be superseded by the constraints of its role as a moderator of Labour and Conservative governments. For, after all, its *raison d'être*, as far as many voters are concerned, is not the need for change, but fear of the rival radicalisms of Mrs Thatcher and Mr Benn. Faced with a Conservative Party which under Mrs Thatcher professes the radicalism of the free market economy, and a Labour Party seeking radical change albeit in an opposite direction, is there room for a

[24] Roy Jenkins, *Home Thoughts from Abroad*, p. 10.

third radical force in British politics? Or is not the Alliance a conservative force, seeking to restore the Butskellite consensus from which the two major parties have departed? Its central policies – support for the EEC, economic modernisation through planning and state intervention, and the adoption of an incomes policy – are just the policies of the consensus of the 1960s. From this perspective, the Alliance appears as restorative rather than radical. It faces the dilemma of whether its centrist stance in the political system is compatible with its professions of radicalism. Is it a formation which will 'break the mould'; or, on the contrary, will it encourage consensus government? The Alliance faces in two directions, and while seeking to dominate the politics of the future, it casts a longing eye backwards towards the past. It is too early to tell whether these two approaches are compatible, or, if they are not, how the tension between them will be resolved.

3

Multi-party politics and the electorate

Centre parties are by no means a new phenomenon in British politics. They have made their appearance at different times in Britain's history when party alignments have seemed to be melting. Between 1885 and 1914, there were a number of different proposals for a centre party – a party which would reject both Irish Home Rule and Little Englandism on the Left and Protection and reaction on the Right. Joseph Chamberlain, Lord Randolph Churchill, Lord Hartington and Lord Rosebery were all mentioned at different times as candidates for the leadership of such a party. During the inter-war period, the Liberals sought to act as a centre party, a party lying between socialism and reaction, but, arguably, their dogmatic attachment to Free Trade prevented them from fully embracing Keynesian ideas of economic reconstruction. An ill-fated attempt to construct such a 'Keynesian' party – Sir Oswald Mosley's New Party – proved to be only a staging-post on the road to Fascism.

Thus, in Britain, although the voter in the centre of the political spectrum is generally believed to decide elections, parties which sought explicitly to represent the centre have been uniformly unsuccessful. Often, the centre has been defined more by what it is *against* – whether Home Rule, Protection or socialism – than by what it stands for. Consensus in Britain has been articulated not by a single party standing for 'moderate values' as against its opponents, but through a party system within which all parties display moderate values.

The difficulties facing a new centre formation in Britain are due in part to institutional factors. There are in fact two institutional barriers blocking the path of a new party today – the electoral system, and the methods by which party politics are financed. The electoral system discriminates against parties without a clearly identifiable socio-economic or territorial basis of support; while the methods by which the parties are financed in Britain make it difficult for a party without intimate connections with companies and trade unions to compete successfully with parties which have ready access to the funds provided by these institutions. The two barriers constituted by the electoral system and the structure of political finance, have made it difficult in the past for the Liberal Party to make a breakthrough, and they are likely to prove equally difficult for the Social Democrats to surmount.

The plurality system of election is widely thought to discriminate against third parties in a two-party system. In fact it discriminates against parties whose support is evenly distributed geographically, but not against those whose support is geographically concentrated. It did not discriminate against the Irish Nationalists in the nineteenth century: indeed it assisted them by extinguishing minority opinion – Liberal and Southern Unionist – and compelling every Catholic who wished his voice to be heard in Irish politics to join the Nationalists. Similarly, in the 1970s, the electoral system has helped the Ulster Unionists in Northern Ireland. In the general election of February 1974, the United Ulster Unionist Coalition secured 11 seats for 1.3% of the total United Kingdom vote, while the Liberals with 19.3% of the vote gained only 14 seats. In October 1974, the Scottish Nationalists with 2.9% of the total vote gained 11 seats, while the Liberals with 18.3% secured only 13.

It is the very evenness of the Liberal Party's support, both geographically and socially, which has handicapped its performance under the plurality system. As we have already noticed, the social profile of the Liberal vote is fairly evenly distributed amongst the social classes, by contrast with the two major parties, and so also is the SPD vote. The vote of the major parties is more concentrated, both socially and geographically. This results in large part from the residential segregation of housing patterns which mirror class divisions. Both the Liberals and the SDP lack such a basis of support, and, therefore, they are at a disadvantage in converting their votes into parliamentary seats. The consequence is that, below the break-even point which lies at around 35% of the total vote, they will be seriously discriminated against by the electoral system.

In *The Economist* (21 February 1981), a calculation was made of the Alliance's potential representation making three assumptions about the basis of its support; that the Alliance gained the whole of the 1979 Liberal vote, that it gained in each constituency 30% of the 1979 Labour vote, and that there was a straight 10% swing from the Conservatives to the Alliance. The result would then be as shown below:

	% share of vote
Lib/SDP Alliance	34.9
Conservative	33.9
Labour	25.9

But the result in terms of seats would be:

Lib/SDP Alliance	142
Conservative	295
Labour	183

Thus, on perfectly plausible assumptions, the Alliance could secure a higher percentage vote than either of the two major parties, and yet remain the third party in terms of seats. If support for the Alliance fell markedly below the level postulated in the above simulation, its share of seats would be very considerably reduced. If, for example, its vote fell to 25.9%, the hypothetical share of the Labour vote in the example above, then, on the same assumptions, it would gain only 20 seats.

It is clear, then, that the electoral system constitutes a formidable barrier for a grouping such as the Alliance which is penalised because of the distinctive social and geographical nature of its support. Yet the very injustice which the Alliance may suffer could constitute a strong argument for changing the electoral system, especially if results such as that of February 1974, when the Liberals gained 14 seats for nearly 20% of the total vote, come to be a regular occurrence. For such results would not be tolerated by the electorate for long. The advent of a strong third formation in Britain would expose the Achilles heel of the plurality system of election. It would emphasise the fact that under this system, the number of seats which a party wins depends not only upon the number of votes which it gains, but upon their geographical distribution, upon where these votes are cast. Gross inequalities of representation would make it difficult to justify the retention of this electoral system.

As the three parties approach to an equal share of the vote, so the relationship between votes and seats, which can be reasonably predictable in a two-party system, will become highly unpredictable and volatile. A small percentage shift in the vote around the 35% mark can produce a very large shift in the number of seats which a party wins. In such a situation the major parties themselves could find it in their interests to reform the electoral system so as to be assured of a stable relationship between the votes which they win and the number of seats they obtain. So, although the electoral system imposes a high threshold upon a third party, it also offers hope to such a party that, if it can maintain the kind of challenge which the Liberals offered in 1974, the injustice of the system will become manifest to enough electors to compel reform; while, if it succeeds in surmounting the threshold, the unpredictability of the system could compel the major parties, in their own interests, to support reform. Electoral reform, were it to come about, would constitute a recognition that the Alliance can no longer be contained; that British politics had become permanently multi-party politics.

The structure of party finance constitutes a second barrier to the electoral success of the Alliance. Britain is quite unique amongst developed Western democracies in the extent to which the two major parties are financed from institutional sources – companies and trade unions. Of the Labour Party's central income, no less than 78% in 1981 was derived from trade union affiliation fees. This is a far higher share than that obtained by equivalent Western European parties, and in none of them do the trade unions form so intimate a part of the party as is the case with the Labour Party. This financial support from the trade unions serves to cushion the Labour Party against a fall in its membership, which in 1952 reached a peak at around 1,015,000 individual members, but by 1981 had fallen to around 275,000. In 1979, an election year, the Labour Party's membership was around 350,000, equal to only 2.5% of those who voted for it, the lowest percentage of any socialist party in Western Europe; and 1979 was, of course, a bad year for the party electorally.

Companies play no formal role in the decision-making process of the Conservative Party as the trade unions do in the Labour Party, and the Conservative Party's central accounts do not distinguish between individual and corporate donations. But unofficial estimates seem to concur in the assumption that company donations account for between 55% and 60% of Central Office income. So it is that the bulk of the contributions made to the central organisations of the two major parties are the result of corporate rather than individual decisions. The parties comprising the Alliance do not receive money from the trade unions, nor do they accept affiliated membership from the unions or any other corporate body; although they will undoubtedly receive company contributions, these are likely to be negligible compared with the payments made to the Conservative Party. This situation may change if industry comes to believe, as it did for a short time after the two elections of 1974, that the introduction of proportional representation should have priority over the election of a Conservative government, since electoral reform could prove a better guarantor of business stability while also ensuring that the Left is kept out of power. The Liberals after 1974 seem to have benefited from such an attitude on the part of industrialists. But the donations which they received appear to have been comparatively small, short-lived and fitful.

Thus the methods by which parties are financed in Britain make it difficult for a new party, not enjoying a privileged relationship with the trade unions, and unable to attract large company contributions, to break through to majority status. In fact, the methods by which the parties are financed, like the electoral system, seem to reward those parties which emphasise one type of political cleavage – class conflict – at the expense of other social cleavages. This constitutes a handicap for the Alliance in its attempts to compete with the two major parties; and it is not, perhaps, surprising that the SDP has proposed to reform the system under which the trade unions contribute to the Labour Party, so that 'contracting out' is replaced by 'contracting in'. Yet, while the Alliance remains a minority formation, it will be dependent upon the major parties for the implementation of such a reform.

II

The importance of these two barriers – the electoral system and the structure of political finance – should not, however, be over-emphasised. Admittedly, they make it difficult for the Alliance to achieve an electoral breakthrough, yet there is nothing inherent in these institutional obstacles which prevents them being overcome if only the Alliance can obtain sufficient support from the electorate. The greatest barrier faced by the Liberals in the past has not been institutional, but rather that they have been unable to win enough votes consistently to overcome the obstacles placed in their path. The source of the failure of the Liberals, therefore, must be sought elsewhere. It lies in their inability to recruit and hold a high and stable proportion of Liberal voters. This in turn flows from the profound historicity of voting patterns, and the slowness with which they change.

The investigation of voting patterns over time is a comparatively recent form of study. Yet, already, there seems general agreement on at least one conclusion – that voting patterns tend to remain stable for long periods of time, and have been remarkably resistant to change. Electoral geog-·raphers such as André Siegfried and François Goguel have shown the astonishing degree of historical continuity in France such that a *département* hostile to the Revolution in 1789 would be likely to support a candidate of the Right one hundred and fifty years later; while a *département* sympathetic to the Revolution would be found supporting the Popular Front in 1936.

Even the ravages of war and destruction are unable to alter deeply rooted habits of electoral behaviour. When the first elections in the German Federal Republic were held in 1949, it was discovered that patterns of support for Christian, conservative and socialist parties mirrored almost exactly voting patterns in the last free elections before Hitler. In Italy despite political instability and an electoral system encouraging the formation of new parties, 92% of the Chamber of Deputies in 1979 was occupied by deputies belonging to parties present in the 1946–48 Constituent Assembly; and these in turn all had their roots in the political traditions of the pre-Fascist era. Parties without such deep historical or cultural roots had a record of almost unredeemed failure. It is habit, rather than the institutions of a country, which constitutes the most serious barrier to a new political formation seeking to make a rapid electoral breakthrough.

In their seminal work on party structures and voter alignments, S. M. Lipset and Stein Rokkan claimed that the basic electoral cleavages in Western Europe were formed when universal suffrage was conceded, which, in most Western European countries, was in the first two decades of the twentieth century, and they have remained remarkably stable since the 1920s. Lipset and Rokkan put forward what has come to be known as the 'freezing hypothesis' that there had been a 'freezing of the major party alternatives in the wake of the extension of the suffrage and the mobilization of major sections of the new reservoirs of political supporters'. For individual voting behaviour was based less upon the appraisal of immediate policy issues than upon the voter's ties with his class, religion, subculture or *famille spirituelle*. 'The voter does not just react to immediate issues but is caught in an historically given constellation of diffuse options for the system as a whole.' Individuals came to identify with particular political parties, and it was party identification which provided the key to the stability of political alignments in Western Europe. Writing in 1967, Lipset and Rokkan could thus conclude that in general 'the party systems of the 1960s reflect with few significant exceptions the cleavage structure of the 1920s'.[1]

In Britain, universal suffrage for men and for women over thirty was granted in 1918; while women between 21 and 30 were given the vote in 1928. It was, moreover, in the 1920s that the Liberals were deposed as the party of the Left by the Labour Party, and the British political system settled down to the pattern of a two-party system based upon class voting. It was class voting which gave to British politics its electoral stability. Electoral behaviour came to display a considerable degree of geographical homogeneity since an elector in Cornwall would tend to vote the same way as an elector from a similar class in Glasgow regardless of national or locational differences. Between 1945 and 1970, except for the general election of 1959, the standard deviation of at least three-quarters of the constituencies lay within 2% of the average swing. Winston Churchill is supposed to have said that on election night he could go to bed after Billericay – Billericay being usually the first constituency to declare. Moreover, because class positions changed slowly, so also did voting patterns, and voters were

---

[1] Seymour M. Lipset and Stein Rokkan (eds.), *Party Systems and Voter Alignments: Cross-National Perspectives* (Free Press, New York 1967), pp. 50, 53, 50.

inoculated against the disruptive effects of new issues, new leaders or last-minute campaign scares.

In the bi-polar political system which resulted, the Liberals had no place; electorally, they lay outside class politics, since their appeal was not basically socio-economic, while ideologically they seemed unnecessary since liberal values had found a home in both of the major parties. It was this combination of a bi-polar structure of class politics together with an ideology of consensus which meant that there was no political space for the Liberals, and it played a far more important role than institutional barriers in preventing the Party from making a break-through.

III

British politics is still marked by the consequences of the realignment which took place in the 1920s, when the Liberal Party was relegated to the position of third party in the system. The attitudes of the electorate towards the Liberal Party remain strikingly different from their attitudes to the Labour and Conservative Parties, and they explain why it is that the Liberals have been unable to overturn the electoral verdict of the 1920s. For the electorate, the Liberal Party still does not appear as a credible contender for power.

As we have already seen, there is no distinctive socio-economic base to the Liberal vote. Its support is not rooted in class, and it has not been possible to correlate the Liberal vote with any other social structural characteristic. To the extent to which voting behaviour is held to be socially determined, therefore, the Liberal vote could be considered as fundamentally unsystematic and unpredictable in nature; and in the Commons, Liberal MPs represent constituencies as different socially as the Isle of Wight and Liverpool Edge Hill, Roxburgh, Selkirk and Peebles, and Rochdale.

The Liberal vote, then, is rootless in socio-economic terms. But neither is the Liberal Party associated in the mind of the electorate with any specific policies, and support for the Party does not seem to be based mainly on support for the Party's policies. The Liberals can be contrasted in this respect with both the Scottish Nationalists and the National Front. The Scottish Nationalists have been identified in the minds of voters with two issues – self-government for Scotland, and use of the oil revenues to aid Scottish economic development. In the mid-1970s, these were policies with which a large number of Scottish voters could positively identify, and support for them played a large part in helping the SNP make its electoral breakthrough in 1974 when it secured 21% and 30% of the

Scottish vote in the February and October elections respectively. Yet, when support for such policies falls, so also will support for the party, and this may be a cause of the SNP's decline from its position of the mid-1970s. The National Front, like the Scottish Nationalists, is identified in the minds of the electorate with specific policies; but, by contrast with the SNP, these policies are held to be so grossly illiberal by the vast majority of the electorate, that they constitute a barrier not an incentive to electoral support for the party. In the case of the Liberal Party, there is neither a very strong positive support for its policies, as with the SNP in the mid-1970s; nor a strong negative repulsion from them, as with the National Front.

In consequence of the Liberals' inability to attract the steady support of any particular socio-economic grouping, and failure to offer distinctive policies which strike a welcoming chord in the minds of the electorate, their regular core of support is far smaller than is the case with the two major parties. Between 1959 and 1979, on average, under 50% of those voting Liberal at one election did so again at the next, as compared with around 75% for the Labour and Conservative Parties. Survey evidence suggests that in the four elections of the 1970s, while 24% of the electorate voted Labour in all of them, and 23% voted Conservative only 2% of the electorate supported the Liberals throughout the decade. Identification with the Liberal Party also is far lower than identification with the Labour or Conservative Parties. In 1979, for example, 68% of Conservative voters identified 'very' or 'fairly' strongly with their Party, while 75% of Labour voters identified 'very' or 'fairly' strongly with the Labour Party. The equivalent figure for the Liberals was only 42%.[2] Thus a much higher proportion of the Liberal vote at each election derives from converts whose support is difficult to retain. These converts find it easy to support the Liberal Party when dissatisfied with either the Conservative or Labour Parties since, as we have already noticed, they perceive the Liberals as lying mid-way between the Labour and Conservative Parties. Moreover, if the Liberal Party does not attract voters primarily because of its policies, neither does it repel them because its policies seem unattractive. The policies themselves constitute neither a barrier nor an incentive to the potential defector.

It is factors such as leadership and style which form the main incentive for voters to switch to the Liberal Party. 'The content of Liberal Party imagery', according to one survey of the Party's vote, 'is distinguished by a lack of specificity ... The Liberal appeal is entirely contained in diffuse images of style: the Liberal Party is "moderate", is "in between the other two", is "good for all the people", "it's time for a change", "they don't

---

[2] Crewe, 'Is Britain's two-party system really about to crumble?', p. 281.

engage in mudslinging like all the rest" and so on.'[3] Support for the Party is therefore diffuse and shallow in nature – it is more in the nature of a protest vote than a considered and permanent commitment. This can be strikingly illustrated by the vicissitudes of the Liberal vote in the two elections of 1974. In February, the Liberals gained 6 million votes – 19.3% of the vote, and in October 5.3 million – 18.3% of the vote. Yet, survey evidence indicates that between February and October, 2.9 million voters – nearly half of the February 1974 Liberal voters – deserted the Party to be replaced by 2.2 million voters who had not supported the Liberals in February, but did so in October. Half a million of these voters were located in the 102 constituencies which the Liberals fought in October but not in February, but the other 1.7 million voters had either voted Labour or Conservative or abstained in February.[4] There is, then, widespread sympathy for the Liberal Party. In 1974 over 8 million – nearly one-quarter of the electorate – voted for the Party at least once; but this sympathy is not translated into permanent identification with the Party. Seventy per cent of those who voted Liberal once in 1974, and over half of those who switched to the Liberals in February 1974, and also voted Liberal in October, had deserted the Party by 1979.[5] The Liberal vote is thus highly volatile, and the Party faces the problem not only of converting more members of the electorate to its support, but also of retaining the support of those whom it has been successful in converting. So far, the Liberal Party has been unable to build up a solid block of voting support which is loyal to it from one election to the next. Liberal voting, rather, is a temporary staging-post for those dissatisfied with the policies or performance of one of the major parties: '... there is barely a Liberal party in the electorate. Rather, the Liberal vote consists of a tiny core surrounded by a much larger, volatile cluster of occasional supporters.'[6]

The birth of the SDP and the formation of the Alliance of course increase the chances of the centre in British politics. Yet the question which has to be answered is whether they change the character of electoral support for the centre. Is support for the SDP and the Alliance likely to prove as brittle as support for the Liberals has been; or, by contrast, is the Alliance likely to be the beneficiary of a new source of socio-economic support, or a new constellation of political issues? Interestingly enough, when the negotiations between the Liberals and the SDP over the allocation of constituencies began in 1981, the SDP insisted

[3] James Alt, Ivor Crewe and Bo Särlvik, 'Angels in plastic: The Liberal surge in 1974,' in *Political Studies* (September 1977), p. 356.
[4] Ibid., p. 348.
[5] Crewe, 'Is Britain's two-party system really about to crumble?', pp. 281.
[6] Ibid., p. 281–2.

upon its rightful share of winnable seats, defining as 'winnable' a seat where the share of the Liberal vote was high. This is an indication that, for its leaders at least, the SDP vote was likely to prove an addition to the Liberal vote, and unlikely to be able to tap any new sources of support. But, of course, such evidence is in the nature of things highly tentative.

Being a new party, it is impossible to determine the answers to questions about the nature of the SDP's support with the same degree of confidence as is possible in the case of the other parties; and indeed there have been hardly any academic studies of the nature of the SDP vote. Such evidence as is available must be treated, moreover, with very considerable caution since the SDP has not yet been in existence long enough for meaningful questions to be asked about the nature of its long-term support; and as the Party has not yet fought a general election, its supporters have only had the chance to display their allegiance in by-elections or local elections. The material, then, is simply not available to allow one to make assertions about the nature of SDP support with any degree of confidence.

Nevertheless, such survey evidence as is available seems to indicate that the SDP faces the same problems as the Liberals in creating a solid block of permanent adherents. We have already seen that the SDP shares the Liberals' lack of a distinctive socio-economic base, and, it will therefore find it difficult to secure electoral allegiance on any basis of group self-interest. In addition, being a new party, the SDP, unlike the Liberals, cannot even claim any inherited attachment; it has had no time to build up committed partisans; and, no doubt, even less of the electorate have an awareness of the content of social democracy than of liberalism. The very limited evidence available indicates that the SDP have, so far, been no more successful than the Liberals in creating a distinctive 'issue space' for themselves; for their appeal too seems based more upon the quality and style of their leaders, together with a distrust of the major parties, rather than upon support for SDP policies, of which the electorate may have only a hazy understanding. At the Warrington by-election fought by Roy Jenkins in 1981, references to the policies of the SDP came far behind more generalised sentiments as a reason for supporting the Party; while at the Glasgow, Hillhead by-election won by Roy Jenkins in March 1982, the SDP actually lay behind the Conservatives and Labour Parties as the party which the electorate preferred for dealing with nine major issues.[7]

It seems then that support for the SDP and the Alliance is no different in nature from support for the Liberal Party in the past. The Alliance, of course, can attract greater support than the Liberal Party since it contains

[7] Ibid., p. 299.

57

leaders who have held high government office – Roy Jenkins is a former Chancellor of the Exchequer and Home Secretary, David Owen a former Foreign Secretary and Shirley Williams a former Education Secretary. The Alliance, therefore, gives the centre in British politics a much higher degree of credibility than the Liberal Party on its own could enjoy. On the other hand, because the SDP lacks committed partisans, its support may hold up less well than that of the Liberals in time of difficulty. There is in fact considerable evidence that Liberal support was less susceptible than that of the SDP to erosion by the so-called 'Falklands factor' which increased the support for the Conservative government in the local elections of 1982, and in by-elections and opinion polls from spring 1982. On the whole, however, the support which the Alliance has obtained shows merely that the SDP in combination with the Liberals has become a more effective vehicle of protest than the Liberal Party on its own could be. It has not yet succeeded in benefiting from any new electoral cleavage; nor has it been able to attach to itself any significant social interest, an advantage perhaps from the standpoint of policy-making, but less so for building up a stable coalition of committed supporters. There is no evidence as yet that the Alliance is near to achieving a fundamental realignment in British politics of the kind which the Labour Party was able to accomplish in the 1920s.

If that was the sum total of what could be said on the subject of the electoral prospects of the Alliance, its prospects would be far bleaker than in fact they are. For its chances of success may owe less to its own positive qualities than to the depth of disillusionment towards the two major parties, a product of the policy failures of successive governments. But there has also been a process of partisan dealignment which is occurring in British politics, a gradual unfreezing of traditional party loyalties from which the Alliance may benefit.

The traditional picture of voting behaviour in Britain is one of stability and geographical homogeneity with the majority of the vote being given to one of the two major parties. Between 1945 and 1970, neither of the two major parties won more than 49% of the vote, or less than 43% of the vote, while the share of the poll gained by the two parties never fell below 87%. We have already noticed that the class basis of political allegiance gave considerable stability to the vote, and prevented too great a geographical diversity in voting patterns. Until 1974, it seemed as if the two major parties commanded two large and loyal armies of disciplined voters who would be likely to support them from one election to another, almost regardless of governmental performance. Elections, therefore, would be decided by the small number of voters who converted to, or defected from, one of the major parties.

This neat and tidy picture has become increasingly inappropriate. The low percentage of the vote secured by the two main parties in the 1970s was quite unprecedented. The Conservative share of the vote in February 1974 – 37.9% – was the lowest which it had received since 1906; while in October 1974 its vote fell further still, to the lowest level in its history as a mass party, and although the Conservative vote recovered somewhat in 1979, its share of the vote was still lower than it had been in any of the other post-war elections – 1951, 1955, 1959, and 1970 – in which it had won a parliamentary majority. The Labour vote in February 1974, although sufficient to put it into government, was the lowest which that party had gained since 1931, and the fall in its share of its vote from 1970 – 5.9% – was the largest drop in support for any Opposition since the war. In October the Labour Party's vote increased, but in 1979 it fell even below its level of February 1974. Moreover, by-election results after the formation of the Alliance in 1981, showed that Labour was unable to capitalise upon the economic difficulties facing the Conservative government, and that it was in danger of falling back even further from its already low base of 1979.

This decline in support for the two major parties seems to be accompanied by a fall in the proportion of the electorate willing to identify *strongly* with either of them, although the proportion of the electorate willing to identify in some manner with the two parties has not itself fallen by very much, and, in any case remains remarkably high by the standards of Western democracies. Party identification fell only 3% between 1964 and 1979 – from 93% to 90% – but the percentage with a 'strong' or a 'very strong' identification declined from 44% in 1964 to 22% in 1979.[8] This decline seems to have been evenly spread amongst different social classes and age groups, but to have gone further and faster within the youngest age group, the newest cohort of the electorate. If it is really the case that the newest age cohort admitted to the electorate is more disillusioned than its elders, then the decline in strong party identification is likely to continue at an increasing rate. But the newest cohort generally has a weaker identification than its elders because it has had less opportunity to acquire strong party loyalties through the act of voting. It may be, therefore, that the lesser degree of identification displayed by this cohort is in large part a generational factor and has little wider significance.

The continuing high level of party identification is a salient warning against predicting a rapid collapse of the two-party system in Britain. Nevertheless, the fall in 'very strong' and 'strong' identifiers indicates

[8] Ivor Crewe, 'Electoral volatility in Britain since 1945', Paper presented to ECPR Joint Session, Lancaster 1981, p. 22.

that there are fewer party stalwarts. It means that the two major parties can no longer count on partisan loyalties automatically working in their favour. The same conclusion follows from a consideration of changing social patterns in Britain.

Class, like party identification, has been a stabilising factor in British politics in the past. Yet there is now considerable evidence that ties between class and party are weakening, and that a larger percentage of voters are no longer prepared to vote for their class-consonant party – Labour for working-class voters; the Conservatives for middle-class voters. The evidence is summarised in table 4. It will be seen that in 1979, the Labour Party was supported by less than half of the working class, and that its lead over the Conservatives amongst the working class had fallen from 28% in 1964 to 7% in 1979. No similar trend is noticeable in the case of Conservative voters; yet there had been a fall of almost one-tenth in the Conservative lead over Labour in classes A and B, while only a little over one-half of the voters in class C1 voted Conservative in 1979. Furthermore, the percentages willing to support their class-consonant party (that is, working-class Labour supporters and middle-class Conservative supporters), has also fallen, as the following figures show.[9]

1964	1970	1979
57%	54%	49%

One reason for this weakening of the class/party link is that fewer members of the electorate conform to class stereotypes. We can list a series of class characteristics which would be possessed by an ideal-type member of the working class or an ideal-type member of the middle class, and then ask what percentage of the electorate conforms to the ideal-type picture. According to Richard Rose, 'An ideal-type British worker would be expected to have, in addition to a manual occupation, a minimum education, trade union membership, a council house residence and subjectively identify as working-class. Reciprocally, a middle-class person would be expected, in addition to a non-manual occupation, to have an above-minimum education, be a home-owner, not belong to a trade union, and subjectively identify with the middle-class.'[10] However, the percentage conforming to these stereotypes was only 23% of the electorate in 1970, and by 1979 it had fallen to 14%. The vast majority of the electorate, therefore, finds itself cross-pressured by conflicting class char-

[9] Richard Rose, *Class Does Not Equal Party: The Decline of a Model of British Voting* (Studies in Public Policy no. 74, Centre for the Study of Public Policy, University of Strathclyde, 1980), p. 19.
[10] Ibid., p. 27.

Table 4. *The weakening of the class/party link*

Class	1979 Con	Lab	Lib	Other	Difference Con–Lab		
Middle	%	%	%	%	1964	1970	1979
A Professional	70	13	14	2	%	%	%
B Business	61	18	17	3			
TOTAL	62	18	17	3	Total +53	+48	+44
C1 Office Workers	53	28	16	3	A+B +19	+17	+25
Working class							
C2 Skilled	41	42	13	4			
D Semi & unskilled	33	50	14	3			
E Welfare recipients	39	48	11	2			
TOTAL	38	45	13	3	−28	−13	−7

Source: Richard Rose, *Class Does Not Equal Party: The Decline of a Model of British Voting* (Studies in Public Policy No. 74, University of Strathclyde, 1980), p. 20.

acteristics, and so the likelihood of voters supporting their class-consonant party is bound to decline. Moreover, fewer voters are willing to place themselves in class categories at all. At the 1979 election, survey evidence showed that less than 50% of the electorate did so;[11] despite the fact that the two major parties were closely associated with a class appeal, Labour's links with the trade unions being emphasised whilst the Conservatives, under Mrs Thatcher, appeared as more stridently 'middle class' than had been the case for many years. The class appeals of the major parties have, paradoxically, not been accompanied by a resurgence of class voting. And, given the social changes which have occurred, they could not have been seriously expected to do so.

Nor does it seem as if class has been replaced by any other social structural determinant of voting behaviour which can bind the voter to his party. Instead, the decline of the class-party link has left a space for other factors to influence voting behaviour. After the 1979 general election, many commentators noticed the divergence in swing between the North and South of England, and the standard deviation of constituency voting was by far the highest in that election than in any since 1945. The average swing to the Conservatives south of a line stretching from the

[11] Ivor Crewe, 'Why the going is now so favourable for a centre party alliance', *The Times*, 23 March 1981.

Humber to the Mersey, including Wales, was 6.4%; while north of this line the average swing was 2.9%. This was not so much a locational effect as a result of differences in the perception of unemployment and inflation. Where unemployment was perceived to be the main issue of the election, the swing against Labour was less, even though the Labour government of 1974–79 had itself presided over a considerable increase in unemployment. Where, on the other hand, the control of inflation was judged to be the main issue, the swing to the Conservatives was larger. There were, in addition, genuine locational effects in voting behaviour. Cities with a large number of car workers, for example, swung heavily to the Conservatives, as did new towns and mining areas. Conversely, constituencies with a large number of immigrants and university towns showed swings smaller than average.

Thus, not only was there less support for the two major parties in the 1970s than in previous decades, but the nature of that support had changed. It was based less upon the stabilising factors of party identification or class solidarity, and more upon short-term factors such as the record of the government or the electorate's perception of political issues. There seems indeed to have been a slow but steady decline in the influence of social factors upon voting behaviour, and it has been replaced by a much greater degree of issue voting.

One result of this shift from class solidarity to issue voting is to highlight the difficulty in which the Labour Party is placed because the main issues with which it is identified – nationalisation, spending on the social services, and maintaining the power of the trade unions – are regarded with increasing hostility even by the Party's own supporters. Table 5 shows how opinion amongst *Labour identifiers* has moved against the Party's main policies. The Labour Party, then, must not only confront the consequences of the social changes discussed earlier. It also faces the problem that a majority, even amongst those who regard themselves as Labour Party supporters, disapprove of the main issues with which the Party is associated. Both its social and its ideological basis is under threat.

The evidence of studies of voting behaviour indicates that there has been a process of political dealignment since 1970. Instead of being able to rely upon solid blocks of support, the parties seem to be faced with an increasingly volatile and sceptical electorate. The attitude of the voter is no longer marked by a high degree of allegiance to the traditional landmarks of class, family or religion. Instead, the voter is sceptical of the pretensions of the parties and disdains the crudity of the rhetoric used to cement party ties. The voter's judgment is based rather on a more hard-headed calculation of the merits of the different parties, founded mainly, although by no means exclusively, upon their success in resolving the major economic

Table 5. *Labour Party identifiers and Labour Party policies*

	1964	1966	1970	Feb & Oct 1974	1979	Change 1964 to 1979
% of Labour identifiers	1964	1966	1970	1974	1979	
In favour of more nationalisation	57	52	39	53	32	−25
Who do not believe that trade unions have too much power	59	45	40	42	36	−23 (1964 to Feb 1974)
In favour of spending more on the social services	89	66	60	61	n.a.	−28
Saying that more social services and benefits are needed	n.a.	n.a.	n.a.	43	30	(1974–79) −13

Source: Ivor Crewe, *The Labour Party and the Electorate*, in Dennis Kavanagh (ed.), *The Politics of the Labour Party*, p. 39.

problems of the day. The parties, therefore, are now judged far more on performance than on their class affiliations; and they are judged more on performance than promise, for issue voting tends to be negative in character – a retrospective judgment on the policies which a government has pursued, rather than a belief in the promises of the manifesto. The vote is a verdict on the past rather than an aspiration for the future.

Because the governments of the 1970s have been seen as unsuccessful in coping with the major economic problems which Britain faces, they have gradually lost the confidence of the electorate. It is this factor rather than the process of social change which is responsible for the *rapidity* of changes in political attitudes; for changes in class feeling occur at a glacially slow rate. If governments had enjoyed more success, or faced less daunting adverse circumstances, they might have been able to counteract the effects of social change. In any case the extent of disillusionment should not be exaggerated; for, as we have seen, identification with the two major parties remains high in comparison with other leading democracies. It would be far too apocalyptic to imagine that the Labour and Conservative Parties are near to total collapse.

What does the evidence of studies of voting behaviour tell us about the possibilities for the Liberal/SDP Alliance and the future of multi-party politics in Britain? The evidence points to dealignment, but not realignment; dealignment from which the Alliance may conceivably benefit, but not to realignment, such as occurred when Labour replaced the Liberals in the 1920s. The gradual unfreezing of traditional loyalties offers a marvellous opportunity to a new political formation which it would not have enjoyed in the 1950s or 1960s. But the Alliance has not yet been able to take advantage of this opportunity to secure a solid core of loyal supporters so that it can take its place as a major party in the political system. For that to happen, it would either have to acquire the support of a new coalition of social forces, as Labour did in the 1920s; or it would have to become identified with a major issue which gave a new dimension to political conflict, and radically altered the cleavage structure. This was achieved by the Democrats in the United States after 1932 when they came to be seen by the electorate as the party best able to deal with the slump; and by the Gaullists in France in 1958 who were seen by the electorate as the party which could ensure governmental stability and national success. There is no sign as yet that the Alliance is anywhere near to emulating this achievement. For this reason, the formation of the Alliance may not lead to the rapid replacement of one major party by another as occurred in the 1920s; nor to a stable three-party system. The role of the Alliance need not be equated with that of Labour in the 1920s as a party about to take its place in a realigned political system. Rather its role may come to bear more similarity to that of some of the new parties which have arisen in recent years in many Western democracies.

In Western Europe, many of these new parties have been of the 'protest' variety – Democrats 66 and Democratic Socialists 70 in Holland, the Centre Democrats and Mogens Glistrup's Progress Party in Denmark, together perhaps with the Green parties in West Germany and France. None of these parties has yet been able to achieve an electoral breakthrough despite some initial successes. Moreover, the history of right-wing breakaways from social democratic or labour parties in Western Europe and Australia shows how difficult it is to supplant parties enjoying an institutional or organisational base and a solid core of party support. In France, the socialists who opposed the Common Programme between socialists and communists were routed in the Assembly elections of 1978, even though the Programme itself was a dead letter by then; in Italy the breakaway PSDI polls consistently less than the Socialists; while in Australia, the Democratic Labour Party (originally known as the Anti-Communist Labour Party) managed to secure 9.4% of the vote in its first electoral test in 1958, but now maintains only the most tenuous political existence. In Denmark, Erhard Jacobsen's breakaway Centre Democrat Party succeeded in attracting 51,000 signatures of support in 1973 (equivalent to half a million in a country the size of Britain) but secured only 7.8% of the vote in the legislative elections of that year.

Admittedly the Alliance is likely to perform somewhat better than these parties, and to remain as a third force in the political system. This is because dissatisfaction with the major parties is far deeper in Britain and therefore more voters will be willing to experiment with an 'unsound' alternative. Moreover, the leaders of the Alliance enjoy more credibility than the leaders of the new parties on the Continent, or past leaders of the Liberal Party, and they are more popular with the electorate than the leaders of the two major parties. For this reason, it is perfectly conceivable that the Alliance might be able to take advantage of short-term discontents so as to propel itself into government. But this would probably be the result of a high degree of alienation from the two major parties rather than enthusiasm for the Alliance itself or its policies. An Alliance government would represent a negative coalition of diverse discontents, rather than a positive desire to 'break the mould' of British politics. A government formed on such a basis would have difficulty in formulating a set of coherent policies equally satisfying to all of its supporters in an electoral coalition containing mutually incompatible elements.

Whether it succeeds in winning a place in government or not, the formation of the Alliance is likely to accentuate trends towards a more volatile and unstable political system. This volatility was, of course, already a feature of electoral reactions in the 1970s well before the formation of the Alliance. By contrast to the 1950s, when opinion between elections seemed to remain fairly stable, the evidence of the polls indicates rapid short-term swings in the popularity and unpopularity of the parties between elections; and this has been especially marked since the 1979 general election.

In such an uncertain situation, short-term factors, perhaps occurring in the election campaign itself, will increasingly come to influence voting decisions. Twenty years ago, the conventional wisdom among students of elections was that events occurring during the election campaign were unlikely to exert any significant influence upon the result. The same cannot be said today. 'Between 1964 and 1979 the proportion of voters who left their final decision until the last week or two of the campaign jumped from 17% to 28%, and the proportion claiming to have thought seriously of voting differently in the course of the campaign rose from 24% to 31%.'[12]

In a political system of this kind, parties may well secure election victories on essentially short-term factors which rapidly evaporate. The mandate argument will lose what little credibility it ever had; indeed, governments will find it increasingly difficult to mobilise an electoral

---

[12] Crewe, 'Is Britain's two-party system really about to crumble?', p. 278.

coalition sufficiently cohesive and long-lasting to enable their policies to be presented with any degree of democratic legitimacy at all. The Commons will come to represent less a mirror of the opinion of the nation, than the result of a well-timed dissolution or the fortuitous exploitation of a campaign issue. In such a political climate, the argument for proportional representation so that a wide variety of interests may be more adequately reflected in the Commons, is likely to be heard with increasing insistence. Indeed the political system and the Constitution itself are likely to come under increasing strain. The rest of this book is devoted to a discussion of these changes. Chapter 4 considers the effects of multi-party politics on the political system, while Part II evaluates the consequences for the Constitution, so many of whose conventions depend upon the implicit assumption of a stable two-party system. When that assumption is removed, the consequences for the political system and the Constitution will be wide-ranging indeed.

4

Multi-party politics and the future

The British political system, then, is likely to become increasingly volatile and unstable. The decline of class feeling and the weakening of the class/ party link have led to electoral dealignment which it will be difficult for the political parties to combat. But it will not be impossible. For politicians are not condemned to passivity in the face of social and electoral trends. They will do their best to adapt to the needs of the day; instead of remaining at the mercy of social change, the parties will seek to take advantage of it. Indeed, the role of the party leader is likely to assume greater importance when old alignments are melting than during a period of stability. He will attempt to forge new electoral coalitions and to redefine old ideologies so as to create new constituencies of support.

Political parties maintain their existence because they represent major cleavages which are persistent and long-lasting. These cleavages may be socio-economic, religious, ethnic or political. Political parties are, as it were, an institutional expression of a country's historical continuity, a mirror-image of the conflicts which past generations have found important. But with the decline of the dominant class cleavage in British politics, a space is opened up for other, hitherto subordinate, cleavages, to make themselves felt. Already, during the 1970s, new issues such as Britain's membership of the EEC and devolution revealed divisions within the parties as well as between them. It is significant that during this decade party discipline began to loosen and cross-party coalitions on such issues as the EEC and devolution came to be formed.

The formation of the SDP goes some way towards the creation of a more rational party structure, in which party distinctions correspond more to divisions of opinion amongst the electorate. The SDP has detached from Labour not admittedly the whole of its Right wing, but that section of the Right which regards Britain's membership of the EEC as the touchstone of social democracy in Britain. Yet, of course, there remain important cross-currents within the major parties. Even the issue of the EEC still divides opinion within the parties rather than between them; for Labour still has a minority of EEC supporters amongst its MPs, while the Conservatives have a minority against. The division of opinion on the EEC represents, in essence, a political cleavage between nationalists and internationalists, separating the centre in British politics – the Labour Right, the Alliance and the bulk of Conservative MPs – from the Left of the Labour Party and a small number on the Tory Right. On this issue the real political division is more one between the centre and the extremes, rather than between Left and Right.

The issue of constitutional reform also divides the centre from the extremes rather than the Left from the Right. The Alliance, of course, is committed not only to proportional representation, but also to devolution, decentralisation, a Bill of Rights and the reform of Parliament. The decentralist/centralist cleavage puts the Alliance, together perhaps with the Scottish and Welsh Nationalists, against the two major parties, although the Alliance will find difficulty in reconciling its decentralist philosophy with its commitment to economic planning and its support for an extension of the Welfare State. On proportional representation, the Alliance is joined by a section of the Tory Left, but by hardly any on the Labour Right, although this could change if the Labour Party is faced with the choice of joining a coalition with the Alliance or condemning itself to perpetual opposition. The strongest opponents of proportional representation are to be found on the Tory Right and the Labour Left, both of whom regard power-sharing as a barrier to the establishment of the kind of society which they advocate.

The economic cleavage also serves to mark off the centre from the Labour Left and Tory Right. For the Alliance shares with the Labour Right and Tory Left a commitment to the mixed economy without fundamental alterations in the ownership of industry or in the balance between public and private expenditure. The Labour Left, on the other hand, is committed to the achievement of a socialist society, while the Conservative Right seeks to create – or re-create – a free market economy in which the balance between public and private expenditure would be very different from what it is today.

There is, finally, a new cleavage emerging in British politics, around what might be called issues of a populist/authoritarian kind – nationhood, immigration, race, crime, law and order – which serve to differentiate the Tory Right from other groups on the political spectrum. These populist/authoritarian issues have been given greater prominence in the Conservative Party since Mrs Thatcher won the leadership of the Party in 1975. They arouse particularly strong if not atavistic emotions, amongst many of the electorate. And, since those who hold strong feelings on such questions come from all social classes and from the supporters of all parties, their exploitation offers an opportunity for the Conservative Party to construct a new electoral constituency, based on opinion rather than socio-economic factors. This cleavage around populist/authoritarian issues may therefore come to assume increasing importance in British politics.

We may now schematise these four issue cleavages – national/international, constitutional, economic, and cultural in the following way.

1. *EEC: National/International*

LABOUR	ALLIANCE	CONSERVATIVE
Left _____ Right		
ANTI-EEC	PRO-EEC	ANTI-EEC

2. *PR: Constitutional*

LABOUR	ALLIANCE	CONSERVATIVE
Left _____ Right		
ANTI-PR	PRO-PR	ANTI-PR

3. *Economic*

LABOUR	ALLIANCE	CONSERVATIVE
Left _____ Right		
SOCIALISM	MIXED ECONOMY	FREE MARKET

4. *Cultural: Populist/Authoritarian*

LABOUR	ALLIANCE	CONSERVATIVE
Left _____ Right		
	LIBERAL	POPULIST AUTHORITARIAN

These diagrams show clearly that the centre – the Alliance – is far more cohesive in terms of political opinion, than either the Labour or Conservative Parties which remain cross-cut by conflicting cleavages. Labour continues to emphasise the once dominant class cleavage, while the Conservatives seek to amalgamate different interests – industrial, financial, agricultural, together with a section of the working class – by means of an appeal to the national interest and the ideology of 'One Nation'. However, these traditional stances no longer coincide either with social reality, or with the natural division of opinion on political issues. The two major parties, therefore, appear less as cohesive agencies of political representation than as uneasy and incompatible coalitions held together as much by the needs of electoral survival as by common political beliefs. With an electoral system which reflected more closely genuine divisions of political opinion, therefore, party fragmentation and realignment might well have occurred before 1981. Under a proportional system, for example, the Liberal vote of 19.3% in February 1974 would have probably led to Liberal participation in a coalition government, and therefore Liberal influence on policy. For a proportional electoral system *reflects* changes of opinion in society; it acts as a seismograph registering fault lines in the political system. The plurality system, on the other hand, *refracts* change so that it cannot be seen by the naked eye until it finally erupts. It is for this reason that the important social and ideological changes which have been occurring in Britain in recent years have not made more impact upon the party system. Yet, even so, the wide gap between a rapidly changing political culture and a relatively unchanging party structure cannot for ever be bridged by the electoral system, and as the gap becomes unbridgeable it is likely to lead to great changes both in the alignment and even in the basic role of the political parties.

II

Changes in party alignment might occur in two different ways, either through the entrenchment of a multi-party system, or through polarisation. Which of these alternatives actually comes about depends upon the coherence and strength of the centre in British politics, and the extent to which the intra-party conflicts in the two major parties can be resolved through skilful leadership. To entrench a multi-party system, the Alliance would have to secure proportional representation. For at present, three major political groupings exist within an electoral system geared to the alternation of two parties in office, and a constitutional structure which also assumes a two-party system. Three groupings reside uneasily in a two-party political system.

With electoral reform, by contrast, the Alliance could quickly become a permanent hinge grouping, open to coalition from Left or Right. It would therefore play a major role in holding the party system together, and through the centripetal pressure which it could exert, help to re-establish that agreement on fundamentals which has always been held to be the hallmark of British democracy. Moreover, as with the FDP in West Germany, the Alliance could re-establish a bi-polar alternation of governing coalitions in place of a centrifugal conflict between two parties with entirely different conceptions of the nature of society and indeed of the conditions of political competition itself. It is in this way that, paradoxically, electoral reform would enable a tri-polar party system to sustain a bi-polar alternation of government. The consequences of a multi-party system of this type would not, however, necessarily prove beneficial. Whether it secured an accurate representation of electoral opinion would depend upon the extent to which opinion remained near the centre of the political spectrum, or whether, under the impact of recession, it moved to the extremes. One danger of a centripetal, tri-polar system would be a growing gap between politics at elite level, where coalitional bargaining and compromise would become important ways of resolving conflict, and politics at electoral level, where disenchantment with consensus politics might set in. If that occurred, it might prove difficult for the electorate to make its views felt. A political system of the West German type can work successfully as long as the opinions of the electorate remain distributed around the centre; and indeed, it may be argued that such a system actually assists in the process of building consensus. But, with a wider distribution of electoral opinion, it could lead to a growing mistrust of politicians, and even to the growth of new extremist parties, outflanking the Labour and Conservative Parties, whose blackmail potential would counteract the centripetal pull of the centre. There would be a danger of immobilism at the centre, and extremism from those outside the political consensus. The argument for a multi-party system, therefore, must depend upon assumptions as to how electoral opinion is distributed, and in particular a belief that worsening economic trends will not lead to a polarisation of opinion.

A presupposition behind this model is that the electorate's basic desire is for political stability, a desire frustrated by the polarisation of the two major parties. The programme of the Alliance which seeks to re-establish consensus, is in large part restorative, catering for this desire for continuity. But if the failures of government shift the electorate in a radical direction, the Alliance may find it difficult to respond. One way in which it has been suggested that the Alliance may adopt a more radical stance is to create a new issue cleavage around the issue of 'powerlessness'. The negative feeling of alienation which is a powerful source of Alliance support could be utilised by a party hostile to the pretensions of the trade unions and big business, and sympathetic to worker participation, the rights of minorities and racial and sexual equality. Such a programme might well prove an analogue to what the nineteenth-century Liberal

Party attempted in the era before, in John Vincent's words; 'popular politics changed from being about power to being about bread'.[1] For the *raison d'être* of the nineteenth-century Liberal Party was an attempt to ensure the self-respect of the nonconformist middle class against the Anglican Church and the landowner; and Gladstone's popularity derived from the fact that he offered 'the possibility of participation ... a sense of power and domination – to people normally entirely subject to circumstances and to other people. The permanent issue behind Midlothian and Reform and Home Rule was what kind of people should have power, in whose name, and in accordance with whose ideas.'[2] So, too, the Alliance might prove the vehicle of the unorganised and powerless to be mobilised against the centres of power in modern society. But such a stance would require a radical and populist assault on Westminster and Whitehall quite alien to the instincts of the leadership of the Alliance or to those of many of its members. For, as John Bright told his wife in 1860, 'argument had never wrested anything from the monopolists of power, political and ecclesiastical, and "something more is wanted to bring about change in this country"'.[3]

III

There is, however, an alternative future for British politics based not on a radicalism of the centre, but a radicalism of the Right. So far, the assumption has been that radical feeling in Britain would be anti-Conservative in nature, directed against the government of Mrs Thatcher and mobilised by the parties of the centre. But it is a fallacy to believe that radicalism is necessarily associated either with the Left or with the centre. Might it not be that modern Conservatism itself becomes radical in nature? This would involve an assault upon the Keynes/Beveridge consensus, through the rolling back of the frontiers of state control and a drastic reduction of welfare provisions.

The basis of the political philosophy put forward by those Conservatives reacting against the consensus politics of the Macmillan era, was a reassertion of Britain's strength in the world, the restoration of a free market economy, and a return to traditional moral values. These policies, if they are to be taken seriously, require radical rather than evolutionary change. For this reason, it would be difficult to regard the Conservative victory of 1979 as a victory for the status quo or for traditional conservatism. The question is whether such a political philosophy is capable of

[1] John Vincent, *Pollbooks* (Cambridge University Press, 1967), p. 49.
[2] Ibid., p. 45.
[3] John Vincent, *The Formation of the Liberal Party, 1857–1868* (Constable, 1966), p. 189.

securing for the Conservative Party a mass base to replace the voting strength which it lost when its central symbols – Empire and Church – ceased to enjoy political resonance; and when it is difficult for the Conservatives to pose as the party of superior competence in managing the economy. The striking popularity of Enoch Powell who, from 1968, championed a similar mixture of nationalistic politics, neo-liberal economics and traditional morality, would seem to show that such a policy mix might indeed prove successful in securing a mass base for a party of the Right. In other democracies, too, parties such as Ronald Reagan's Republicans, Jacques Chirac's Gaullists and Menachem Begin's Likud, have deserted conservatism for a militant and radical populism whose appeal can be directed to sectors of the electorate hitherto resistant to the appeal of the Right. If the Conservative Party were to adopt such a stance, it would, of course, have distanced itself considerably from the Party of Baldwin or Macmillan, and its doctrines would come to owe little to those propounded by Burke and Disraeli. In the past, the Conservative Party has been dominant in British politics when the electorate has desired stability and calm, and the hegemony of Salisbury, Baldwin and Macmillan alike was based on the skilful exploitation of this feeling. The Conservatism of the radical Right, by contrast, is a response to instability and cultural frustration, born of dissatisfaction and a widespread feeling of powerlessness and anomie.

Although it is difficult to assess trends amongst a large number of different democracies with very disparate historical traditions, it would hardly seem that, in a comparative perspective, the prime beneficiaries of economic crisis and social upheaval have been the forces of centrism and moderation. A radicalisation of the electorate under the pressures of economic decline could, therefore, take strange and unfamiliar forms. Indeed one consequence of the economic recession which followed the Yom Kippur War of 1973 has been a loss of faith in Keynesian economics, and a much greater scepticism as to the role of government in economic affairs. In a number of democracies, monetarism has become a new economic orthodoxy, despite the fact that it has not so far been conspicuously successful in achieving economic recovery. However, those parties of the Right which have embraced the creed of free market economics have done so as much for moral and cultural reasons as for economic ones. The belief which unites Ronald Reagan, Margaret Thatcher, Jacques Chirac, Franz Josef Strauss and Menachem Begin is that the free market provides the only framework within which the values of individual choice and responsibility can flourish; and these values are held to be not only a means to economic progress, but good in themselves. For this reason, the failure of governments of the Right to secure economic recovery has not undermined the ideology upon which parties of the Right have based their actions; nor has it yet made the economics of the free market unfashionable.

Moreover, the economic philosophy of parties of the Right has been buttressed by a cultural appeal – called earlier populist/authoritarian. For the area of individual responsibility and choice covers a much wider field than the economic, and many politicians of the Right believe that 'permissive' reforms of the abortion, homosexuality and criminal laws have weakened the incentive to individual responsibility. The issues of immigration and race also give rise to fears that national identity is being eroded. This mixture of nationalism, free market economics, with a reassertion of the values of choice and responsibility – frequently linked, as in the United States, with religious revivalism – has become the basis of the appeal of the Republicans in the United States, the French Gaullists, Strauss' Christian Social wing of the West German Christian Democrats and Menachem Begin's Likud. It is perfectly possible that the British Conservative Party may come to adopt a similar approach. The euphoria which followed the victory in the Falklands in 1982, and the attempt by many Conservatives to link military success to the moral virtues of neo-liberalism – individual responsibility, self-discipline, and deferred gratification – may prove a harbinger of what is to come.

The assumption behind such a stance is that the electorate, far from desiring the restoration of consensus, seeks the dismantling of what it regards as the creation of a liberal elite divorced from the people. The politics of powerlessness is less likely to be an instrument of the Alliance which seems ill-equipped to act as an instrument of radical populism capable of battering down resistance in Westminster and Whitehall, than of a radicalised and populist Right differing as much from traditional conservatism as modern liberalism differs from that professed by Adam Smith or J. S. Mill.

In the absence of economic recovery such a strategy might prove to be a logical one for the Conservative Party to pursue. It offers the hope of creating a new cross-class electoral constituency supporting the Party, united less around economic issues than around cultural and nationalist ones. A period of economic restrictionism, such as Britain appears likely to experience, seems likely to increase cultural tensions, for it will no longer be possible to resolve conflict through the ameliorative influence of economic growth. Conservatism could base itself upon cultural frustrations rather than the cautious empirical approach to politics which has generally characterised it in the past.

There is no evidence as yet that parties of the Right have been able to construct a majority electoral coalition around the exploitation of such populist/authoritarian issues. Governments in Western democracies are still mainly judged by their success in managing the economy, and economic failure is still the main reason why governments lose elections. But if the electorate comes to believe that governments are relatively impotent in economic matters, then issues of nationalism, culture and race may come to the fore. Indeed, economic failure may come to be blamed less upon the ineptitude of government than upon an internationalist liberal elite, a permissive moral code or the erosion of national values by alien racial minorities. If that happened, there could be a decisive movement of electoral opinion towards the Right. This would not necessarily mean that right-wing parties would always be in power; what it would mean is that the political agenda will be set by parties of the Right, and parties of the Left would have to adapt themselves to this situation; just as, from 1945 to the mid-1970s, the basic agenda of politics in Britain was set by the Left, and in particular by the post-war reforms of the Labour government, so that parties of the Right had to accept these achievements if they wished to compete electorally. By contrast to the post-war period, however, the dominance of the Right could lead to polarisation, not consensus; and the centre, far from coming to be the pivot of the system, could easily be swept away. Such a transformation of the political agenda in the direction of the radical Right has not yet occurred in Britain. But there is no inherent reason why it could not happen.

IV

A further possibility, and perhaps the most likely, is that neither of these changes – a movement towards the centre or a polarisation of politics through the building-up of a radical Right – will prove sufficient to secure the hegemony of one particular political grouping. Instead, transient coalitions will form around particular issues, and party lines will remain fluid. There will be new and stable political alignments only if the factors of instability and volatility in voting behaviour which have caused dealignment are strictly temporary phenomena. Yet there is no reason to believe that they will be speedily reversed. What is far more probable is that their continuation will alter the *nature* of party politics in Britain, undermining the centrality of party in the political process. Changes in electoral perception will affect the *role* even more than the alignment of parties in Britain.

During the period of mass suffrage, parties have been central to democracy. They have been the basic form through which political representation has taken place. It is parties which have created the political agenda, and, by communicating to and mobilising the mass electorate, it is parties which have secured the adherence of voters to political programmes which they have proposed. The fundamental purpose of party activity has been conceived to be the organising of public opinion, and the clarification of political choice. Both of these purposes presuppose that parties are themselves cohesive and stable institutions, so that they are capable of organising the electorate into different political camps. And, just as Bagehot defined the Cabinet as 'a *hyphen* which joins, a *buckle* which fastens, the legislative part of the state to the executive part of the state',[4] so we might, by analogy, claim that party in Britain as in other Western democracies has been the hyphen which joins the electorate to government, the transmission belt between the demands of the people and the response of the state.

In the modern democratic state, the basic form of the political party has been the 'catch-all party', the party which, disdaining religion and ideology alike, seeks, after the fashion of a commercial organisation, to maximise its 'revenue', its vote. The concept of the 'catch-all party' is derived from the German–American political sociologist, Otto Kirchheimer, whose analysis lies within the context of a political sociology derived from Max Weber, and is designed to show the falsity of the view that the development of industrial society will inevitably lead to the intensification of class conflict. For Kirchheimer as for Weber, capitalism could develop without perpetual crises, and class divisions were only one of the forms of social stratification within a modern industrial society. Indeed, economic progress would tend to the dissolution of rigid social divisions, and this would be bound to affect political parties. For those parties which clung to older ideologies when social distinctions and the political views based upon them were becoming more fluid, would inevitably narrow their potential constituency: so also would parties which clung to a religious basis in an increasingly secularised world. The party of ideology, therefore, or what had been called the party of mass integration, which, like the German Social Democrats before the First World War, looked after its adherents 'from the cradle to the grave' was, on this view of the evolution of industrial society, doomed to electoral decline. Kirchheimer declared:

Modern industrial society has contributed to breaking down barriers among various elements of the new employed middle class, the skilled workers, the middle ranks of the white collars, and the civil service ranks. Similarities of situation and expectations outweigh existing traditional distinctions, even though we are far from the unified middle class society stressed by some authors ... the struggle between the independent old middle class and the employed new middle

---

[4] Bagehot, *The English Constitution, Collected Works*, vol. 5, p. 212.

class is more a struggle for larger shares of similar social welfare provisions than a clash of incompatible programmes. The impact of this change in social structures permeates all political parties, whatever their official label. The lower degree of social polarisation is to be seen in other groups as well as among the middle classes ... The consequences are more rational party structures, less bound by ideology. This fact eases inter-party relations and increases the parties' potential to develop – below a thin veneer of ideology – many features of an interest-market.[5]

The majority, though by no means all, of the political parties in Western Europe have followed the path predicted by Kirchheimer. Religious parties have become secularised, and socialist parties have become Revisionist. Parties such as the German Christian Democrats, and even, to some extent, the Italian Christian Democrats, have in practice become secularised conservative parties, while the MRP in France has merged into the conservative UDF. Most socialist parties in Western Europe have followed the example of the German Social Democrats, who at Bad Godesberg in 1959 abandoned any pretence of Marxism, and became a party dedicated to maintaining and improving the mixed economy. The British Labour Party is exceptional in retaining through Clause 4 its commitment to socialism. Kirchheimer believed that

Such parties face the same difficulties in recruiting and holding intensity of membership interests as other political organisations. Yet, in contrast to their competitors working within the confines of the existing political order, they cannot make a virtue out of necessity and adapt themselves fully to a new style of catch-all people's party. This conservatism does not cost them the confidence of their regular corps of voters. On the other hand, the continued renewal of confidence on election day does not involve an intimate enough bond to utilise as a basis for major political operations.[6]

Writing in the context of 'two old class mass parties, the French and the Italian Communist parties', Kirchheimer's remarks provide with uncanny accuracy a diagnosis of the problems besetting a party such as the Labour Party which has refused to acknowledge the facts of social change. Of course, the majority of governing parties in Western Europe have been willing to adapt, as they must if they are to survive electorally. During an era in which intellectual and social developments alike have cast doubt upon the explanatory value of religion and ideology, so also the political parties of the West have come to reflect this transformation. They, like so much in the modern world, are children of an age of relativism.

[5] Otto Kirchheimer, *Politics, Law and Social Change* (Columbia University Press, 1969), pp. 271–2.
[6] Otto Kirchheimer, 'The transformation of the Western European party systems', in J. LaPalombara and M. Weiner (eds.), *Political Parties and Political Development* (Princeton University Press, 1966), p. 361.

The 'catch-all' party, then, seemed a rational response to the processes of development in advanced industrial societies. Yet in jettisoning ideology, and developing, as Kirchheimer put it, 'many features of an interest-market', the parties at the same time weakened their relationship to particular social groups which had offered them a loyal clientele and therefore a stable basis of support. Parties ceased to be able to rely upon social solidarity, and were forced to depend upon success in governing if they were not to lose support to their opponents. How in such circumstances could parties hope to retain loyal supporters?

The concept of party identification was an attempt to explain how party loyalty could remain in the absence of powerful solidarity structures, since the electorate would support the policies or be attracted to the 'image' for which the party stood; and, although it has weakened in Britain over the last two decades, party identification still remains higher than in many comparable democracies. Nevertheless, even in Britain, party identification is no longer sufficiently strong for the parties to be able to rely upon the loyalty of a stable and relatively immobile segment of the electorate willing to place party allegiance before a pragmatic conception of the public interest. That, after all, is no more than is implied by the notion of the 'catch-all party' and the social changes which have brought it about. In place of an electorate divided into discrete segments, each of which consists of party stalwarts, the electorate becomes fluid and volatile. It can no longer be mobilised by parties lacking a record of political success, such as has eluded parties in Britain since the 1950s.

Yet, does not the centrality of party in the institutional structure of Western democracies depend precisely upon the assumption of a fundamentally loyal and stable electorate? As the stark divisions of the industrial era come to be replaced by the fragmentation and even the balkanisation of society into numerous competing and shifting groups, how can stable political alignments be formed; and if they cannot be formed, what role can parties play in an advanced industrial society? These questions are raised by the social context within which the 'catch-all party' has been given life, and they are posed with particular sharpness in the case of Britain where social conflict is given its cutting edge by precipitate economic decline and the seeming incapacity of governments to do anything to ameliorate it.

What is happening in Britain, as in other advanced democracies, is the gradual detachment of public opinion from party choice. The parties no longer come to be seen by the electorate as guides, they are no longer central in the formation of the political agenda; while their pedagogic function comes to be taken over by the mass media which can communicate to the electorate in a more balanced and informative way than the parties have ever been willing to do. Nor is the 'catch-all party' in general cohesive enough to be a wholly successful agency of representation; for, in the absence of an ideological base, its unity is established through a process of bargaining and accommodation between its constituent parts, and it is no longer held together through the cement of shared belief.

For these reasons, parties have found themselves ill-equipped to cope with the pressures for participation made by an increasingly educated electorate voting on the basis of issues rather than party loyalty. In Britain, party membership has declined by 2 million since the 1950s, while the electorate has increased by 15 million. This decline in membership has occurred despite developments in education and leisure which have increased membership of pressure groups and voluntary activities. The demand for participation in political decisions, therefore, has been satisfied not by the parties but by pressure groups of various kinds, not only interest groups representing particular occupations, but also single-issue groups dedicated to reforms in, for example, education or housing policy as well as feminist groups and the anti-nuclear movement. Because the parties are unable to cope with social change, social fragmentation has been accompanied by political fragmentation, and it has become more and more difficult for the parties to aggregate the various demands made upon them.

One response to these changes, as we have seen in our analysis of developments in the Conservative Party, is for parties to revert to ideology in an attempt to create new stable coalitions of support which can be retained over long periods of time. For the 'catch-all party' finds it difficult to retain the support which it 'catches', while recent electoral developments in Britain and the United States have shown that ideology is by no means the bar to electoral success which it had seemed. Only through the development of a new ideological appeal, it might be suggested, can parties build up the loyal support which might enable them to govern successfully. Such would be the cry not only of Ronald Reagan and Margaret Thatcher, but also of Tony Benn and François Mitterrand. But there is as yet no evidence that, for example, the Republicans or the Conservatives have been able to create the realignment which they have sought. What they have done is to take advantage of what could be a purely temporary disenchantment with their political opponents. They have taken advantage of dealignment, but not succeeded in creating realignment. They have not been able to overcome the trends leading to the weakening of parties which have affected most if not all Western democracies.

Parties, whose function it was to guide the processes of social change, have become to an increasing extent the victims of social modernisation. How will the conflict between a relatively unchanging political structure and a rapidly changing political culture be resolved? It is perfectly possible for the parties to recover their old position if only they can discover the secret of economic revival, or construct an electoral coalition more lasting than a ramshackle agglomeration of support lasting for no more than one or two elections. What is more likely, however, is that parties will lose their crucial importance as agents of representation, and pressure groups and referendums will come to fulfil some of the functions which were formerly fulfilled by parties. Indeed, the more the electorate bases its choice on issues rather than upon party loyalty, the more suited single-issue groups and referendums would be to further the process of democratic choice. It may be that the political party which assumed its main functions during the era of mass suffrage was but a creature of a particular age, and that in a post-industrial society its functions will become severely attenuated. Already, indeed, not only in Britain, but in many other Western European countries, 'there is a pervasive sense of living through a period of transition in which the old forces that provided stability, governmental capacity, and legitimacy have been played out and new ones have not yet come to maturity'.[7]

To carry the analysis any further would indeed be to step too far into the realms of speculation. What should, however, be clear is that the prospects for either a stable two-party system or a stable political realignment in Britain look almost equally remote. Instead, Britain seems likely to enter a period of volatility and uncertainty where the guidelines of the past will become almost wholly irrelevant. The politics of stable majorities and single-party government is not by any means an immutable feature of the British political scene. Indeed, the period of bi-polar alternation of power from 1945 has been the longest in British history in the period of mass suffrage. This type of politics may increasingly come to be seen as the product of a particular political culture, historically rooted, and now passing away. For the British polity, this will leave the fundamental dilemma of how strong government can be secured with weak parties; and for the British Constitution, the problem of how its conventions can be adapted to a system of many parties and shifting coalitions. It is to the second of these questions that the rest of *Multi-Party Politics and the Constitution* is devoted. The first question is one that no political scientist has yet begun to answer. For it relates to a future which has yet to be born.

[7] Suzanne Berger, 'Politics and antipolitics in Western Europe in the seventies', *Daedalus* (Winter 1979), pp. 47–8.

Part II

The constitutional consequences

5

Forming a government: the lessons of history

I

The central consequence of multi-party politics will be that single-party majority government can no longer be assured. This of itself is not so novel as is sometimes supposed. The alternation in power of two single-party majority governments has been the exception rather than the rule in British politics. Before 1945, the British Constitution frequently accommodated itself to coalitions and minority governments, and politicians were forced to contemplate the problems which would arise in the event of no single party gaining power. Indeed, between 1900 and 1945, single-party majority government occurred for only 10 years out of 45 – between December 1905 and January 1910, between November 1922 and January 1924, and from October 1924 to June 1929.

The political climate in the 1980s and 1990s could, however, prove very different from anything which politicians have faced before in the twentieth century, with the exception perhaps of the years between 1922 and 1931. There are, as Chapter 1 showed, two reasons for this. The first is that the formation of the Social Democrat–Liberal Alliance may be producing a tri-polar party system revolving around a sizeable central grouping willing in principle to form a coalition with either the Labour or Conservative parties. Such a tri-polar system existed between 1922 and 1931, but only as a transitional stage until Labour replaced the Liberals as the second party of the state. In other multi-party situations, by contrast, the allegiance of third parties has been taken for granted. The Irish Nationalists could, after 1886, be relied upon to support the Liberals, while the Liberal Unionists were very unlikely to desert the Conservatives. Such parties, therefore, did not disturb the predominantly bi-polar nature of British politics. There were still only two candidates for government – the Conservatives with their allies (Liberal Unionist, Liberal National or National Labour) and a party of the Left – the Liberals until 1922, Labour after 1931. This type of situation is, of course, much easier to manage than a tri-polar system where the permanent allegiance of the central grouping to any single party can never be assured.

Furthermore, this new central grouping – the Alliance – seeks not only to play a part in government, but also to change the very rules of the game, by introducing proportional representation which would make 'hung' Parliaments the norm except on those rare occasions when one party might attain more than around 47% of the vote. Such disagreement about the rules under which elections should be conducted has occurred once in the past, during the years 1922 to 1931, when the Liberals – still potentially a party of government – were not only committed to proportional representation, but seemed to enjoy some chance of achieving it. But this period of tri-polar politics did not in fact last long enough for guidelines to be established which could reliably regulate any system of multi-party politics in the future.

The formation of the Alliance is not, of course, the only reason why hung Parliaments will become more likely. Changes in electoral behaviour would have made single-party government less probable even if the Social Democratic breakaway had never occurred. For it has now become much less likely that the plurality system of election will continue to be able to fulfil its function of giving an overall majority to a single party.

We have already seen that the two major parties have in recent years become more solidly entrenched in their areas of electoral strength –Labour in the North and urban areas, the Conservatives in the South and rural areas. This, as Curtice and Steed have shown, is the result of systematic and cumulative variations in electoral swing since 1955, such that rural areas have increasingly swung to the Conservatives and urban areas to Labour.[1]

A consequence of this change is that there are fewer marginal seats in Britain today than in the past. In 1955, the number of marginals (defined as seats where the Conservative share of the vote was between 45% and 55%), was 166; in 1979 the figure had dropped to 108; while in October 1974, it was as low as 98. A given swing, therefore, has led to a smaller turnover of seats in recent elections than it did twenty or thirty years ago. In 1955, each 1% swing led to 17 seats changing hands; whereas Curtice and Steed estimate the equivalent figure now to be around 10. The 'cube law' which states that if the ratio of the vote for the two leading parties in an election was A:B, the seats would be divided between them in the ratio $A^3:B^3$, no longer offers an accurate prediction of the working of the

1 John Curtice and Michael Steed, 'Electoral choice and the production of government: the changing operation of the electoral system in the United Kingdom since 1955', *British Journal of Political Science*, (1982), 249–98.

British electoral system. The exaggerative effects of the system are much less than they were, and, given the existence of the Alliance and other groupings in the Commons, a greater swing is needed to secure a given overall majority, and thus avoid a hung Parliament.

Curtice and Steed calculate that a swing of between 0.82% and 5.55% away from the Conservatives after 1979 would produce a hung Parliament, or a Parliament in which one party has an overall majority of under 20, probably insufficient to survive mid-term by-election defeats. In fact, six of the ten general elections since 1950 have produced swings within this range of 0.82% and 5.55%. The spatial distribution of electoral opinion, therefore, makes a hung Parliament more likely than it was before the 1970s.[2]

It is important to note that the Curtice/Steed analysis is based upon the assumption that support for third parties remains at its 1979 level. But, of course, with the formation of the SDP and the Alliance with the Liberals, as well as the increase in the number of constituencies in Northern Ireland, this assumption is an implausible one. If third-party support comes to be higher than it was in 1979, then the range of swing leading to a hung Parliament would be considerably wider. So it can be argued that the Curtice/Steed analysis actually *understates* the likelihood of a hung Parliament, rather than exaggerating it.

On the other hand, the greater volatility of the electorate could lead to electoral swings being much larger than they have been for most of the post-war period. The swing to the Conservatives in 1979 was the largest to any party since 1945, while the swing in 1970 was larger than any since 1950. It may be that the electorate has become more prepared to switch its allegiance *en masse* just at the time when the political system requires such behaviour if it is to continue to produce single-party governments.

Nevertheless, despite these countervailing pressures, it is perfectly possible that hung Parliaments will become a more frequent feature of the British political scene; and, if the Alliance can take advantage of a favourable bargaining position in only one such hung Parliament, to secure proportional representation, Parliaments without single-party majorities will become regular rather than exceptional.

Parliaments in which no single party enjoys an overall majority will give rise to novel and serious constitutional problems whose implications have as yet barely been considered by politicians. Conventions of the British Constitution concerning the formation of government and the dissolution of Parliament, which have been hitherto unquestioned, will come under critical scrutiny. The Constitution will be in a state of flux,

[2] Ibid., pp. 270, 293.

and it may well be some time before new conventions are developed to meet new and perhaps recurrent conditions. Before this process hardens, there will be a wide penumbra of uncertainty surrounding the behaviour of both politicians and the Sovereign. It will become more difficult to prescribe how they ought to act in situations which will be far from clear and straightforward either to participants or outside observers.

Multi-party politics will affect the Constitution in a number of different ways. First, it will make the formation of government more complicated, since there will often be more than one potential government capable of surviving in the House of Commons. Second, it might imply that the Prime Minister's right to a dissolution of Parliament can no longer be taken as automatic, something which it has in practice become since the development of the two-party system. Third, the increased likelihood of coalition or minority government will influence conventions relating to Cabinet responsibility and the relationships between government and Parliament. Existing conventions governing these relationships may not survive unscathed during a period when governments will have to rely upon agreement either between coalition partners, or between the Cabinet and Parliament. In each of these areas, the development of multi-party politics will place the Constitution under strain.

II

The conventions regulating the relationship between government and Parliament, and the role of the Sovereign *vis-à-vis* her government are, in general, perfectly clear in a two-party situation. The basic principle defining the relationship between government and Parliament is of course that the government must enjoy the confidence of Parliament. We may call this the principle of parliamentarism. Furthermore, the government is a collective entity, and the Cabinet lives by the convention of collective responsibility, so that its members cannot be picked off by the Opposition one by one. In normal times, of course, when the parties are united, the two-party system ensures that governments are defeated not in the Commons, but by the electorate. Only twice in this century – in October 1924 and March 1979 – have governments been defeated on issues of confidence. Normally it is the voters rather than the Opposition who decide whether the government enjoys the confidence of the country.

In a multi-party system, by contrast, the working of such conventions becomes unclear. It will not always be obvious who should be asked to form a government; nor whether the government of the day, if it represents only a minority of the Commons, should automatically be entitled to a dissolution. Where there is doubt, the Crown could be placed in an uncomfortable position, and the use of her prerogative powers could become the subject of controversy.

A constitutional monarch, while his acts cannot be personal or arbitrary, is nonetheless not a mere automaton, 'a mandarin figure which has to nod its head in assent, or shake it in denial, as his Minister pleases'.[3] He has the advantage of a far longer and more continous political experience than the politicians with whom he deals. 'The principles of the English Constitution', declared Disraeli, 'do not contemplate the absence of personal influence on the part of the Sovereign; and if they did, the principles of human nature would prevent the fulfilment of such a theory.'[4] The Sovereign enjoys Bagehot's famous trinity of rights – the right to be consulted, the right to encourage and the right to warn; and these can give considerable influence to a sagacious head of state.

Yet, as well as influence, the Crown in Britain also enjoys certain prerogative powers, essentially residual in their nature, but powers which could *in extremis* be used to guard the Constitution against abuse – as, for example, if a government sought in peacetime to prolong the existence of Parliament beyond the statutory period of five years. But the central purpose of the Crown's prerogative powers are to ensure the smooth functioning of Parliament; and the main powers which the Sovereign still retains – the nomination of a Prime Minister, and the summoning and dissolution of Parliament – are designed to secure this end.[5]

Of course, a constitutional monarch cannot exercise these prerogative powers at her discretion. For the Sovereign's position depends upon her remaining strictly neutral in political matters and above the party battle. This can be achieved only if the Sovereign acts on the advice of ministers who are willing to assume responsibility for her actions. But the act of nominating a Prime Minister is unique amongst the Crown's powers since necessarily it cannot always be taken upon advice by her present ministers. Indeed, it would be absurd to ask a Prime Minister just defeated in the Commons or at the polls for his advice as to a successor.

The request for a dissolution, unlike the choice of a Prime Minister, is an act which the Sovereign can take on advice. But there remains some doubt as to whether a Prime Minister 'advises' a dissolution, with the

---

[3] Baron Stockmar to Prince Albert, 1854, quoted in Robert Blake, 'The Crown and politics in the twentieth century', in Jeremy Murray-Brown (ed.), *The Monarchy and its Future* (Allen and Unwin, 1969), p. 11.

[4] Quoted in Frank Hardie, *The Political Influence of the British Monarchy: 1868–1952* (Batsford, 1970), pp. 44–5.

[5] Barry Nicholas, 'Le chef d'Etat dans les régimes parlementaires contemporains', in *Parlement et Gouvernement: Le Partage du Pouvoir* (Actes du Colloque de Florence, October 1977).

implication that the Sovereign cannot constitutionally refuse; or whether he can only 'ask' for a dissolution, with the Sovereign being entitled to refuse. In his memoirs, Harold Macmillan insists that in 1959 he 'asked' for a dissolution so as to show respect for the prerogatives remaining to the Crown, although, of course, there could be no question of a dissolution being refused in the circumstances of that year.[6] There are, as we shall see, grounds for arguing that the Sovereign still retains the discretion to refuse a dissolution. But it remains doubtful whether she should ever exercise this discretion except in highly pathological circumstances.

In the ordinary course of events, however, the actions of the Sovereign in nominating a Prime Minister and deciding whether to grant a dissolution create no problems. The normal practice is for the Sovereign to grant a dissolution whether the Prime Minister who asks for it enjoys a majority in the Commons or not. There is, indeed, no case of a Prime Minister being refused a dissolution since before the Great Reform Act of 1832; although Sovereigns have, on occasion, seriously contemplated refusing to grant a dissolution.

The choice of Prime Minister has come to be regulated by simple and straightforward rules presented in their most authoritative form by the constitutional lawyer, Sir Ivor Jennings in his book, *Cabinet Government*. According to Jennings, 'It is an accepted rule that when a Government is defeated, either in Parliament or at the polls, the Queen should send for the Leader of the Opposition.'[7] This is the only way in which the Sovereign can satisfy the principle that not only should she 'in fact act impartially, but that she should appear to act impartially'. There is no case since the advent of universal suffrage when the Sovereign has failed to send for the Leader of the Opposition following the defeat of a government either in the Commons or at the polls. A corollary of the rule, therefore, is that 'before sending for the Leader of the Opposition, the monarch should consult no-one. If she takes advice first, it can only be for the purpose of keeping out the Opposition or its recognised leader.'[8]

Where a government resigns for some other reason, there are also clearly stated rules regulating the Sovereign's conduct, although they cannot be equally precise. When a Prime Minister dies in office, or retires, the major parties each have a recognised procedure for electing a new leader, so the Sovereign is not required to use her discretion. When, however, a government resigns through internal dissension, there is no clear procedure through which a successor is chosen, and no obligation

6 Harold Macmillan, *Riding the Storm 1956–1959* (Macmillan, 1971), p. 750.
7 Sir Ivor Jennings, *Cabinet Government* (3rd edition, Cambridge University Press, 1959), p. 32.
8 Ibid., pp. 32, 40.

upon the Sovereign to call for the Leader of the Opposition. Her actions, however, must still be guided by the rule that she has to find a government capable of surviving in the House of Commons.

In a multi-party system, the rules laid down by constitutional authorities such as Jennings lose a good deal of their value, for they will cease to prescribe unique solutions. If, after a general election, a government retains the largest number of seats, but lacks an overall majority, has it been 'defeated' or not? Is a minority government which may have been in office for only a short time entitled to a dissolution as and when it pleases? What is the meaning of the principle of parliamentarism, that the government must enjoy the confidence of the Commons, in such a situation? Does it mean that the government commands the support of a majority in the House, or merely that no majority *against* it can be found, no majority prepared to bring it down? The principle of parliamentarism no longer uniquely defines which party should form a government, especially if the parties are internally divided when a number of possible coalition arrangements might be possible. It is in these circumstances that the Sovereign's discretion comes to be enlarged while the rules which guide her use of this discretion cease to provide authoritative landmarks. In such circumstances there is always the danger that the Sovereign's actions may appear partial to politicians who believe that they have been placed at a disadvantage by them; and if the Sovereign comes to be accused of partisanship, she could be embroiled in the kind of political controversy which could prove perilous to the institution of constitutional monarchy.

III

In any constitutional crisis caused by the advent of multi-party politics, the actions both of the Sovereign and of leading politicians are likely, in the absence of clear constitutional guidelines, to be governed by precedent. For in Britain, legitimacy is conferred not by the inherent logic of publicly accepted rules codified in a constitution, but by habits – Sidney Low's 'tacit understandings' – which become sanctified through experience. Legitimacy is conferred not by logic but by history.

To understand the nature of the problems which multi-party politics is likely to pose for the working of the Constitution, it is therefore first necessary to consult the lessons of historical experience. Unfortunately, however, there is a paucity of relevant precedents upon which to draw. The precedents which have been laid out by constitutional authorities such as Jennings are of limited use because they relate to two quite different political worlds – those before 1867, the dawn of the age of mass suffrage, and those after 1867. Yet for different reasons, neither of these is likely to resemble the political world of the future.

Before 1867, politics was in a sense multi-party politics. For the Commons consisted not of two highly organised and disciplined parties, but of a number of inchoate and shifting groups whose outlines were not often wholly clear even to close observers of the political scene. It was a political world where, in the absence of a wide suffrage or organised parties, there was a much greater degree of independence on the part of the individual MP. The Commons was thought of less as a body representative of the people, than as an instrument for sustaining the Queen's Government. Leading politicians, drawn almost wholly from the landed aristocracy, were entirely united upon the need for the Queen's Government to be carried on. Dissolution was regarded not as an appeal to the country to decide upon a new government, but as an unpopular, expensive, trouble-making last resort to escape an otherwise insoluble parliamentary deadlock.

Precedents from such an era, although still of *some* relevance, must clearly be qualified by an awareness of the radically altered atmosphere of contemporary politics. Post-1868 precedents are founded on a quite different conception of the role of government and Parliament. The government is held to represent the people, who normally speak through highly organised political parties. One party generally dominates the government which it forms either alone or with allies; weak governments or hung Parliaments are rare and brief, so premature dissolutions become uncommon and the general assumption is that hung Parliaments are merely an interregnum before a two-party system re-establishes itself.

In a transition period such as the present, the argument will be about the relevance of particular precedents. Those who believe that a multi-party system will remain a permanent feature of politics are likely to look upon pre-1868 precedents with more sympathy than those who are not so convinced. But any attempt to cite older precedents will be suspect unless the changed political environment is borne in mind. The argument will always be about whether, on balance, the older precedents are relevant, or whether the rather rigid and mechanical rules gradually built up since 1868 and codified by Jennings are the relevant ones. In form an argument about constitutional rules, in reality, it is, as we shall see, a dispute about party interests rather than abstract morality.

The precedents which are likely to prove most helpful as a guide to the future are those derived from the brief periods of multi-party politics in the democratic age. For this purpose, analysis of the hung Parliaments of the last period of party realignment in the 1920s, is particularly valuable. But the experience of the years 1974–79 when on two separate occasions the government lacked a majority, is also a useful pointer to what might happen in the future. The bulk of the analysis, therefore, is concentrated upon the experience of these two periods. Earlier precedents will only be cited where these seem to retain continuing relevance.

IV

Since 1918, only three out of eighteen general elections have failed to produce a clear winner – the general elections of 1923, 1929 and February 1974. On each occasion, serious constitutional difficulties might easily have arisen, embroiling the monarchy in the power-play of party advantage. That they were, in the event, resolved satisfactorily owed as much perhaps to luck as to the foresight and judgment of the politicians involved.

On all three occasions, there was some dispute as to whether it would be right for the government – Conservative in each case, as it happens – to meet Parliament, or whether, not having succeeded in gaining a majority, the government was under a duty to resign immediately. In 1923, the Conservatives remained the largest single party after the general election, although they were some 50 seats short of an overall majority. In 1929 and February 1974, the Conservatives were the second largest party, but on each occasion they secured more votes than their competitors. In 1923, the question of who the King should call to the Palace after the Prime Minister resigned, was explicitly broached; while the question of whether a minority government was entitled to a dissolution at a moment of its own choosing became of considerable importance both in 1923–24 and in 1974.

The events following the general election of 1923 were highly complex, and the situation which arose is full of interest as a case study of the problems which can arise in a hung Parliament. They are, therefore, worth discussing in some detail. But first the background to the extraordinary election of 1923 must be appreciated.

V

In 1922 the Conservative/Liberal Coalition led by Lloyd George which had ruled Britain since 1918 was overthrown by a revolt of Conservative back-benchers who refused to accept the advice of their leaders that the Coalition should continue. A purely Conservative government was formed under the leadership of Bonar Law, and Parliament was dissolved in October 1922. Bonar Law's leadership of the Conservatives was, however, by no means secure, since the majority of leading Conservatives, including such figures as Austen Chamberlain, Lord Birkenhead (formerly F. E. Smith), Lord Balfour and Sir Robert Horne, remained loyal to the Coalition. They hoped and believed that Bonar Law would fail to secure an overall majority for the Conservative Party. It would then become apparent that the experiment of resuscitating an independent Conservative Party had failed, and a new coalition between Conservatives and Liberals would be the only way of meeting the socialist threat.

The Liberal Party was also divided, between the supporters of Lloyd George, who, like Austen Chamberlain and Birkenhead, hoped for a revival of the Coalition, and the independent Liberals under the leadership of Asquith who had opposed the Lloyd George Coalition from the Opposition benches since 1918. But it was the Labour Party which had become the official Opposition in 1918. It was the most united of the three parties, and, having adopted a socialist constitution in 1918, it was in no mood to form a coalition with either of the 'capitalist' parties. It sought a socialist majority in its own right, but most of its leaders believed that a long period of education and propaganda would be necessary before that majority could be secured.

In the event, the general election of 1922 gave the Conservatives an overall majority of 37, albeit on only 38.2% of the vote, a consequence of the fact that the Conservatives were competing with three other parties – Lloyd George Liberals, independent Liberals, and Labour. However, the Conservative government of 1922 was destined to prove an ill-fated one, for in May 1923, only six months after assuming office, Bonar Law was found to be suffering from incurable cancer of the throat, and he immediately resigned. Most of the leading Conservatives who might have hoped to succeed him were disqualified as supporters of the Lloyd George Coalition, and the succession went to the relatively unknown Chancellor of the Exchequer, Stanley Baldwin. After six months as Premier, however, Baldwin told the Conservative Party Conference that unemployment was the gravest domestic issue which the country had to face, and that 'if we go pottering along as we are we shall have grave unemployment with us to the end of time'. The remedy, in his view, lay in a protective tariff keeping out those imports likely to damage British manufactured goods. Unfortunately, however, Baldwin was prevented from applying this remedy because of a pledge given by his predecessor Bonar Law that there should be no fundamental change in the fiscal arrangements of the country. 'I am not a man to play with a pledge', Baldwin told the Conference. 'I am not a clever man. I know nothing of political tactics, but I will say this: Having come to that conclusion myself, I felt the only honest and right thing as a leader of a democratic party was to tell them, at the first opportunity I had, what I thought, and submit it to their judgment.'[9]

Baldwin therefore decided to seek the dissolution of a Parliament which was barely a year old. George V tried to dissuade him from this course and indeed went so far as to register a formal protest:

> I then pointed out to him that I strongly deprecated a dissolution at this moment as I had implicit confidence in him and in the Conservative Party now in power, and I considered that as most countries in Europe, if not in the world, were in a chaotic and indeed dangerous state, it would be a pity if this Country were to be plunged into the turmoil of a General Election on a question of domestic policy which will arouse all the old traditional bitterness of the hard fought battles between Protection and Free Trade: also that it was quite possible that his majority might be reduced, or that he might not get a majority at all.
>
> I was therefore prepared to take the responsibility of advising him to change his mind, and I was also prepared for him to tell his friends that I had done so.

But Baldwin was not to be moved.

> He answered that he had gone too far now and that the Country expected a dissolution.[10]

Parliament was dissolved on 13 November, and the election announced for 6 December.

Baldwin's declaration for Protection had the immediate effect of reuniting the two sections of the Liberal Party around the historic cause of Free Trade, and Asquith and Lloyd George came together at public meetings to exchange insincere pleasantries. The leading Coalitionists in the Conservative Party – Austen Chamberlain and Birkenhead – had, perforce, to come to terms with Baldwin, and sustained him as unwillingly as Lloyd George accepted Asquith's leadership.

Labour, the most united of the three parties, fought the election on the basis that socialism was the true answer to Protection. But it did not seriously expect to win. Indeed, according to Beatrice Webb, 'So far as I know, no member of the Labour Party, certainly not any Front Bench man, foresaw the possibility of a Labour Government arising out of the election',[11] and most expected either a continuation of the Conservative government or a renewal of Conservative/Liberal coalition.

Memories of the Lloyd George Coalition, however, and the taint of corruption which adhered to it – Baldwin had regarded the Lloyd George Cabinet as a 'thieves' kitchen' – made most politicians unwilling to

[9] Richard W. Lyman, *The First Labour Government 1924* (Chapman and Hall, 1957), pp. 20–1.
[10] RA GV K 1894/2, quoted in Harold Nicolson, *King George V: His Life and Reign* (Constable 1952), p. 380.
[11] Lyman, *The First Labour Government*, p. 69.

contemplate a renewal of the experiment. Moreover, there was in both the Conservative and Labour Parties at this time a widespread mistrust and fear of Lloyd George. Thomas Jones, Deputy Secretary to the Cabinet from 1916 to 1930, recorded that at Baldwin's Worcestershire home, there was an 'L.G. obsession ... I came across a picture of Lloyd George as Chancellor of the Exchequer defaced. How they do hate him', while the second Labour government of 1929 'like their predecessors, are apparently haunted by the spectre of Ll.G. never absent from the Cabinet Room'.[12] This hatred of Lloyd George on the part of both Baldwin and MacDonald made it very difficult for the Conservative or Labour Parties to contemplate either coalition with the Liberals, or even a tacit understanding with them to sustain a minority government; and the politics of the 1920s cannot therefore be understood without appreciating the widespread antagonism both to coalition and to Lloyd George personally.

The electorate, to the surprise of many, rebuffed Baldwin and denied him a mandate for Protection. The result was as follows:

Conservatives	258 seats
Labour	191 seats
Liberals	158 seats
Others	7 seats

Such a distribution of seats allowed, in the abstract, for a wide variety of possible governments. The Conservatives might seem to have a legitimate claim as the largest single party; but they had failed to obtain a mandate for Protection. Therefore, perhaps Labour as the largest anti-Protection party, should be allowed to govern. Yet Labour had not fought the election solely on a negative programme of hostility to Protection but on its socialist programme; and the electors had given even less of a mandate to socialism than to Protection.

Since the election had been fought on the issue of Protection, there was an argument for the two Free Trade parties – Labour and the Liberals – joining together in a coalition. But Labour saw the Liberals as being a 'capitalist' party, and therefore hardly better than the Conservatives; and there were, in addition, powerful social factors predisposing Labour to a dislike of the Liberals whom they regarded as haughty and patronising in manner.

Socialism, however, had been repudiated at the polls even more decisively than Protection, and there seemed to be a stronger case for an anti-socialist coalition composed of the Conservative and Liberal Parties

---

12 Thomas Jones, *Whitehall Diary*, vol. 1 1916/1925 (Oxford University Press, 1969), p.256; vol. 2 1926/1930 (Oxford University Press, 1969), p. 196.

than for a Free Trade one. The Liberals, although the smallest of the three parties, would seem to be the only party whose programme had not been rejected by the electors; and, as the only party which could co-operate with either of the other two, it would seem to have been put in a particularly strong position by the result of the election. Certainly Asquith saw the situation in much this light. But, as events were to show, the Liberals were quite unable to take advantage of their pivotal role, and their high hopes were to be rapidly dashed.

It was possible, therefore, to argue for any of a range of governments –Conservative/Liberal Coalition, Labour/Liberal Coalition, or minority Conservative, Labour or Liberal governments – depending upon which principle of government formation one believed to be the most important. The outcome, however, would be settled not by determining the relative validity of different principles of government formation, but by the complex process of political manœuvering which began as soon as the election results were known.

VI

The election was held on Thursday 6 December, and the result known the next day. Baldwin returned to London on the Friday, and told his friend Geoffrey Dawson, the editor of *The Times*, that he would resign immediately and would probably be succeeded by a Conservative/Liberal coalition, possibly led by Asquith, in which he, Baldwin, might well participate. On the 8th, Baldwin saw the King's Private Secretary, Lord Stamfordham, and told him that although he 'had come to no decision', his inclination was 'not to meet Parliament but to resign'. 'He had asked the country for a mandate for Tariff Reform, this had been refused, and the honourable thing would be for him to resign at once.' As regards his successor, 'it seemed to him that there were only two alternatives – a Liberal/Conservative Government or a Liberal/Labour Government'. Stamfordham reports Baldwin as saying:

The latter seemed to him almost impossible, as the Labour policy was primarily based upon the two principles of a Levy on Capital and Nationalisation. Also, he did not believe that Labour would coalesce with a Government of which Mr Lloyd George was a member. But he thought that Mr Asquith might form a Coalition with the Conservatives, although there again Mr Lloyd George might be a difficulty.[13]

Baldwin was encouraged in his inclination to resign immediately not only the Premiership but also the leadership of the Conservative Party, by the

[13] RA GV K 1918/14.

Conservative Party Chairman, F. S. Jackson, and his immediate predecessor, Sir George Younger. Their advice was not wholly disinterested, however, since there seems to have been a move in the Conservative Party at this time to replace Baldwin as Party leader by Austen Chamberlain, and so prepare the ground for another Conservative/Liberal Coalition – a reversal, as Cowling puts it, of the verdict of the Carlton Club which had destroyed the Lloyd George Coalition.[14] The Marquess of Lincolnshire, a former Liberal Minister (as Earl Carrington) and confidant of Asquith, wrote in his diary on 8 December with emphasis, '*The general opinion is that Baldwin has made such a mess of it that he must go at once*', and on 18 December, '*There is a Chamberlain–Birkenhead intrigue going on backed by the "Daily Mail"*'.[15] Lord Birkenhead, who lunched with Lord Derby (the Secretary of State for War in Baldwin's Cabinet) on 10 December, told him that Baldwin would resign, that the King would then send for Lord Balfour, the only living Conservative ex-Prime Minister, to seek advice. Balfour would say that Austen Chamberlain should be sent for; and, according to Birkenhead, Balfour thought that this was 'the right course to pursue as it gave the King one other alternative before sending for Ramsay MacDonald'.[16] There was some possibility that Asquith and the Liberals would support a reconstituted Conservative government, and in this way the nation could be saved from the perils of socialism. Certainly the general belief was that, having wantonly thrown away a Conservative majority, Baldwin could not remain as Party leader let alone Prime Minister; and Randolph Churchill, the biographer of Lord Derby, comments that 'It is interesting to notice in Derby's correspondence, and in that of other leading Tories of the time, how for the first two or three weeks after the Party's defeat in the Election there was an unchallenged assumption that Baldwin could not survive the catastrophe.'[17]

However, no sooner was the intrigue launched than Baldwin killed it by the simple expedient of deciding to remain in office and meet Parliament. For, by Monday 10 December, on the same day that Birkenhead told Derby of the plot, Baldwin saw the King and told him that he had decided not to resign. His decision was clothed in the rhetoric of constitutionalism. His supporters, Baldwin said, thought that he should meet Parliament, 'and that former precedent did not apply in this instance, in which the question at issue was one concerning not two but three Parties, and that the House of Commons was the proper place for the choice of the Electorate to be made known'.

---

[14] Maurice Cowling, *The Impact of Labour 1920–1924* (Cambridge University Press, 1971), p. 335.

[15] Diary of Marquess of Lincolnshire, MS Film 1110, pp. 344, 347.

[16] Randolph S. Churchill, *Lord Derby 'King of Lancashire'* (Heinemann, 1959), p. 544.

[17] Ibid., p. 562.

The King approved of this decision, and indeed Lord Stamfordham wrote a memorandum which revealed that the King had seen Balfour on 8 December and told him that, 'If Mr Baldwin wishes to resign, the King will refuse, on the grounds that he is still the head of the largest Party in the House of Commons and for every reason, constitutional and otherwise, it would be right and proper for the Government to meet Parliament and leave it to the representatives of the people to decide whether or not they will support the Government.'[18]

Comments of this type have led some commentators to accept an exaggerated interpretation of the King's role. The King could hardly 'refuse' to accept Baldwin's resignation if Baldwin insisted on going. All that he could do would be to advise him strongly against resigning, and, as he had done when attempting to dissuade him from dissolving Parliament, back up his advice with a formal protest, allowing Baldwin to tell his colleagues that the King objected to the course he was taking. It is therefore quite wrong for Maurice Cowling, whose account of the crisis is by far the best, to write of 'The King's *decision to make Baldwin stay in office.*'[19] (My italics.) The King was in no position to make such a decision and, in any case, Baldwin had already decided to meet Parliament when he met the King on 10 December, and so the King did not even have to persuade him to adopt what he believed to be the correct course.

After telling the King of his new-found resolve to meet Parliament, Baldwin added that he was 'absolutely opposed' to Coalition. He had, after all, played a prominent part in destroying the Lloyd George coalition fourteen months before, and had no wish to be involved in another one. The King responded by asking whether a working arrangement with the Liberals might be possible, and Baldwin said that he would find out.[20] The Cabinet met on Tuesday 11 December and unanimously approved of Baldwin's decision that the government meet Parliament in five weeks' time on 15 January.

With this, the first phase of the crisis was over, and the intrigue against Baldwin collapsed. His continued leadership of the Conservatives, at least until the government met Parliament, was now assured. Had Baldwin resigned immediately after the election, on the other hand, the King might well have sought to ascertain whether another Conservative could have formed a government and secured Liberal support. Baldwin's decision, therefore, limited the options available to the Liberals. If they wished to prevent Labour forming a government, they would have to come to an arrangement with Baldwin, rather than any other Conserva-

18 RA GV K 1918/34; RA GV K 1918/25.
19 Cowling, p. 365.
20 RA GV K 1918/34.

tive; and since the Liberals had only just fought an election opposing Baldwin's policy of Protection, this would be a difficult course for them to take. On the other hand, if the Liberals voted against Baldwin, they would be putting Labour into power, something which many Liberal electors had not envisaged when they had voted Liberal to preserve Free Trade. In making up their minds what to do when faced with the expected no-confidence motion from Labour therefore, the Liberals were put in a most unenviable position.

Asquith, however, was in no doubt as to his course of action. On 18 December he addressed the Liberal MPs assembled at the National Liberal Club, making what one observer called 'the speech of his life'.[21] He began by declaring that Liberal members 'were not sent here by your constituents to play the part of soldiers of fortune to settle squalid fights'. He declared that if either Protection or the capital levy were submitted to the Commons, they would be defeated by a majority of more than 200. Neither the Conservatives nor Labour, therefore, had a chance of retaining or obtaining office unless they abandoned for the time being the principal position which they fought the election to obtain. 'Whoever may be the incumbents of office, it is we who really control the situation.'

Asquith then made it clear that he would do nothing to assist the Conservatives. 'The days of the present Government are numbered. They will go, and they will go with short shrift ... Their record is an almost unbroken one of impotence and humiliation.' In the Debate on the Address when Parliament reassembled, Asquith made clear the reason why the Liberals would turn the government out.

There may be many theories, I have no doubt there are, why we have been sent here by the electorate in such strange proportions. But there is one theory which will not hold water for a moment; and that is, that we were sent here to maintain the present Government in office. It was their election, not ours. It was they, not we, who threw down the challenge. It was they again, not we, who invited the judgment of the electorate. They have got it.[22]

The Liberals, then, would support Labour's amendment declaring no confidence in the government. The consequence would be that the King would send for Ramsay MacDonald, the leader of the Opposition. Labour, however, was determined to govern on its own, without recourse to coalition. How, then, could the Liberals hope to gain advantage from this situation? At the National Liberal Club meeting, Asquith revealed his thinking. He made it clear that he thought a minority Labour government would have no right to a dissolution if it was rapidly

[21] Diary of Marquess of Lincolnshire, p. 352.
[22] H.C. Debs, vol. 169, cols. 310–11, 17 January 1924.

defeated in the Commons. The King could legitimately refuse a request to dissolve for the third time in a little over a year. Asquith claimed:

the Crown is not bound to take the advice of a particular Ministry to put its subjects to the tumult and turmoil of a series of general elections so long as it can find other Ministers who are prepared to give it a trial. The notion that a Ministry which cannot command a majority in the House of Commons ... a Ministry in a minority of 31 per cent ... in these circumstances is invested with the right to demand a dissolution is as subversive of constitutional usage, as it would, in my opinion, be pernicious to the general and paramount interests of the nation at large.

Either, therefore, Labour would govern with the support of the Liberals which would indeed make the Liberals the arbiters of government; or Labour would be defeated in the House, and seek a dissolution which would be denied to them. 'Father asks me to say', wrote Asquith's daughter Violet Bonham-Carter to Winston Churchill, 'that there are an immense number of Dominion precedents for refusing one [i.e. a dissolution] under such conditions.'[23] Asquith would then be summoned to form a government which would be supported by the Conservatives.

Asquith gave Stamfordham his views on how he imagined the situation would develop. He saw the Labour Party's position as a difficult one, and began his conversation with Stamfordham by saying rather patronisingly that in MacDonald's position, he, Asquith, would decline office 'on the grounds that he and his Party were not yet fit to undertake the responsibility'. But if MacDonald did form a government, the Liberals would sit on the Opposition benches. Stamfordham reported:

The next step that he foresaw would be that Mr Ramsay MacDonald comes to the King and asks for a Dissolution: indeed Mr Asquith believes that in accepting office Mr Ramsay MacDonald will very probably ask His Majesty to promise a Dissolution in the event of an early defeat of the Government in the House of Commons ... Mr Asquith considers the King would be constitutionally justified in giving an absolute refusal ... there can be no possible justification for a third Election within a year; and, if on the King's refusal to dissolve Parliament Mr Ramsay MacDonald resigned, and his Majesty sent for Mr Asquith, the latter would accept all responsibility for the King's action. No doubt he himself would have difficulties: but he thought that the Conservatives, without entering into any general undertaking, would support his Government, which would not embark upon any extravagant legislation; and in this way the King's Government might be carried on for another Session or even longer.[24]

Asquith's approach caused some alarm both to the Labour Party and to the King. Labour's suspicions were immediately aroused that Asquith's

---

[23] Violet Bonham-Carter to Winston Churchill, 26 December 1923, in Martin Gilbert, *Winston S. Churchill*, (Heinemann, 1979), Companion vol. 5, pt. 1: The Exchequer Years 1923–1929, p. 87.
[24] RA GV K 1918/67.

speech at the National Liberal Club was part of an 'Establishment' plot to deny Labour fair play, and that a Labour government defeated in the Commons would be denied the right which other governments had enjoyed, of an immediate dissolution. Asquith's remarks, therefore, gave rise to the expression of some anti-monarchical sentiment. The Rev. Campbell Stephen, a prominent figure on the Labour Left, declared that if Labour was refused a dissolution, the monarchy would be in danger. George Lansbury, speaking at Shoreditch Town Hall in January 1924, reminded the monarch that 'Some centuries ago a King stood against the common people and he lost his head.' MacDonald in a speech at Elgin in December voiced his 'suspicion that between now and January ... there was going to be a serious attempt to wangle the Constitution so that the democracy of this country might not have fair play given to them'.[25]

The King, understandably enough, did not thank Asquith for implying that he would deviate from the role of strict constitutionality by denying to Labour what he had given to the other parties. Hugh Dalton, whose father was Canon of Windsor, reports a conversation which he had with Stamfordham at Windsor Castle on 26 December. According to Stamfordham, 'The King frightened by Glasgow speeches, including especially one by Campbell Stephen, saying that if J.R.M [i.e. MacDonald] is refused a dissolution, that will be the end of the Monarchy. The King had rung up S [i.e. Stamfordham] about this from Sandringham. S blames Asquith for raising the constitutional aspects of the right to obtain a dissolution in his recent speech.'[26]

Whatever the constitutional value of Asquith's approach in the abstract, his speech ignored political realities. If he were to defeat a Labour government as soon as it had taken office, the Liberals would be accused of frivolity in precipitating an unnecessary election, especially if Labour contented itself with moderate policies as it intended to do. No one could predict with certainty whether or not the King would grant a dissolution in such circumstances, but his inclination was to ensure that the Labour government be given every privilege that previous governments had enjoyed. The King was particularly anxious to dispel the view expressed by Campbell Stephen and Lansbury that he was hostile to Labour; and he told J. C. C. Davidson, a confidant of Baldwin, on 21 January after the Conservatives had been defeated in the Commons, that 'it was essential that their rights under the Constitution should in no way be impaired'. 'I must confess', Stamfordham wrote to St Loe Strachey, editor of the *Spectator*, '... at the present moment I feel that His Majesty should do his utmost not to hamper in any way Ramsay MacDonald in,

[25] Lyman, *The First Labour Government*, p. 85.
[26] Dalton diary: I: 4: 26 December 1923.

what we must all admit will be, a task of almost incalculable magnitude. And I expect that the King would be interpreting the general feeling of the people of the country that, true to British ideas, the Government, whoever they may be, should have a fair chance ...'[27]

Nor was there any reason to believe that the Conservatives would support an Asquith government when Asquith had been responsible for turning them out of office. Asquith 'rather took for granted', Stamfordham confided to the Archbishop of Canterbury, 'that the Conservatives would help keep him in office, although without any agreement'. The Conservatives, Winston Churchill predicted, with rather more prescience than Asquith, would not 'act as bottle holders to those who kicked us into the street three months ago and deliberately erected this Socialist monstrosity'.[28]

In fact, the first Labour government which took office in January 1924, after Baldwin had been defeated on an amendment to the Address, lasted until October, when the new government in turn was defeated on a Liberal amendment to a Conservative motion which MacDonald chose to regard as a matter of confidence; and the Conservatives rather than the Liberals were to be the beneficiaries of MacDonald's fall.

VII

The defeat of the first Labour government raised the issue of whether the King could refuse a dissolution to a minority government. The King took exceptional care to sound out the attitudes of the party leaders before granting MacDonald a dissolution, and fortunately the situation was so clear-cut that his actions could not be questioned. But George V's method of approach to the problem offers an excellent illustration of how a constitutional monarch resolved what might otherwise have proved an intractable decision.

The motion which was to destroy the Labour government was to be debated on 8 October 1924. But MacDonald was well aware before that date that he faced defeat, and he gave advance notice to the King through a letter to Stamfordham written on 2 October. He warned that in consequence of two motions tabled by the Conservative and Liberal Parties – one relating to a treaty with the Soviet Union which had recently been presented to the Commons, the other on the abandonment

---

[27] Robert Rhodes James, *Memoirs of a Conservative* (Weidenfeld and Nicolson, 1969), p. 191. Stamfordham to Strachey, 14 December 1923, Strachey Papers S/14/12/23. Partially quoted in Nicolson, *King George V*, p. 384.

[28] RA GV K 1918/68; Winston Churchill to Violet Bonham-Carter, 28 December 1923, in Gilbert, *Winston S. Churchill*, p. 89.

of the 'Campbell case' – a prosecution against the *Workers' Weekly*, a Communist newspaper – it might be necessary to ask the King to dissolve Parliament. He also wrote to the King saying that 'coalitions stink so much in the nostrils of our people that to try one now, would be a colossal blunder. I see nothing for it but another appeal to the country as quickly as possible.'[29]

Because MacDonald had given this advance warning, the King, through Stamfordham, was able to discover whether there was an alternative government able to command the confidence of the House of Commons. The extra time available meant that the King could come to a definite decision by the time MacDonald was defeated, and could tell him immediately whether or not he was prepared to grant a dissolution.

On 7 October, Stamfordham arrived in London from Balmoral to consult informally and confidentially with the political leaders as to what course of action the King should pursue. His first visit at 10.45 a.m. was to Sir Ronald Waterhouse, the Prime Minister's Principal Private Secretary, who reported on MacDonald's views which Stamfordham forwarded in a letter sent the same day to the King.

MacDonald clearly did not believe that his right to a dissolution was automatic since Stamfordham's letter contained a number of reasons which MacDonald had put forward as to why he should be given a dissolution. MacDonald first alluded to the precedent of November 1923. Baldwin, he declared, had been granted a dissolution 'when he had an actual majority in the House of Commons, one may say, to gratify a whim of his own viz. protection whereas the PM in a minority is defeated on a question of non confidence'. 'To refuse a General Election', MacDonald (as reported by Stamfordham) continued, 'would only be to postpone it – unless a coalition government were formed which is an improbable if not impossible contingency and if practicable the new Government would only last a few months at most and would then go to the country on their own programme which would certainly be regarded as unfair by the Labour Party.' Moreover, MacDonald argued, 'Refusal of dissolution would be regarded as a slap in the face to the Labour Party who in office form the best buffer to Communism. This anti-Communism undoubtedly represents the *present* Labour mentality – to affront it might result in a rapprochment to Communism in the future.'[30]

After obtaining the Prime Minister's views, Stamfordham then saw Baldwin whose advice was clear and to the point. 'As to a Baldwin–Asquith combination', Stamfordham reported to the King, 'the former said this was not *now* feasible, whatever it might be after a General

29 RA GV K 1958/1; K 1958/4.
30 RA GV K 1958/13.

Election ... If the King sent for him he could not form a Government and speaking for himself he did not see how the King could refuse Dissolution.'[31] After this interview, Stamfordham telegraphed in code to Hardinge, his deputy who was at Balmoral, 'Livy entirely drunk and frivolous. Shall report Virgil's condition later on.'[32] Hardinge was thus able to pass on to the King immediately the news that Baldwin would not himself form a government.

Stamfordham's last call was upon 'Virgil' – Asquith – whom he saw at 3 p.m. Asquith's constitutionalism now came up against the facts of political life. For, according to Stamfordham, Asquith 'thinks on the whole very difficult for the King to refuse dissolution though to ask for it on the Campbell question is very unreasonable'. Asquith argued that although the King had 'the unquestioned "prerogative"' to refuse dissolution, he would have to bear in mind the precedent of the dissolution granted to Baldwin in 1923 'upon really weak grounds'. 'Mr Asquith', according to Stamfordham, 'said an arrangement *might* be possible to help the Conservatives if they took office – but this could only be a temporary makeshift – and that come what may a General Election within a few months is inevitable ... he concluded by stating that on the whole it would be difficult for the King to refuse the Prime Minister's request if it is made ...'[33]

George V now knew with certainty that no alternative government could survive in the House of Commons. Neither Baldwin nor Asquith believed that they could form such a government, and both agreed that the request for dissolution should not be refused. When MacDonald saw the King on 9 October, the day after his defeat in the Commons, and requested a dissolution, the King was in no doubt as to his proper course of action. In Stamfordham's words, 'His Majesty did not hesitate to grant the Prime Minister's request, as he had ascertained that no-one would undertake to form a Government and moreover it was realised that, even if such an arrangement were possible, a General Election was inevitable in the immediate future.'[34]

The King, however, did not content himself simply with granting MacDonald's request; he also made a formal protest. 'While acceding to Mr MacDonald's request for a Dissolution, the King deprecated the necessity for it, and expressed his regret that the Country should be put to the turmoil and expense of a General Election, and also that the Appeal to the Electorate could not have been made upon a more vital

[31] Ibid.
[32] RA GV K 1958/11.
[33] RA GV K 1958/13.
[34] RA GV K 1958/19.

issue than that of the abandonment of the prosecution of a Communist newspaper.'[35] The King subsequently sent MacDonald a memorandum to this effect so that it could be placed on record.

The ensuing general election ended, for the time being, the uncertainties of multi-party politics, for the Conservatives secured a large overall majority with 419 seats, while Labour was reduced to 151, a loss of 40 seats, and the Liberals proved to be the main losers being reduced from 159 seats to 40 – a punishment perhaps imposed by erstwhile Liberal voters for having put a Labour government in office.

VIII

The constitutional crises of December 1923 and January 1924, together with the aftermath in October 1924 are endlessly instructive, revealing with great clarity the political dynamics of a multi-party situation. The first point of interest is, of course, Baldwin's decision not to resign but instead to meet Parliament. His opponents within the Conservative Party could not force Baldwin to go, even though he had been denied a mandate which he had asked for, and thrown away a Conservative majority which could have dominated Parliament for another four years. Many Conservatives – perhaps a majority – would have preferred another leader who might have been able to continue in office, perhaps in alliance with the Liberals, but their views were of no avail.

Under some constitutions where multi-party politics is an accepted feature of political life – Denmark, for example – there is a convention that the Prime Minister resigns after an election if it is at all unclear whether he can carry on; or he may retain office as a caretaker with only limited powers until a new government is formed. In Britain there is, of course, no such convention. The British system of government does not require the Prime Minister to resign immediately after an election. The British Constitution still knows nothing of elections as a method of choosing a Prime Minister; it relies upon the House of Commons to transmit the views of the electorate.

This gives the incumbent Prime Minister enormous influence in the confused situation after an election in which no single party enjoys an overall majority. For, until the Prime Minister resigns there is no vacancy. He is able, as Baldwin did, to secure his position within his party, since his resignation entails also the resignation of the administration as a whole; and there can be no guarantee that another member of his party will be asked to form a government before the Leader of the

[35] RA GV K 1958/9.

Opposition is called. So the Prime Minister has an immensely strong tactical position, which Baldwin did not hesitate to exploit to the full by beating off the challenge against him from within the Conservative Party, and placing the Liberals in the embarrassing position of putting a Labour government into office.

Asquith's dilemma also raises interesting questions. Did he allow a strong bargaining position to slip through his fingers? The assumption on which he acted in putting Labour in office was, as we have seen, that Labour would be compelled to come to terms with him, otherwise it would be replaced by a Liberal minority government. Asquith, as Maurice Cowling has noted, was, in contrast to Baldwin thinking in static rather than dynamic terms, 'not realising the pulling power the Labour Party would have once it had established that it could govern'.[36] He failed to appreciate that Labour, far from wishing to re-create a 'Progressive Alliance' with the Liberals wanted to drive them out of Parliamentary politics altogether. This aim at least Labour shared with Baldwin; for the Conservatives believed, with some justice, that the bulk of the Liberal vote was now anti-socialist and would revert to them upon the demise of the Liberals.

Asquith's strategy would have worked only if no single party had been able to obtain an overall majority at a further election in 1924. Then another rapid dissolution might well have been regarded as unwarranted, a multi-party system could have become entrenched, and either the Labour or Conservative Parties would have been compelled to come to terms with the Liberals. As it was, however, the multi-party Parliament of 1924 proved to be only a transitional stage in the return to the two-party system which, both Labour and the Conservatives assumed, was natural, desirable and inevitable.

Two alternative strategies were open to Asquith, neither of them very palatable. He might first have attempted to make an agreement with a Conservative Party purged both of Baldwin's leadership and of the incubus of Protection by declaring that he would co-operate with any Conservative leader who would support Free Trade. This would give the Conservatives an incentive to replace Baldwin, but it might also arouse resentment that the Liberals were trying to dictate who the Conservative leader should be. Moreover, this strategy might appear as a conspiracy by the two 'capitalist' parties to deny Labour its 'rights'. It might thus serve to intensify class conflict and alienate Labour from the Constitution. Indeed, Baldwin was not alone amongst Conservatives in thinking that there was nothing the Left would like better than an arrangement between the Conservative and Liberal Parties to keep Labour out.

[36] Cowling, *The Impact of Labour*, p. 350.

The second alternative would have been for Asquith to allow Labour to govern, but only under conditions negotiated between the Liberal and Labour Parties. Asquith did not entertain this idea because he believed that it was in Labour's self-interest to co-operate. 'How', Lloyd George asked, speaking of Asquith after the 1924 electoral debacle, 'could he have conjectured that the leader of a great party would have behaved like a jealous, vain, suspicious, ill-tempered actress of the second rank?'[37] 'Looking back', Lloyd George told C. P. Scott, editor of the *Manchester Guardian*, 'he said he felt that the real mistake of the past session had been not the putting of Labour into office but doing so without any understanding or conditions. I confess, he said, it never occurred to me that we could be treated as we were treated. I took for granted that the relations of the two parties would be analogous to those between the Irish and Liberal parties in the Home Rule period.'[38]

But it is not clear that it would have helped the Liberals to have made their support of Labour conditional if MacDonald was determined not to accept any conditions at all. MacDonald had, after all, been summoned by the King to form a government. He was not asked, as he might have been under some constitutions, if he could form a government *supported by a majority in the Commons*. St Loe Strachey, the former editor of the *Spectator*, believed indeed that neither MacDonald nor anyone else should have been given the task 'who has not got pledges of support from leaders representing more than half the house'.[39] If such a condition had been imposed, MacDonald would have had to consult with the Liberals and seek terms. As it was, MacDonald inherited the full plenitude of power as Prime Minister even though he held only a third of the seats in the Commons, and just over 30% of the vote. If he did not wish to accept Liberal co-operation, there was very little the Liberals could do about it, other than defeat him in the House. And if that happened, MacDonald would be very likely to secure a dissolution. There is no reason, therefore, to believe that the strategy suggested by Lloyd George with the wisdom of hindsight, would have been any more successful than that actually followed by Asquith.

The Liberals, it is clear, were not in so strong a position as they had believed. For the assumptions of parliamentary government in Britain are dualistic in nature, and a third party cannot easily make its views felt in the process of government formation. In particular, third parties cannot control the basis on which votes are taken in the Commons, but must

---

37 John Campbell, *Lloyd George: The Goat in the Wilderness* (Cape, 1977), p. 108.
38 Quoted in Chris Cook, *The Age of Alignment: Electoral Politics in Britain 1922–1929* (Macmillan, 1975), p. 194.
39 Strachey Papers, 8 December 1923, S/13/15/40.

vote for or against motions initiated by Government or Opposition. There are no constitutional provisions facilitating conditional verdicts, but rejection of the government is interpreted, *ipso facto*, as endorsement of the Opposition.

Finally, the constitutional difficulties of 1923/4 show how delicately the Sovereign needs to tread if his actions are not to become the subject of political controversy. There is no doubt that George V's approach to the problem of government formation and dissolution showed a masterly understanding of the nature of constitutional monarchy. The King was careful to do nothing to give the impression that he was unwilling to call on Labour to form a government and he took no step which could have been interpreted as encouragement of a Conservative/ Liberal combination to keep Labour out. Once MacDonald was installed as Prime Minister, the King was determined to ensure that he enjoyed the same rights as any other Prime Minister. Although he deprecated a second premature dissolution in October 1924, the King acceded to MacDonald's request, because through his Private Secretary he had already assured himself that no alternative government was feasible. It does not, of course, follow that if an alternative government *had* been available, the King would necessarily have refused Mac- Donald his request to dissolve. The fact that it would have been consti- tutionally possible for him to refuse did not mean that it would necessarily have been right to do so. That would have depended on a number of contentious judgments. The King would have faced a dif- ficult problem, since he would have had a genuine discretion with no clear precedents to guard his behaviour. On balance, perhaps, the safest course might still have been to give MacDonald a dissolution so as to avoid the slightest suspicion that the King was biassed against the Labour Party. But that, of course, is speculative, and no one can know what the King would have done in such circumstances.

IX

The outcome of the crisis of December 1923 to January 1924 was the installation of the first Labour government. It is not clear that such a result was more in accordance with the norms of democratic government than a number of other possible outcomes. For the MacDonald govern- ment, 117 short of an overall majority, replaced a Conservative govern- ment which was only 50 short of that target. As Cowling concludes, the decisions which put MacDonald in office were not made 'out of a feeling that MacDonald had a right to govern which, as leader of the second party in the House of Commons, he manifestly had not. They [i.e. the

Conservative and Liberal leaders] made their decisions because they supposed that a MacDonald government would provide tactical advantages for themselves and restore personal fortunes while giving MacDonald no opportunity to do serious damage to the social order.'[40] The decisions, although clothed in the language of constitutionalism, were in the last resort political ones made by men concerned as much with party – and personal – advantage as with the niceties of constitutional government.

In December 1923, the key decision had been that made by Baldwin not to resign immediately. In 1929, the Parliament elected in 1924, having nearly run its course, was dissolved, and the election, held on 30 May produced another hung Parliament. The result was as follows:

Labour	288 seats
Conservatives	260 seats
Liberals	59 seats

The Conservatives, although having fewer seats than Labour, had a larger share of the vote:

	Votes	*Share of vote*
Labour	8,389,512	37.1%
Conservatives	8,656,473	38.2%
Liberals	5,308,510	27.7%

This time, Baldwin, after contemplating meeting Parliament, decided to resign immediately. He told Stamfordham that 'He had appealed to the people to trust him, as in 1924, and they had refused. He was beaten and he accepts it and thinks this sporting attitude will count in his favour next time. If he hangs on they will say, "Here is this man clinging to office, he won't take his defeat, he is trying to prevent the Labour Party from enjoying their victory."'[41] Yet there was also a political reason for Baldwin's immediate resignation. For if he had attempted to meet Parliament in 1929, it would have looked as if he was seeking to make terms with the Liberals, now led by Lloyd George, and this he was determined not to do. Thomas Jones, the Deputy Secretary to the Cabinet and a confidant of Baldwin's, describes Baldwin's process of thought:

On Friday afternoon, 31st, S.B., Mrs Baldwin, and Duff [i.e. Duff Cooper, a junior minister in the government] had gone down to Chequers to consider

---

[40] Cowling, *The Impact of Labour*, p. 382.
[41] Keith Middlemas and John Barnes, *Baldwin* (Weidenfeld and Nicolson, 1969), p. 527.

quietly whether he should resign at once, or wait for the meeting of Parliament under the Amendment to the Address to be moved by the Labour Leader. On Saturday several of his colleagues visited Chequers, including Davidson, Eyres-Monsell (the Chief Whip), Austen Chamberlain, and Sam Hoare. I arrived at 11.30 on Sunday morning in favour of his meeting Parliament. We talked it out in the study. I found him in a state of great nervous tension, the Ll. G. Obsession weighing heavily upon his mind. Austen was in favour of meeting Parliament; so was Winston. I said very little, but he spoke with great rapidity – most unusual with him, and only possible when roused by Ll. G. It was Ll. G. who had put the Socialists into office, and it was Ll. G. who throughout the day dominated our discussion. What would he do? As the day wore on I moved round to the view that the P.M. ought to resign straight away. Duff strongly held this opinion. What we all feared was that Ll. G. might keep S.B. in office for a week or a month, and humiliate him and his party in every conceivable way. S.B.'s instinct was to go out at once ... If this were not done there would be a scream from Labour that S.B. was denying them the fruits of victory.[42]

The discussion was hardly couched in constitutional terms, and there was no suggestion that Baldwin would be acting unconstitutionally if he were to meet Parliament. The discussion was a tactical one – how would Lloyd George and the Labour Party react? Had he not been so loth to enter into any kind of arrangement with Lloyd George, Baldwin might well have decided to meet Parliament. Instead he could afford to resign immediately, since, by contrast to 1923, he was not faced with any challenge to his leadership. Moreover, because the Conservatives were not the largest party in the Commons, there was no danger of the King calling another Conservative to the Palace who might, unlike Baldwin, be prepared to bargain with Lloyd George and construct a majority government.

Baldwin could, it seems, have decided to meet Parliament as he did in 1923 so as to place on the Liberals the onus of installing a Labour government, but, as the extract from Thomas Jones's diary shows, Baldwin did not trust Lloyd George to act as straightforwardly as Asquith had done. Asquith had immediately declared himself in 1923 as intending to turn the Conservatives out. Lloyd George, on the other hand, might allow the Conservatives to continue in government on sufferance extracting every last ounce of political advantage from the situation. As John Campbell has put it, Baldwin rated 'the fear of being humiliated by Lloyd George higher than the possible advantage to be gained by letting the Liberals be seen to install Socialism in office'.[43]

The truth is that whether a Prime Minister decides to meet parliament or not in a situation in which no single party enjoys an overall majority depends not upon any abstract constitutional rules, but upon whether the Prime Minister wishes, for tactical reasons, to test the *grounds* on which

---

[42] Thomas Jones, *Whitehall Diary*, vol. 2. 1926/1930, p. 192.
[43] Campbell, *Lloyd George*, p. 242.

the Opposition seeks to displace him. This was the course taken by Lord Salisbury after the general election of November 1885 which left him in a minority of 86 against the Liberals, with the Irish Nationalists also returning 86 members. He decided to meet Parliament so as to exhibit the fact that the Liberals could only come to power with the support of the Irish Nationalists. It was to lessen this tactical disadvantage that the Liberals chose to defeat the Conservative government in January 1886, not on an Irish issue, but on the 'three acres and a cow' amendment, an issue of purely domestic policy. Similarly, in 1892, Lord Salisbury, although left in a minority of 40 against the Liberals and Irish National-ists, decided to meet Parliament since he hoped to extract from Gladstone the particulars of the Home Rule Bill which he intended to introduce, and discover how it differed from the first version which had been defeated in the Commons in 1886.

In 1885, 1892, 1923/4 and 1929, the Prime Minister decided on political rather than constitutional grounds whether or not he should meet Parliament. Of course, one of the factors involved in making an estimate of the situation would be his judgment of whether meeting Parliament would make him appear 'unsporting' and unwilling to accept the verdict of the electorate. But that again is a political and not a constitutional argument.

X

This conclusion can be strengthened by moving forward half a century and analysing the most recent occasion when a general election has produced a hung Parliament, February 1974. The election had been called by Edward Heath to counteract the miners' industrial action against his government's statutory incomes policy. The electorate, however, did not give Heath his mandate, and the result of the election was as follows:

Labour	301 seats
Conservatives	297 seats
Liberals	14 seats
Others	23 seats

As in 1929, the Conservatives had won a greater share of the total vote than Labour. The Liberals, although they secured only 14 seats, gained nearly one-fifth of the popular vote, and this seemed to give them a moral claim to some sort of consideration in the formation of a govern-ment.

Votes	Share of vote
11,639,243	38.0%
11,868,906	38.8%
6,063,470	19.3%
1,762,047	3.9%

When the results were known on Friday 1 March, Heath, instead of resigning immediately, approached Jeremy Thorpe, the Liberal leader, and made an offer of coalition with full Liberal participation in government. Such a coalition would, of course, still not have commanded a majority in the Commons, for one of the peculiarities of the situation was that no two parties acting together (apart from Labour and the Conservatives) could secure such a majority; but the Heath move would at least have made the Conservative/Liberal coalition the largest single grouping in the Commons. Negotiations continued until Monday 4 March when the Liberals rejected Heath's offer, and Heath resigned. Harold Wilson then formed a minority Labour government.

Heath's action in refusing to resign immediately once the election results were known was criticised as 'bordering on the unconstitutional' by Lord Crowther-Hunt (*The Times*, 4 March 1974), a Labour peer and Fellow in Politics at Exeter College, Oxford, shortly to become constitutional adviser to the Wilson government. Crowther-Hunt's reasoning was based on the fact that there was no twentieth-century case of a Prime Minister failing to resign after an election which left his party only the second largest in the Commons.

But it is doubtful whether one can build a constitutional principle upon the precedent of 1929. For, as we have seen, close examination of this precedent is insufficient to establish the conclusion that the Prime Minister is under any obligation to resign if his party is not the largest in the Commons; and there are contrasting, though admittedly earlier, precedents from 1885/6 and 1892.

Indeed, having once decided not to resign immediately, Heath might well have been better advised to meet Parliament. He would probably not have incurred much further criticism, and he might well have gained some tactical advantage by forcing the Liberals to be seen installing Labour in office. This had been the tactic adopted by Baldwin in 1924. Indeed, there was even the possibility, albeit a slim one, that Heath would not be defeated on a vote of confidence when the House met. This possibility is sufficient, surely, to dispose of Crowther-Hunt's assertion that Heath was acting unconstitutionally. For, so long as there was any uncertainty as to whether there was a majority against him, Heath was surely entitled to test the possibility. Whether meeting Parliament would have been politically wise is, of course, another question, and there is no doubt a case to be argued on both sides. But Heath's actual resignation immediately after the negotiations with the Liberals had failed, flowed from his political judgment and not from any constitutional necessity.

The negotiations with the Liberals may have had an important constitutional consequence. For Harold Wilson's minority Labour government faced the possibility of immediate defeat on an amendment to the Address on the Queen's Speech. If that happened, would he be able to secure a dissolution, or would the Queen refuse a dissolution and summon Edward Heath, now Leader of the Opposition, to form a government?

In a speech at High Wycombe on 15 March 1974, ten days after his government was formed, Wilson warned the Conservative and Liberal Parties that, if they defeated him on the Address, they would face an immediate general election.

Frustrated and resentful at the advent of a Labour Government, the Opposition parties have, apparently, decided to continue the manoeuvering they first set in hand while the election results were still being declared ... I believe that the British public ... will be impatient of any further manoeuvering designed to put back into office the administration which almost had to be dragged from office 10 days ago.

As a realist I recognise that if the Opposition parties are determined to play around with the future of this nation they are in a position to do so.

I want to give this warning: That if *they* are realists they will recognise that they will do so at their electoral peril. The Labour Government will not emulate the Conservatives in a desperate attempt to hold on to office, for we believe the electorate will know how to respond. The British public will not lightly forgive politicians and parties who, having been rejected by the voters, seek to prevent the Labour Government from taking the measures necessary for the nation's survival ... If Mr Heath and Mr Thorpe are determined to play the role of wreckers, it is the British people, in the first place, who will have to face a heavy bill for damages. But they and their parties will not be immune from the consequences of their own frivolous irresponsibility.

This masterly speech seems at first sight the opening shot in a new electoral campaign, but it also contained a veiled warning to the Opposition that Wilson had confidence in being granted a dissolution if he was forced to ask for one. It appears that this belief was conveyed by an informal and oblique channel – certainly not Wilson himself – to the Conservatives.

At any rate, the speech had its desired effect, and the Conservative threat to defeat him on the Address evaporated. For the Conservatives had no desire to precipitate a general election which they believed might be won by Labour with an overall majority. The Conservatives, therefore, failed to divide the House on an amendment which they themselves had tabled! Indeed they abstained on all major votes in the Commons until June 1974, because they did not wish to provide Wilson with an excuse to go to the country. Wilson was thus able to dissolve at a time of his own choosing in September 1974, and to gain a narrow overall majority in October.

Did Harold Wilson have any grounds for being confident that he would be granted a dissolution? It is highly unlikely that he would have been given a guarantee in advance by the Queen that if defeated on the Queen's Speech he could secure a dissolution. Indeed, in his book, *Final Term*, Wilson states that 'neither Mr Heath nor I had, or could have had, any idea what the Sovereign's response would have been to so quick a request for a second election'.[44] Wilson's confidence, therefore, must have been based on other considerations.

It is not difficult to reconstruct what might have been his chain of reasoning, or the arguments which might have been put to him by his constitutional advisers. For the Conservatives had already enjoyed one opportunity to form an administration and they had been unsuccessful. The failure of the Heath–Thorpe negotiations meant that it was unlikely that any alternative government could be formed in the existing House of Commons. The Queen, therefore, could not have gone back to Heath without being accused of favouring him. Had Heath been asked to form a government again, only subsequently to be defeated on a confidence motion or on *his* Queen's Speech, he would have sought a dissolution at a time of his choosing, with all the advantages which an incumbent enjoys. That would have rendered the Queen liable to accusations of partisanship. Therefore she could not afford to refuse Wilson's request for a dissolution, but would have to grant it.

The interesting question then arises whether this chain of reasoning would still have held if the Heath–Thorpe negotiations had not taken place, Heath having resigned immediately upon learning of the result of the election. It would then no longer have been quite so obvious that no alternative government was available. In theory, therefore, the Queen might have summoned Heath to the Palace and asked him to form a government if Wilson had been defeated on the Address. But the Queen would still have been unwise to do so unless she had been given an assurance that an alternative government was viable. Otherwise, she would again be put in the position of appearing to favour Heath. She could not, therefore, afford to rely upon speculation that an alternative government *might* survive; if she was to break with precedent to the extent of refusing a dissolution for the first time for over 150 years, she would have to be absolutely certain. The only way in which she could

---

[44] Harold Wilson, *Final Term: The Labour Government 1974–1976* (Weidenfeld and Nicolson and Michael Joseph, 1979), pp. 15–16.

have obtained this certainty would have been if Heath had entered into negotiations with Thorpe (and perhaps with other minority parties also) and made the result public knowledge. Otherwise, the Queen would have been unwise to refuse a dissolution.

XI

Whether the Prime Minister of a minority government can secure a dissolution as MacDonald did in 1924 and Wilson hoped to do in 1974 is of vital importance to him. For if he can, he is absolved from the necessity of negotiating with other parties to avoid parliamentary defeat. Instead he will, as Wilson did, seek a tactical dissolution so that he can secure an overall majority. The pressure, therefore, is directed at the Opposition parties rather than at the government; whereas if the Prime Minister knew that he would be unlikely to obtain a dissolution, the pressure would be upon him and not upon his opponents. Thus the ability to obtain a dissolution yields a great accretion of strength to the Prime Minister and his government.

The situation would be very different if there were fixed-term Parliaments with no possibility of dissolution. Such a constitutional change is favoured by some who wish to see an increase in the influence of Parliament *vis-à-vis* the executive. That hope would be frustrated by the possibility of a tactical dissolution; but if Parliament could not be dissolved at all, the Prime Minister would have no alternative but to enter into negotiations with other parties in the House.

The ability to secure a dissolution, then, increases the power of the Prime Minister over his opponents. In particular, it weakens the position of a small pivot party such as the Liberals seeking to make best use of their bargaining position in a hung Parliament. It is, therefore, in the interest of the major parties that the right of dissolution be automatic; correspondingly it is not in the interest of the smaller ones that this should be so.

It is a significant illustration of the extent to which the conventions of the British Constitution favour the major parties that in 1974, as in 1923/4, the Liberals, who seemed in such a strong bargaining position, were unable to exert any influence upon government, and their hopes soon evaporated. In theory, one might have thought, the Liberals as the centre party should have been all-powerful, free to determine the political agenda by offering to combine with either Labour or the Conservatives. Yet in each case they were decisively outmanoeuvered.

Asquith's tactics in 1923/4 have been the subject of much criticism in retrospect; yet, as we have seen, it is difficult to suggest what other course

114

of action he might have taken which would have produced a better result. Jeremy Thorpe too has been criticised for being so ready to meet with Edward Heath in 1974. His position, it has been argued, would have been stronger if, instead of exploring an arrangement with the Conservatives which he should have known would prove unacceptable to Liberals who had just fought an election campaign against the Conservative government, he had held himself in reserve, waiting to see what the Queen's Speech contained before committing himself. Such an approach, it may be said, would have put pressure on the other parties to come to terms with the Liberals. Harold Wilson would not have been able to claim that he had 'won' the election, nor could he have formed a minority government with the assurance that it would survive. The Liberal Party's bargaining position would, therefore, have been very considerably strengthened.[45]

But, in practice, the Liberal Party would probably once again have come up against the constitutional bias towards the major parties. For the Liberals would not have been in the position of choosing which government to support. There would already be a government in existence. If Heath had decided to meet Parliament, the Liberals would have been faced with the same choice as Asquith in 1924 – whether or not to support a Labour no-confidence motion. In practice, the Liberals would have found it difficult not to support such a motion without alienating many of their leading activists whose instincts were strongly anti-Conservative. Indeed, the main reason why Thorpe did not accept coalition with the Conservatives in March 1974 was precisely the fear that he could not carry the Liberal Party with him. Therefore, it would not have been a practical option for Thorpe to have voted against a no-confidence motion, and to keep the Conservatives in office. He would have had to support such a motion. Harold Wilson would, of course, have been fully aware of this. Therefore he would not have needed to make any offer to the Liberals, just as MacDonald did not in 1923/4. He could simply have taken office as head of a minority government after the Conservative defeat and secured a dissolution at a time of his own choosing.

Alternatively, if, in the circumstances postulated, Heath had decided to resign, which seems more likely, Wilson would have been called immediately to the Palace and would have formed a minority government. In this situation also, as we have seen, he would probably be able to choose when he went to the country.

It appears then that the Liberals' seemingly strong bargaining position was as deceptive in 1974 as it had been in 1923/4. In a multi-party

[45] This argument has been put forward by Michael Steed in his Introduction to Arthur Cyr, *Liberal Party Politics in Britain* (John Calder, 1977).

situation, the conventions of the British Constitution make for minority government rather than majority coalitions. This weakens the position of a centre party, and therefore also the centripetal forces in the political system. Thus the ability of the Prime Minister of a minority government to secure a dissolution entails two important consequences. First, it strengthens the position of the Prime Minister against Opposition parties. Secondly, it strengthens the position of the major parties against the smaller parties, and in particular against a pivot party of the centre.

But if proportional representation established multi-party politics on a permanent basis a wholly different situation would arise. Then the advantage of being able to secure a tactical dissolution would lose much of its value, since it would be less likely that a dissolution in itself would make a great deal of difference. A government might gain or lose support, but it would still not be able to govern on its own, and would be forced to seek an accommodation with other parties. There would therefore be pressure on minority governments to secure sufficient support to obtain a majority in the Commons. This would, of course, give much greater weight to pivot parties of the centre, and it explains why such parties have a good deal more influence in Continental countries using proportional systems than they are able to enjoy in Britain.

With proportional representation, the political dynamics of government formation would be entirely different from those at work in 1923/4 and 1974. The centre would enjoy a pivotal position, *vis-à-vis* the major parties; and a party of the centre would acquire more leverage upon government than a corresponding party of equivalent electoral strength displaying a more extreme ideological viewpoint. In multi-party systems, the tremendous power of pivot parties is well illustrated by the roles of the West German Free Democrats (FDP) or the Dutch Christian Democratic Appeal (CDA), which are able and willing to co-operate with either Left or Right. Conversely, parties such as the Italian Communist Party, or, in Denmark, Mogens Glistrup's Progress Party, with which no major party will co-operate, remain in a political ghetto. Thus votes cast for non-co-operative parties do not carry the same weight as votes cast for their more co-operative competitors, since the former are far less likely to be able to influence the process of government formation. Proportional representation can ensure that each vote carries the same weight in adding to a party's strength in the legislature; but it cannot ensure that each party enjoys the same weight in the process of government formation. This would depend more upon the attitude of the party towards co-operation with others, and its acceptability by others as a suitable party with which to co-operate.

But the advent of proportional representation or permanent multi-party politics would do more than alter the relative strength of the political parties. It would also affect the whole process of government formation. It would, in particular, render the role of the Sovereign far more difficult than it is at present. For, since she will generally have a good deal more discretion than she enjoys under a two-party system, she will, to this extent, become more exposed to the accusation of partisanship, and will need to show a considerable degree of skill to avoid the problems which will arise. It is to a consideration of these problems and how they might be resolved that the next chapter is devoted.

6

Forming a government: the rules of the game

I

If multi-party politics were to become permanently entrenched in Britain, then many of the conventionally accepted constitutional rules would cease to provide unambiguous guidance either to the Sovereign or to political leaders. In such circumstances, the principle of parliamentarism, that a government must command the confidence of Parliament, may not dictate a unique solution to the problem of government formation. As the example of the 1923/4 crisis shows, there is likely to be more than one party or coalition capable of forming a government. The action of the Sovereign in asking one party leader rather than another to form a government, could easily exert an important influence upon the result. There will be a danger, therefore, that the Sovereign may come to be accused of political bias, or become embroiled in coalition negotiations. Some of the constitutional monarchies of the Continent have adopted new institutional procedures designed to avoid this possibility; but, as we shall see, these have in some respects increased rather than reduced the difficulties of the process of government formation. For the responsibility for maintaining the monarchy as an institution above party politics rests less with the Crown itself than with the political parties. It is they who must develop procedures and practices designed to ensure that the complex process of government formation can occur without the Crown's neutrality being compromised.

The problems that are likely to arise may be of three specific kinds. The first is the difficulty of determining who should be asked to form a government when no single party enjoys a majority in the Commons. The second is the problem of determining what *type* of government should be formed in such circumstances – whether a coalition or a minority government; while the third arises when one or more of the parties are split and their leadership does not have united support for the course which they wish to pursue. All three situations pose great difficulties for the Sovereign and political leaders alike.

The central difficulty is that whoever is *first* asked by the Sovereign to form a government will enjoy a considerable advantage. One reason for this is that he will have authority to offer posts. Partly for this reason, there is only one party leader this century who has been asked by the Sovereign to form a government, and failed – Bonar Law in 1916. But that failure occurred not because Bonar Law was *unable* to form a government, but because he judged that it would be *imprudent* to form one in which Lloyd George did not hold the leading place. There can be little doubt that Bonar Law could have succeeded if he had genuinely sought the Premiership in 1916.

On other occasions, opposition to the candidate designated by the Sovereign has rapidly evaporated. In December 1905, following the resignation of the Conservative government. Edward VII called on Campbell-Bannerman, the Liberal leader, to form a government. Campbell-Bannerman was regarded by many other leading Liberals as too elderly and uninspiring to be Prime Minister. Asquith, Haldane and Grey had in September entered into the so-called Relugas Compact by which they pledged themselves not to enter the government unless Campbell-Bannerman went to the Lords. However, the offer of the Chancellorship of the Exchequer to Asquith was sufficient to destroy the compact, and Campbell-Bannerman found no difficulty in forming a government.

Attlee in 1945 was similarly able to head off with ease a challenge to his leadership by Herbert Morrison. Morrison, after Labour had won the general election, demanded that a party meeting be called to vote on the leadership; only after that should the victorious candidate present himself to the Palace to kiss hands. Attlee quashed this intrigue by going to the Palace immediately upon being summoned by the King, and accepting the King's commission to form a government. Finally, in 1963, Lord Home was to find no difficulty in forming a government even though some of his colleagues had earlier considered refusing to serve under him. These colleagues, except for Iain Macleod and Enoch Powell, accepted Cabinet posts partly because they calculated that if Home were to fail, the damage to the Conservative Party would be very great. Thus, even though Home may well not have been the first choice of the majority of Conservative MPs or of his Cabinet colleagues, he was able to kiss hands as Prime Minister.

None of these three cases is strictly analogous to the situations which might arise under multi-party politics. The examples of 1905 and 1945 show only that it is difficult if not impossible for party dissidents to prevent the Leader of the Opposition from forming a government, especially if, as in 1945, he has just led his party to victory in a general election. The 1963 example relates to the resignation of one Prime

Minister and his replacement by another, a situation which, for all four political parties, is now regulated by internal party rules, thus ensuring that the Queen is not involved in the process. Nevertheless, these cases do show the advantage which can be derived from being asked to form a government, and therefore being able to appear as the candidate in possession.

Moreover, once an administration has been formed, the electorate may not take kindly to the government being dismissed by the House of Commons before it has had a chance to put its policies into effect. The voters' response in such circumstances might well be to endorse the government in a subsequent general election. Therefore the other parties represented in the Commons will have to think carefully before defeating it. For this reason, also, the incumbent Prime Minister will enjoy a considerable advantage over competitors from other parties. It is particularly important, therefore, that the Crown should not be put in the position of appearing to be giving an advantage to one contender at the expense of his rivals.

II

In a multi-party situation, there will be controversy not only over who is asked to form a government, but over what type of government is formed – whether a minority government or a coalition. The principle of parliamentarism may be ambiguous not only because there is more than one party or coalition capable of forming a government, but also because the very meaning of the phrase 'commanding the confidence of Parliament' is ambiguous. It can mean either that a government commands the positive support of a majority in the Commons; or, a weaker interpretation, that there is no majority against it. Which of these interpretations should the Sovereign follow in the process of government formation?

In 1923/4, as we have seen, George V was perfectly prepared to ask MacDonald to form a government without requiring him, as St Loe Strachey would have liked, to seek pledges of co-operation from leaders of other parties to ensure that he had the positive support of over half of the House. The principle underpinning government formation in this case was that MacDonald enjoyed the confidence of the Commons because there was, until October 1924, no positive majority against him. But he never enjoyed a clear majority in the House.

In August 1931, by contrast, when MacDonald's second Labour government resigned, the King, acting on the advice of Opposition leaders, sought a government which could command a positive majority in the House so that it could take firm measures to deal with the economic crisis. For this reason, he did not ask Baldwin, the Conservative leader, to form a minority government; nor – and here his action was more controversial – did he ask Arthur Henderson, the Foreign Secretary and second in command in the Labour Party, whether he could form a minority Labour administration. Instead he asked MacDonald to form an all-party National Government, a government which Labour opposed, but which was still capable of commanding a majority in the Commons.

The King's choice was in part conditioned by the view that a majority government was essential if Britain was to remain on the gold standard. But George V's actions during the 1931 crisis have remained a subject of controversy amongst historians. The question of whether, in the event of a hung Parliament, there should be a minority or a coalition government is a highly political one. It would be best, therefore, for the Sovereign to be protected, insofar as that is possible, from having to decide it.

III

The final source of difficulty in the process of government formation arises when a party is divided, with one section being willing to enter a coalition with other parties, while another section is opposed to such a scheme. In such a situation, the Sovereign would need to be careful that her actions did not unwittingly give rise to accusations that she was benefiting one section of a party rather than another. Such an accusation was levelled at George V in 1931, even though he was careful to act throughout on the advice of the party leaders. Hostile critics claimed that he was personally responsible for the formation of the National Government, splitting Labour, and condemning it to a crushing defeat in the general election. If the King had simply accepted Ramsay MacDonald's resignation instead of asking him to form an all-party coalition such a result would not have occurred.

A critic eager to make a case against George V might claim that he neglected to consider the effect of his actions upon the party system. Ramsay MacDonald, after all, was Prime Minister not by virtue of any personal qualities he may have possessed, but because he was the leader of the Labour Party. Yet the King acted as if MacDonald could be detached from the party which he headed. Such an assumption fitted the preconceptions of eighteenth-century political life but hardly accorded with those of the twentieth. George V acted as he did because in common with much of the political and financial leadership of the country, he believed that Britain faced an emergency which could be alleviated only by economy measures of the kind which MacDonald had proposed. Since

MacDonald could not persuade his Cabinet to approve these measures, it was, in the view of the King and the leaders of all three parties, imperative to secure a government which was able to carry them out. This, however, involved a political decision concerning the type of government which should be formed, and it is doubtful if George V's use of his prerogative to this effect in 1931 would be acceptable today.

Earlier in his reign, in 1916, George V had been able to avoid appearing to intervene in an intra-party conflict by using the device of an all-party conference. In December 1916, Asquith resigned as Prime Minister, and the King asked Bonar Law, as leader of the largest party in the Commons, to form a government. Bonar Law, in turn, after a vain attempt to secure the support of Asquith, decided that it would not be sensible for Lloyd George to hold the second place, and reported failure to the King. At the suggestion of Balfour, the only other living ex-Prime Minister, the King then summoned the three party leaders – Asquith, Bonar Law and Arthur Henderson – together with Balfour and Lloyd George, to a conference at Buckingham Palace to resolve the crisis. The central purpose of this conference was to discover whether it was possible to construct an administration which, by retaining the services of Asquith and those Liberals who followed him, could succeed in maintaining national unity. To gain this end, it was suggested that either Bonar Law or Lloyd George should be asked to lead a wartime administration, depending upon which of these individuals Asquith could be induced to support. When it became apparent, however, that Asquith was not prepared to accept a subordinate place, Lloyd George was asked to form a government and succeeded in doing so without difficulty.

In this situation, the conference method proved of great value in clarifying the views of political leaders at a time when the parties were divided. It is very doubtful, however, if such a method could be used today. For if the Sovereign were to summon a conference, this would have to be done in the full glare of media publicity and speculation which could itself damage the Crown's position as an institution above politics. Today, the Sovereign would be more likely to adopt a passive role, waiting for the parties to settle their differences and for some clear indication that agreement had been reached before summoning anyone to form a government. The parties will be expected to make their own dispositions before a Prime Minister is designated. The party leaders could themselves, if they so wished, hold a conference without involving the Palace. In 1974, after all, Heath and Thorpe were able to negotiate perfectly well under their own auspices; there was no need to include the Palace.

Nevertheless, even if the party leaders do all they can to avoid implicating the Sovereign in party matters, it is perfectly possible that she may, on occasion, have to make a real choice amongst competing contenders for the premiership. There may be occasions when there will be more than one course of action which can be justified as being constitutionally correct, so that it will not necessarily be sufficient defence for the Sovereign simply to say that she has acted on advice.

Can there be any way of protecting the Crown's position in such a situation? Can any rules be laid down to guide the Sovereign's use of her discretion other than the rather formalistic principles enunciated by constitutional authorities such as Jennings? Or, alternatively, should the monarchy be protected by institutional reforms of the type which have taken place in the constitutional monarchies of the Continent such as the Netherlands and Sweden?

IV

What is particularly striking about the British monarchy as compared with the constitutional monarchies of the Continent is the almost complete absence of information about the way in which the Sovereign exercises her prerogative powers; nor indeed is there any settled doctrine laying down how the Sovereign *ought* to exercise them. As Bagehot remarked, 'There is no authentic explicit information as to what the Queen can do, any more than of what she does.'[1] This secrecy is in fact part of the essence of constitutional monarchy as it has developed in Britain. It serves to protect the institution of royalty. If royal actions were to become public, debate and argument about them would be inevitable, and the Crown could thus be brought into the arena of party politics. A constitutional monarch, therefore, can only exercise her powers if there is some uncertainty as to what their precise scope should be. For this reason, there is no definite way of answering the question – what are the proper limits of royal discretion in the process of government formation?

There is a sharp dichotomy between what Bagehot called the 'dignified' or theatrical elements of monarchy and the 'efficient' or working functions of that institution. For, whereas the dignified aspects of the monarchy must be, by their very nature, public, the Crown's involvement in the process of government formation remains almost entirely secret. As Bagehot understood, this secrecy 'is ... essential to the utility of English royalty, as it now is. Above all things our royalty is to be reverenced, and if you begin to poke about it you cannot reverence it.

---

[1] Bagehot, *The English Constitution, Collected Works*, vol. 5, p. 243.

When there is a select committee on the Queen, the charm of royalty will be gone. Its mystery is its life. We must not let in daylight upon magic.'[2]

There are also positive advantages both for the Sovereign and for the institution of constitutional monarchy in not clarifying options. For, once precedents are categorised, they may be treated as binding and so *limit* the use of the prerogative; or, they may be used by those hostile to the Sovereign to limit her freedom of action, and even to attack the institution itself. The Queen in any case cannot be *bound* by precedent; she must use her discretion as she thinks best in the light of specific circumstances which cannot be predicted. In an unwritten and therefore uncertain Constitution, it is peculiarly difficult to lay down rules to guide the Sovereign's actions in hypothetical situations.

Hitherto, one of the essential purposes of preserving some ambiguity concerning the Sovereign's precise powers has been the feeling that these powers would probably need to be used only in an emergency situation, and that no one could foretell what such a situation might be like. With multi-party politics, however, the Sovereign's intervention may not be confined to irregular or emergency situations, but could become a regular feature of the political scene. Like the constitutional monarchs of the Continent, the Queen could become more closely involved in the government-formation process. Are there any lessons from the experience of Continental monarchies which could be of use to the monarchy in Britain as it attempts to cope with a novel and dangerous situation?

V

Norway is the Continental country in which the process of government formation operates least controversially. But this is due more to two specific characteristics of the Norwegian political system, neither of which is present in Britain, rather than to any inherent features of the process itself. First, the Norwegian multi-party system divides neatly into two blocs – socialist and anti-socialist – with no party seeking to form an alliance with a party from an opposing bloc. In such a situation, government formation will be easier than in a tripolar system where more than one coalition arrangement is possible. In Norway, it is usually obvious which bloc is able to form a government after an election, and allegiances are generally highly stable. Difficulties have arisen only when, as in 1971 and 1972, the two-bloc system has been

[2] Ibid.

cross-cut by other territorial issues – specifically by the EEC issue which divided both Right and Left.

The King, for the first time in Norway's post-war history, was then faced with a genuine choice of candidates for the premiership, and in 1971 was compelled to adopt a new procedure to protect his position. He asked the president of the lower house – roughly equivalent to the Speaker of the Commons – to negotiate with the parties on his behalf. Unfortunately, however, this was not as helpful as he might have hoped since it was never entirely clear whether the mandate which the president was given required him to negotiate specifically for a majority government or whether a minority government would be acceptable. In 1972, after Norway unexpectedly rejected EEC entry in a referendum, an anti-EEC government had to be formed, even though the parties hostile to the EEC represented only a minority of the Storting (parliament). The King, however, was not on this occasion involved, and the necessary negotiations were conducted by the parties themselves.

There is a second reason why the process of government formation generally works more smoothly in Norway than it would be likely to do in Britain. The Norwegian political parties are far more cohesive and less internally divided than their British counterparts. This facilitates the process of coalition building, and minimises the possibility of party splits. This means that the Crown will not become involved in making a judgment on whether a particular coalition is viable or not. In Britain, by contrast, where party cohesion is weaker, it will be more difficult to predict in advance whether a party leader can carry his followers with him when negotiating a coalition with another party. This adds an extra complication to the government-formation process which is absent in Norway.

VI

The question then arises whether the hitherto informal methods of government formation in Britain can survive such difficulties; or whether it would be better to adapt from Continental practice innovations whose purpose has been to protect the Crown from political involvement. The most radical of these innovations has been adopted in Sweden where the role of the monarch in nominating a Prime Minister has been entirely delegated to the Speaker of the Riksdag, the Swedish single-chamber parliament. Such a change has also been proposed for Britain by Tony Benn in the September/October 1982 issue of the *New Socialist*, a Labour Party journal.[3] However, as Swedish experience shows, giving the power

[3] 'Power, Parliament and people', in *New Socialist*, Sept–Oct 1982.

of nominating the Prime Minister to the Speaker tends to raise more problems than it solves.

The 1974 Instrument of Government which is in effect the Swedish Constitution, deprives the monarch of any role in the formation of government, and Article 1 of the Instrument declares that 'All public power in Sweden emanates from the people.' In place of the monarch, the Instrument designates the Speaker as responsible for initiating the government-formation process. The procedure is clearly described in Chapter 6, Articles 2 and 3 of the Instrument:

Art. 2. When a Prime Minister is to be designated the Speaker shall convene representatives of each party group within the Riksdag for consultation. The Speaker shall confer with the Vice Speakers and shall then submit a proposal to the Riksdag. The Riksdag shall proceed to vote on the proposal, not later than on the fourth day thereafter, without preparation within any committee. If more than half of the members of the Riksdag vote against the proposal, it is thereby rejected. In any other case it is approved.

Art. 3. If the Riksdag rejects the proposal of the Speaker the procedure as prescribed in Article 2 shall be resumed. If the Riksdag has rejected the proposal of the Speaker four times the procedure for designating the Prime Minister shall be discontinued and resumed only after elections for the Riksdag have been held. Unless ordinary elections are in any case to be held within three months, extra elections shall be held within the same period of time.

Already in the short life-time of the Instrument, the convention seems to have been accepted that when the Speaker nominates a Prime Minister, he will at the same time specify the precise party composition of the government to be formed. But this convention is not, of course, inherent or essential to the Swedish method of conducting the government-formation process.

The new procedure was introduced by a Social Democratic government in Sweden as a compromise between those who wished to abolish the monarchy entirely and those who were content with the status quo. The monarchy was retained but its political role was entirely nullified. The Swedish king no longer enjoys those prerogative powers which other constitutional monarchs enjoy and which are generally thought to give life to the institution of constitutional monarchy. Yet the new Instrument has done little to resolve the problems of government formation which arise in a multi-party system. Indeed, it may even have aggravated them. There are two dangers, neither of which has been entirely avoided in Sweden. First, there is the danger that the role of the Speaker may become politicised, while second, the Speaker is much more likely than the monarch to be tempted to misuse his power.

The Instrument does not regulate the election of the Speaker, but there has in the past been a tacit tradition in Sweden that he should come from the majority bloc and be a generally respected member of the Riksdag. The new Instrument was first put to the test in 1976 when, for the first time for 44 years, a non-socialist coalition succeeded in winning power. The three non-socialist parties comprising the coalition were, as it happens, willing to retain the Social Democratic Speaker, Henry Allard, who was widely respected. By the time of the 1979 election, however, Allard had resigned from parliament. The non-socialist coalition which now had a majority of only one in the Riksdag were determined to elect a Speaker from amongst their number, and proposed a leading member of the Conservative Party. The Social Democrats, however, indicated that they were not prepared to accept a Conservative Speaker and put up their own candidate. To everyone's surprise, the Social Democrat's candidate was elected, since one of the non-socialist members of the Riksdag defected to the Social Democrats on this issue; the latter's motivation, it is generally thought, was jealousy at his not himself being the government coalition's candidate for the Speakership.

Delegating the monarch's role in nominating a Prime Minister to the Speaker thus raises the question of how the Speaker is to be selected. In Britain, the Speaker is a figure entirely removed from party politics. He has, admittedly, not always been chosen by agreement between the parties. But, even when there has been a contested election, he has been accepted by the other parties, and it is the custom after a general election for a new government to support the re-election of the existing Speaker even when he had been elected under the auspices of the government's political opponents. In 1945 Labour, although returned with an overwhelming majority, and although there had never been a Labour Speaker, decided to support the re-election of Clifton Brown, a former Conservative. Similarly in 1964, Labour supported the re-election of the former Conservative Sir Harry Hylton-Foster, and in 1974 likewise supported the re-election of the former Conservative minister Selwyn Lloyd. Correspondingly the Conservatives in 1970 supported the re-election of the former Labour back-bencher Horace King and agreed to the former Labour minister George Thomas being re-elected in 1979. Were the Speaker to be chosen for a single parliament only, he would be dependent on the government for re-election; the Opposition parties would become suspicious of him, and this would weaken his authority.

Once elected, the Speaker withdraws entirely from political involvement. 'He serves only the House of Commons, regardless of which faction might be temporarily in control of it ... From the moment of his appointment he withdraws completely from political activity and ceases to belong to any political party ... Even in his private life he must observe discretion in his associations with practising politicians.'[4] This abstention from political action is what makes possible the continuity of the Speakership and prevents the Speaker being dependent on either government or party. Upon retirement, the Speaker goes immediately to the Lords where he sits on the cross benches and continues to abstain from party activities.

The principles upon which the British Speakership are based are not fully accepted, even in those Commonwealth countries such as Canada, Australia and New Zealand whose conception of parliamentary procedure owes so much to the Westminster Model. In 1956, for example, in Canada, during a debate on a motion of censure on the Speaker, the Prime Minister, Louis St Laurent, revealed his lack of understanding of the nature of the Speaker's office by declaring that the Speaker still retained the confidence of the *majority* of the House. He failed to grasp that the Speaker is the protector of the rights of every member of the House, and not just the rights of the current majority.

In most European parliaments, there is explicit recognition that 'presiding officers in general maintain their political associations, although they act impartially in discharging the duties of the Chair.'[5] In Britain, by contrast, the office of the Speaker is conceived of as largely 'judicial' in nature, and he is regarded as an official of the whole House. He is fundamentally a servant of the House rather than a source of political authority in his own right.

The question is whether such a conception of the Speaker's position could survive him being given the task of nominating a Prime Minister, or whether it would lead to a confusion of roles to the detriment of his authority as a protector of the rights of all MPs. The Swedish example is not encouraging in this regard, for before 1974 the election of the Speaker was uncontentious, generally uncontested and a product of all-party agreement. These conventions have clearly not survived the new Instrument of Government.

If the Speaker was required to involve himself in the process of government formation, he would need to be well-informed about internal developments within the parties. This would subject his impartiality to very considerable strain. The election to the Speakership would inevitably become politicised. The government of the day would insist that a Speaker from its own side of the House be elected at the beginning of each Parliament, and Opposition parties would have less confidence in him. The speaker himself, owing his position to the governing party, might well come to see himself as a party representative rather than a

---

[4] Philip Laundy, *The Office of Speaker* (Cassell, 1964), p. 7.
[5] Ibid., pp. 378, 441.

servant of the whole House. He might be tempted to exercise political initiatives of his own, and this would lead to further controversy about his position. In Sweden in 1979, the non-socialist parties faced problems in reconstructing their three-party coalition after the general election. It is reported, although in the nature of things it cannot be documented, that the Speaker told Thorbjörn Fälldin, the putative leader of the three-party coalition that if he did not hurry, the Speaker would call upon Olof Palme, the Social Democratic leader, to form a government! Such an initiative would hardly be possible on the part of a constitutional monarch.

Since the position of the Queen depends upon her impartiality, she is far less likely than a Swedish-style Speaker to be tempted into controversial or partisan actions. She has the double advantage of being a generally respected symbol of the state, and, through the activities of her Private Secretary (as the example of Lord Stamfordham in 1923/4 shows) being able to inform herself of the state of political attitudes. The Speaker would not enjoy such advantages, and his unique position, built up through centuries of constitutional development, could be rapidly destroyed.

The Swedish Instrument of Government does not therefore assist the process of government formation in the complex situations of multi-party politics which are likely to arise. Like all constitutions, it proves a set of formal rules which cannot by their very nature provide for situations where there is a choice of solutions and the Speaker has to exercise his discretion. The Speaker is given, potentially, the powers of a presidential head of state in countries such as West Germany or Italy. He will be more tempted to misuse his power than a constitutional monarch who dare not display any appearance of partisanship. Moreover, the Sovereign is likely to have a longer and more continuous political experience than any parliamentarian, and, through her advisers, she can keep in closer touch with the parties than the Speaker will be able to do. It is unlikely, therefore, that a reform of the Swedish type could do much to resolve the peculiar constitutional problems raised by multi-party politics; and even in Sweden, there are many who are doubtful of the merits of a reform which owed more to political prejudice than to serious argument as to its constitutional merits.

VII

The second possible innovation to protect the monarchy from the exigencies of multi-party politics is the introduction of an *informateur* to conduct negotiations on the monarch's behalf. The *informateur* is a person selected by the monarch because of his general acceptability to the main political parties with the task of discovering through interviews with leading politicians the various possibilities with regard to government formation. He will then report to the monarch and usually suggest the name of a *formateur*, the particular individual who can be entrusted with the task of actually forming a government.

The *informateur* was first appointed to assist in government formation in Belgium in 1935. In the post-war years he has become an important part of the process in both Belgium and the Netherlands and has also been used on occasion in Denmark and Norway. In the Netherlands, it has been customary in recent years to appoint successively a number of *informateurs*. Indeed, in 1977, when the process of government formation took a record 207 days, no less than nine *informateurs* were appointed. In 1977 and 1981, furthermore, two *informateurs* were appointed at a time – one for each of the two major parties involved in the negotiations.

The *informateur* is mentioned in neither the Belgian or Dutch Constitutions, nor in the Constitutions of Denmark or Norway. The idea developed entirely naturally. When the monarch asked a particular candidate to form a government and he was unable to do so, he would *inform* the monarch of the name of someone who could in fact undertake the task. The institution, as it has developed in Belgium and the Netherlands, is now part of a complex and highly ritualised process and it is indispensable to the formation of government.

In the Netherlands, *informateurs* are drawn from a variety of sources. In 1958 and 1972/3, ministers in the outgoing government acted as *informateurs*, while in 1958 and 1967 former Prime Ministers were asked to perform this task, and in 1965 the *informateur* was the leader of the largest party group in parliament. As well as active politicians, elder statesmen and provincial governors with no political ambitions have been used in this role. However, it is only in the Netherlands that the *informateur* need not be a member of the legislature.

In Belgium, the *informateur* has always been a member of one of the two chambers and an active politician. In Norway, only the president of the lower house has been an *informateur*, while in Denmark, the *informateur* has always been a member of the single-chamber parliament, the Folketing. The Danish Speaker was asked to act as an *informateur* in 1975, but has not otherwise been called upon, and the position is generally given to an elected politician who may himself be a candidate for office. In 1981, the *informateur* was the Prime Minister still in office – Anker Jørgensen – who in the end remained as Prime Minister of a coalition government; and on other occasions it has been a party leader.

The task of the *informateur* also varies with the constitutional traditions of different countries. In Denmark and Sweden, he tends to play a rather passive role, contenting himself with registering the opinions of the party leaders, and reporting them to the monarch. In Belgium and the Netherlands, by contrast, he plays a more active role and attempts to secure agreement both on the distribution of posts and the composition and programme of the government.

VIII

It may seem that the *informateur* is far too remote from anything in British experience to be worth considering as a means of protecting the monarchy. Yet someone very like an *informateur* was in fact used by Queen Victoria in the early part of her reign when politics was characterised by a multiplicity of loosely organised groups and factions rather than the highly developed party system of today. Victoria was accustomed to ask an elder statesman to sound out other political leaders to discover what political combinations might be possible, and to report back to her. In the first years of her reign, the Duke of Wellington was employed for this purpose; while in the 1850s, the 3rd Marquess of Lansdowne was asked to sound out opinion. In 1855, for example, after the defeat in the Commons of the coalition government headed by Lord Aberdeen, Lansdowne was called to the Palace, and agreed to see 'first Lord Palmerston, then the Peelites, and lastly Lord John [Russell], and come to Buckingham Palace at two o'clock prepared to give answers upon the question what was feasible and what not'. As Lansdowne 'was seventy-five years old, and crippled with the gout' he was not himself a possible candidate for the premiership. After Russell had tried to form a government and failed, Lansdowne was again called in and reported to the Queen that Sir James Graham, a leading Peelite, had told him that 'the country was tired of Coalitions, and wanted a united Cabinet'. Lansdowne's conclusion was that the Queen should not let it appear that she had any personal animosity towards Lord Palmerston (who was in reality her *bête noire*), but should summon him to form a government after Lord John Russell had failed, a course of action which the Queen did in fact follow.[6]

Use of an elder statesman for this purpose ceased after the 1850s. This was not only because the 1867 Reform Act led to a more clear-cut and disciplined party structure, but also because in 1861 the Queen for the first time secured the services of a Private Secretary who could negotiate

[6] A.C. Benson and Viscount Esher, *Letters of Queen Victoria 1837–1861* (John Murray, 1907), vol. 3, pp. 109, 119.

on her behalf. Unknown to the Constitution, the Private Secretary acts as a link between government and the Sovereign, and it is part of his duty to ascertain the state of political opinion much as Lord Stamfordham did in 1923/4. He can therefore perform the tasks which the Duke of Wellington and the Marquess of Lansdowne undertook in the nineteenth century, and to some extent protect the Crown from direct political involvement in inter-party bargaining.

Yet, of course, the Private Secretary cannot go so far as an *informateur*. He is an official of the court who can enquire but not probe. He cannot, as an *informateur* would do, play an active role in helping to secure the formation of a coalition government. He registers opinion without being able to influence it, and must take particular care not to let it appear that the Queen favours any particular type of government. The Private Secretary's value, therefore, is very great in a situation such as that of 1923/4, an occasional hung Parliament in what remains basically a two-party system with clear-cut results. But his position would become a much more difficult one if multi-party situations became a regular occurrence in Britain.

The role of the *informateur* has developed in an evolutionary way, rather than as a result of conscious planning. It is difficult to see how else it could come about, and highly doubtful whether it will be introduced into Britain in the near future. The problem is that there is hardly in Britain that degree of consensus which would make the institution of the *informateur* workable. For he must be someone acceptable to MPs in all parties. He must possess the qualities both of an elder statesman trusted by all, and also of a shrewd and experienced politician who can sense which political combinations are possible and which are not. It is doubtful whether the parties would be able to agree on an individual whom they could trust and who also displayed these desirable qualities.

Nevertheless, it is perfectly possible that an *informateur* might come to be used if Britain adopted proportional representation and it became clear that hung Parliaments were likely to prove a permanent feature of political life. Even if this were to happen, however, this would not absolve the Sovereign from the exercise of her discretion, since the choice of an *informateur* could easily become just as controversial as the nomination of a Prime Minister. In Belgium and the Netherlands, in particular, the monarch has considerable discretion in the choice of an *informateur*, and it is not difficult to imagine how a skilful monarch could influence the choice of government through appointing a particular individual as *informateur*. So, although the *informateur* may become necessary when negotiations become especially complicated, he does not entirely shield the Crown from the process of decision-making. The *informateur* is essentially a facilitator, and he cannot usurp the functions of the head of state.

IX

The problem of government formation, then, cannot be resolved by institutional reform. To delegate the Sovereign's powers to the Speaker would admittedly protect the Crown from accusations of political bias, but only at the cost of creating new difficulties which are likely to prove far more acute and dangerous; while the *informateur* could operate only in a political system containing a greater degree of political consensus than at present exists in Britain, and in any case would not wholly shield the Crown from political involvement. Is it possible, however, to protect the Crown by codifying accepted practice so that there is clear and public guidance on how the Sovereign should act? This is, admittedly, quite contrary to the spirit of British practice, which prefers that the precise scope of the prerogative be left undefined. But the case for explicitness is that it might enable the Sovereign's powers to be exercised without arousing political controversy. There might be agreement both on the specific situations in which the Sovereign had the right to act, and also on the precise scope of her discretion. 'Residuary discretions', claims S. A. de Smith, 'which become exercisable in an atmosphere of political crisis inevitably expose the person who exercises them to partisan criticism.'[7]

Many of the constitutions of the New Commonwealth countries (with India being the most significant exception) instead of following the British practice of leaving the scope of the head of state's discretion undefined, offer guidance on who should be nominated as prime minister when no single party has an overall majority. These constitutions are based broadly on the Westminster Model, and so they may offer a clue to the rules which would be appropriate in the British context. Since Britain has no written constitution, it would not, of course, be possible to entrench these rules; if they were merely conventional, they could not bind, while if statutory, they could be repealed by Parliament at any time. Nevertheless, they might come to be regarded by the Crown and by political leaders alike as reasonable guides to behaviour. If that happened, the Sovereign's discretion would be narrowed, but so also would be the danger of her being exposed to partisan criticism.

Most of the New Commonwealth constitutions which adopt this approach offer a similar formula for determining how the power of nominating a prime minister should be exercised. In Nigeria, Sierra

---

[7] S.A. de Smith, *The New Commonwealth and its Constitutions* (Stevens, 1964), p. 83.

Leone, Kenya and Malaysia, there is a requirement to appoint a member of the lower house who is 'likely to command the support of a majority of the members' of that house. In the constitutions of Guyana, Malta and Jamaica, there is a requirement to choose the candidate who is 'best able to command the support [or, in the case of Jamaica, the 'confidence'], of a majority of members' of the lower house. The 1962 Uganda Constitution, by contrast, lays down a series of instructions to the President, who must first appoint the leader of the largest party in the Assembly; and then, if this candidate fails, the leader of the next largest party; and so on until the leader of every party which has more than 20 seats has been asked. If the formation of a government is still not possible, then the Constitution provides for a caretaker government to be led by the last Prime Minister – or, if he is no longer a member of the Assembly, or unavailable for any other reason, the leader of the largest opposition party. Even the powers of the caretaker government are carefully defined. It is to remain in office for three months, even if a vote of no-confidence is passed against it, but it can pass no legislation except to declare a state of emergency. Parliament is, however, dissolved after three months unless the government has succeeded in securing the support of the Assembly by then.[8]

While a codification of this type might well assist the Sovereign and political leaders in the process of government formation, it would also distort past practice which cannot be reduced to simple rules. Precisely because the British Constitution is an elastic structure, it is extremely difficult if not impossible to lay down rules according to which the Sovereign should act. Indeed, what may seem to be procedural rules often have a hidden substantive content. For example, in each of the New Commonwealth Constitutions discussed in the last paragraph, the government-formation process is intended to produce a government which enjoys the support, or confidence, of a parliamentary *majority*. But that would not be a fully accurate summary of the purpose of the process in Britain. For in 1923/4, 1929 and March 1974, the Sovereign nominated a Prime Minister who did not command a majority in the Commons; in each case, the candidate satisfied only a lesser criterion, that there should be no majority *against* his party. Indeed, the conventions of British parliamentary life even put a premium upon the formation of a minority single-party government when there is a hung Parliament, rather than a majority coalition. The injunction to the Queen, therefore, could not be

8 Constitution of Nigeria 1963, s 87 (2); Constitution of Sierra Leone 1961, s 58 (2); Constitution of Kenya 1963, s 75 (3); Constitution of Malaysia 1957, s 43 (2) (a); Constitution of Guyana 1966, s 34 (3); Constitution of Malta 1964, s 77 (5) (c); Constitution of Jamaica 1962, s 70 (1); Constitution of Uganda 1962, s 62 (4), (5), (6), (7), (8).

that she should necessarily look for a majority government – for that would be a distortion of past practice – but rather that she should look for a government which can *survive* in the Commons – and that is a very different requirement.

Yet it would not be satisfactory to codify this rule either. For the Sovereign has not *always* sought a Prime Minister who can survive in the Commons rather than one who can command a majority. The example of 1931 shows how the normal conventions can seem entirely inappropriate in the middle of an economic crisis. There is no clear or easily stated rule derivable from past practice laying down when the Sovereign should seek a majority government and when a minority government will suffice. The practice in Britain has been to leave such decisions to be determined by the actual situation. The answer cannot, it is said, be predicted in advance. Whether or not this approach is thought to be a good one or not, it follows that any attempt to codify the rules not only abridges them but also *distorts*. Indeed, the implication of any attempt to codify rules is that Britain should adopt a written constitution which would define and perhaps entrench that which has been hitherto left flexible and elastic.

Yet countries with written constitutions do not avoid the kinds of uncertainty which are implicit in British practice. In monarchies such as Denmark, Norway, the Netherlands and Belgium, the constitution plays a purely formal role. On the process of government formation, it offers nothing more than emblematic statements. The Norwegian Constitution contents itself with saying, 'The King himself chooses a Council of Norwegian citizens, who must not be under thirty years of age. The Council shall consist of a Prime Minister and at least seven other members.' Article 4 of the 1953 Danish Constitution declares similarly that 'The King shall appoint and dismiss the Prime Minister and the other Ministers. He shall decide upon the number of Ministers and upon the distribution of the duties of government among them.' The Netherlands and Belgian Constitutions declare simply, 'The King appoints and dismisses his Ministers.'

It is true that, supplementing the constitution, various rules of the game have come to be accepted in other constitutional monarchies. These rules dictate whom the head of state should consult and in what order. They have become particularly highly formalised in Denmark, but there, as in other countries, it is mainly the early stages of the procedure which have been reduced to formal rules. Generally the conventions dictate that the head of state sees all of the parties, or in Belgium only the larger parties, in order of size. But it is at the ensuing stages of the process that problems arise for the head of state; and these are not regulated by convention. They cannot, therefore, provide a rule by which the Sovereign can know how to use her discretion.

The difficulty with the argument for codification is that it presupposes the very consensus which it seeks to create. Where there is a consensus on what ought to be done, codification will be a way of making public the agreed rules of the game. But in Britain, there is disagreement both on the proper scope of the monarch's discretion and upon the relative merits of coalition and minority government. The first conflict divides the Left from the centre and Right; while the second divides the Liberal/SDP Alliance from the Labour and Conservative Parties.

In March 1974, when the issue arose of whether the Queen could refuse a dissolution to the Prime Minister of a minority government, a Labour left-winger, Norman Atkinson, supported by the Tribune Group, wrote to the Leader of the House, Edward Short, saying that the monarch had no right of any kind ever to refuse a dissolution. Indeed, the general view of the Left in Britain is that the prerogatives of the monarch should not be used, and that where discretion is unavoidable, the Queen's powers should be delegated to the Speaker. But such a narrow conception of the Sovereign's role is hardly shared by many outside the ranks of the Left.

The Liberal/SDP Alliance, through its support for proportional representation, actively favours coalition government. If a general election produced no overall victory for one party, the Alliance believes that a coalition would produce better government than a minority government which, like that of 1974, sought an early tactical dissolution. Most Labour and Conservative leaders, on the other hand, would argue that a coalition could mean, as in West Germany, submitting to dictation from what might be the smallest of three political groupings represented in the Commons. Believing in the two-party system, they would not wish to surrender its benefits without a fight; and therefore, they would incline to single-party minority government rather than coalition.

Where there is no consensus on the role of the head of state, a set of codified rules will merely embody in statute or convention a victory for one side in what is essentially a political debate. Contrasting convictions about the way in which the British political system should work cannot be settled by fiat through codifying one set of conventions at the expense of another.

The situation would be different, of course, if the politicians were able to reach agreement on the procedures to be followed in the event of a hung Parliament. In that case, a code of conduct could be drawn up and made publicly available. If such agreement cannot be reached, however, a code of conduct drawn up by politicians or academics would be prescriptive rather than merely descriptive of past practice, and it would have authority only amongst those who agreed with it.

The exercise of discretion on the part of the head of state, therefore, cannot be excluded wherever there is the possibility of more than one government being formed in a multi-party situation. This discretion is thus an irreducible element in multi-party politics. It cannot be conjured away by institutional reforms, and can be codified only at the cost of distorting and making rigid what is flexible and so inevitably uncertain. In an ideal world, politicians would respect the electorate's right to decide that no single party deserves an overall majority in the Commons; and this would entail working out new constitutional norms to meet novel situations. But, of course, that ideal world has little connection with the Britain of the 1980s where party self-interest is overlaid with wide ideological disagreements. However, the duty of safeguarding the Constitution belongs less to the Sovereign than to the politicians. It lies with them to develop conventions and understandings which can preserve the values of constitutional monarchy in a multi-party system, and ensure that the monarchy is not unwittingly brought into the arena of party politics. Yet, although the vast majority of politicians are supporters of constitutional monarchy, it would be difficult to deny that the challenge of developing such conventions could well be one which they are unable to meet.

7

Minority government

I

If a general election fails to give one party an overall majority of seats in the Commons, single-party majority government will be impossible. The consequence, therefore, must be either a minority government or a coalition which can command a majority in the House. In Britain, minority governments rather than coalitions have been the norm in such situations. Coalitions when they have occurred have been the result either of war – as between 1915 and 1918, and from 1940 to 1945 – or economic crisis as with the National Government in 1931. They can occur to meet emergency situations, but not as a response to the exigencies of parliamentary arithmetic compelling two parties to join together to secure a majority in the House of Commons.

There have been five minority governments in Britain in the twentieth century. From 1910 to 1915, a minority Liberal government was dependent upon the generally reliable support of Labour and the Irish Nationalists for its parliamentary majority. Three Labour governments were in a minority position: in 1924, 1929 and February 1974. In October 1974 Labour succeeded in gaining a small overall majority, but this was gradually eroded through by-election defeats and defections, so that by April 1976 the party found itself in a minority again, and remained so until defeated in the general election of May 1979.

One reason for the prevalence of minority government rather than coalition in Britain has already been analysed in the previous chapter. It lies in the conventions regulating the process of government formation. After a general election in which no party has been able to gain an overall majority, the Sovereign is not required to nominate a Prime Minister who can secure a majority in the Commons, but rather one who can survive as leader of the largest (or in 1924 the second largest) minority party.

The Prime Minister then acts as if he had a majority, and his government drafts a Queen's Speech embodying its proposals for legislation. If defeated on the Address, the prevailing assumption is that the Prime

Minister of a minority government can secure a dissolution of Parliament, even though the vote on the Address is, in a sense, one on the investiture of the government. As the course adopted by Harold Wilson in March 1974 seems to show, the Prime Minister of a minority government is almost certainly correct in his assumption that he will be granted a dissolution in such circumstances. Thus the conventions associated with the process of government formation and dissolution make it likely that minority government rather than coalition will be the result of a hung Parliament. It is possible, however, to envisage different conventions which would encourage the search for a majority. Indeed, in the constitutional monarchies of north-western Europe, the search is always for a majority government in the first instance, and only when it has been shown that no majority government is possible is the attempt to construct a minority government undertaken.

In Belgium and the Netherlands, the monarch conceives his task as being the nomination of a Prime Minister who can secure a majority in the legislature. A government once formed has to secure a positive vote of confidence from the lower house, and, since the negotiations preceding the formation of a government are thorough and exhaustive, the vote of confidence is invariably obtained. There is therefore a premium on the formation of majority coalitions. In Britain, on the other hand, there is no pressure on the leader of the largest party to negotiate with other parties to construct a majority, for he can enjoy power as head of a minority government without compromising his party's ideals. This would not be possible under the procedures followed in the Continental democracies where, if no party has an overall majority, consultations must be held between the leaders of the parties before the monarch nominates a Prime Minister. The initial search is for a majority government, and a minority government is regarded as a second-best alternative to be tried only after consultations have shown that no majority government is possible.

II

The chances of survival of a minority government depend in part upon whether or not the Prime Minister is able to secure a dissolution at a time of his own choosing. Where he cannot do so, either because as in Norway there is a fixed-term parliament, or, because as in Israel, a dissolution can be refused by the head of state if there is an alternative government available, then there is strong pressure on the government to come to terms with the other parties. For the latter can afford to defeat the sitting premier with impunity if the consequence is merely the resignation of the government and its replacement by another from the same parliament. Thus Harold Wilson's position in March 1974 would clearly have been very different if he had been unable to secure a dissolution in the event of defeat on the Address. Instead of challenging his opponents to defeat him, he would have had to seek agreement with them before producing the legislative proposals embodied in the Queen's Speech. The Speech could not have been drawn up unilaterally by a minority government, but would have had to be the result of power-sharing. Yet in 1974, because Wilson believed that he 'had a dissolution in his pocket' – a belief shared by the other parties – he was able to govern as if he already had a majority and await a suitable moment to make that majority real through a tactical dissolution. The power to dissolve Parliament can therefore be a powerful weapon in the hands of a minority government, especially against small parties which will probably lack the means to fight frequent general elections.

Moreover, the Prime Minister of a minority government has a good deal of leeway in deciding when he should go to the country. He is not compelled to dissolve if defeated in the House, even on a three-line whip, and he can, within limits, decide for himself what is to count as an issue of confidence. In February 1924, for example, Ramsay MacDonald declared that his government would resign only if defeated on what it regarded as a substantial issue, but he offered no criteria by which anyone could determine how such an issue was to be recognised. He noted:

I have a lively recollection of all sorts of ingenuities practised by Oppositions in order to spring a snap division upon a Government; so that it might turn it out upon a defeat. I have known bathrooms downstairs utilised, not for their legitimate purpose, but for the illegitimate purpose of packing as many Members surreptitiously inside their doors as their physical limitations would allow. I have known an adjoining building, where there happens to be a convenient Division bell, used for similar purposes. I have seen the House, practically empty when the bells began to ring, suddenly transformed into a very riotous sort of market-place by the inrush of Members, doing their best for their nation, for the House of Commons and for their party, to find a Government napping, and to turn it out upon a stupid issue.

I am going out on no such issue ... The Labour Government will go out if it be defeated upon substantial issues, issues of principle, issues that really matter. It will go out if the responsible leaders of either party or any party move a direct vote of no confidence, and carry that vote ... on matters non-essential, matters of mere opinion, matters that do not strike at the root of the proposals that we make, and do not destroy fundamentally the general intentions of the Government in introducing legislation ... then a division on such amendments and questions as those will not be regarded as a vote of confidence.[1]

Although in the nine months during which it held office, the first Labour government was defeated ten times in the Commons, it treated none of

[1] H.C. Debs, vol. 169, col. 749, 12 February 1924.

these as 'issues of confidence'. When it finally decided to regard the prosecution of the *Worker's Weekly* as a matter of confidence, this was the result of an explicit Cabinet decision. The decision was taken on tactical grounds, to avoid defeat on the government's proposed treaty with Soviet Russia which was to be debated shortly afterwards. There was no inherent constitutional reason why the issue of the prosecution should have been regarded as, in MacDonald's words, something which strikes 'at the root of the proposals that we make', and as destroying 'fundamentally the general intentions of the Government in introducing legislation'.

In March 1974, likewise, Harold Wilson made it clear that his minority government would not regard a defeat in the House as constituting, *per se*, a reason to dissolve. He announced:

The Government intend to treat with suitable respect, but not with exaggerated respect, the results of any snap vote or snap Division ... In case of a Government defeat ... the Government will consider their position and make a definitive statement after due consideration. But the Government will not be forced to go to the country except in a situation in which every Hon. Member in the House was voting knowing the full consequences of his vote.[2]

According to this doctrine, no issue would be treated as one of confidence unless the government had so informed the Commons before the vote. What this meant in practice was that the government itself would decide what was an issue of confidence and would then graciously inform Parliament of the fact. This decision would, of course, be taken on essentially tactical grounds. In the event, Harold Wilson's minority government of March–October 1974 was defeated seventeen times before Parliament was dissolved. The subsequent Wilson/Callaghan governments of October 1974 to March 1979 (which were in a minority only after April 1976) were defeated 42 times, although on the three defeats on issues central to government policy – the 1976 and 1977 Expenditure White Papers, and the 1978 vote to reject the use of sanctions against employers breaching pay guidelines – defeat was followed by a request for a vote of confidence. The government could have dissolved at a relatively favourable time in autumn 1978, but chose not to do so and was defeated on a direct motion of no-confidence in March 1979.

Thus the ability of a government to decide for itself what is to count as a vote of confidence greatly assists a minority government to stay in office and correspondingly handicaps its opponents. A minority government is able to retain the tactical initiative and choose to dissolve at a time when it believes, from opinion poll and other evidence, that it can secure a

2 H.C. Debs, vol. 870, col. 70, 12 March 1974.

majority. This is a powerful inducement to a minority government to avoid compromise with other parties, and seek an overall majority of its own.

But the conventions surrounding government formation and dissolution in Britain are not the only reason for the greater historical incidence of minority government as compared with coalition. Two other factors must be taken into account. The first is that the ideological traditions of the parties have not inclined them to believe in the sharing of power. In 1924, both Baldwin and MacDonald preferred to drive out the Liberal Party rather than explore the possibility of securing a coalition with them. In 1974, Wilson set himself adamantly against deals or bargains with non-socialist parties; while in its October 1974 manifesto, the Labour Party declared that coalition would be a 'cruel farce ... If we believe, as we must, in our own independent political philosophies', it asserted uncompromisingly, 'there is no meeting point between us and those with quite different philosophies.'

The second factor underpinning the prevalence of minority government has been the belief on the part of political leaders of all parties that hung Parliaments are simply an aberration, a brief and painful interlude between single-party majority governments. To form a coalition with a weaker party, then, is unnecessarily to admit it to the perquisites of office, and increase its credibility. Preservation of the two-party system, on the other hand, ensures that each of the major parties will in due course enjoy its full share of power and patronage.

III

A number of techniques are available to a minority government anxious to ensure its survival against a potentially hostile majority in the House of Commons. The first method is to negotiate a formal written pact with minor parties of the kind agreed between the Labour government and the parliamentary Liberal party during the period March 1977 to July 1978. The second is to conclude a more informal and unwritten understanding which is neither published nor made public. It is difficult, in the nature of things, to find clear documentation of such understandings, but there may possibly have been such an agreement between the Labour government and Lloyd George between 1930 and 1931, or at least from spring 1931 until the fall of the government in August; and there may have been an understanding in 1978–79 between the Labour government and the Ulster Unionists that the latter would not allow the government to be defeated before legislation had been passed increasing the number of parliamentary constituencies in Northern Ireland.

In the absence of such understandings, a minority government will seek to survive through securing ad hoc majorities on particular measures. This may involve negotiations before legislation is introduced into Parliament in order to ensure that it is acceptable to a majority of members. But the majority will be a different one on different issues, and the negotiations which result can be quite complex and involved. This method of governing is more characteristic of a country such as Denmark – where it is known as governing by means of 'jumping majorities' – than Britain, where governments are generally unwilling to discuss draft legislation with other parties, and Oppositions are on the whole hostile to the idea of assisting the government to survive, even if this gives them some temporary influence over legislation.

The most usual way in which minority governments have survived in Britain, however, is not through any positive agreement or understanding with other parties, but through fear on the part of the latter that the defeat of the government will lead to an election which they wish to avoid. The Opposition parties may find it difficult to combine against the government; one Opposition party may seek to avoid giving another a tactical advantage by allowing a dissolution at a time convenient to the latter; or they may themselves fear punishment in an election. A government cannot, however, rely upon this negative approach for very long. If it wishes to survive for a long period of time, it must be willing to negotiate with other parties. That would involve surrendering its unilateral control over the parliamentary timetable, and sharing legislative power with one or more Opposition parties. Such a price, however, is one which minority governments in Britain have rarely been prepared to pay.

How a minority government decides to secure its survival has depended essentially upon tactical considerations. Each minority government in Britain has adopted a different approach to the problem of survival depending upon its conception of the relative strength of the political forces against it, and upon how long it has sought to remain in office. The longer a minority government has wished to stay in power, the more it has been compelled to enter into negotiations with other parties.

IV

In the case of the first Labour government, Ramsay MacDonald was bound by a resolution of the 1922 Labour Party Conference which had declared 'against any alliance or electoral arrangement with any section of the Liberal or Conservative Parties'. The Glasgow Independent Labour Party, representing Labour's Left wing, sent a telegram to Mac-

Donald saying 'No coalition under any circumstances. Labour alone is competent and willing to govern'. Labour's National Executive, supported by the TUC, asked MacDonald to 'accept full responsibility for the government of the country without compromising itself with any form of coalition'.[3] When Richard Lyman was writing his monograph in the 1950s on the first Labour government, he was able to interview C. P. Trevelyan, the only surviving member of that administration, who stressed 'that here was only one generally accepted thing in all the confusion and flux of the time – the party's determination to avoid the Liberal embrace. Labour's leaders realized that for them to share office with the Liberals would mean a new lease of life to the older party, whereas the attainment of power was dependent upon the destruction of the Liberals'.[4] For this reason, according to Snowden, the Chancellor of the Exchequer, 'There was little or no preliminary consultation between the Government and the Liberal leaders on legislation which it was proposed to introduce.' The government, Snowden complained, 'never really accepted the limitations of its Minority position'.[5] Being convinced, perhaps, that the 'inevitability of gradualism' would lead to a socialist majority, it felt no incentive to do so.

MacDonald did not seek in 1924 to put forward an ambitious legislative programme for which Liberal support would have been necessary. On the contrary, the first Labour government was an extremely cautious one, and the more radical Liberals were urging it to do more, rather than trying to restrain its excesses. MacDonald's aim was not so much to place socialist legislation on the statute book as to prove to the electorate that a Labour government could be as respectable and safe as a government of the old parties. Because the government was so cautious, it was difficult for the other parties to throw it out immediately without allowing MacDonald to complain to the electorate that he had been denied fair play. The Conservatives had to wait for the government to show itself as extremist, while the Liberals, chronically short of funds, were frightened at the thought of an immediate general election. For this reason, the Labour government was able to survive for nine months despite the absence of any agreement or understanding with the other parties.

The first Labour government was, in Beatrice Webb's words, to be merely 'a scouting expedition in the world of administration – a testing of men and measures before they are actually called to exercise majority power'.[6] MacDonald did not perhaps expect the government to last long,

---

[3] Lyman, *The First Labour Government*, pp. 88–9.
[4] Ibid., p. 89.
[5] Philip Snowden, *An Autobiography* (Nicholson and Watson, 1934), vol. 2, pp. 631–2.
[6] Lyman, *The First Labour Government*, p. 92.

and when, in October 1924, the Conservatives and Liberals were able to act together in voting to censure the government's handling of the prosecution of the Communist newspaper, the *Workers Weekly*, MacDonald chose to regard it as a vote of no-confidence and dissolved Parliament.

V

In the case of the second Labour government, by contrast, a number of attempts at co-operation were made. The government formed in June 1929, was only 20 short of an overall majority, but soon ran into electoral difficulties, with the result that from January 1930, MacDonald wanted to avoid a dissolution which would probably be followed by an overall Conservative majority and another full term in opposition for the Labour Party. Although a formal and public alliance with another party would have been impossible because the Labour left would have accused him of betraying socialism, nevertheless, in the debate on the Address in 1929, MacDonald appealed for co-operation.

I wonder how far it is possible, without in any way abandoning any of our party positions, without in any way surrendering any item of our party principles, to consider ourselves more as a Council of State and less as arrayed regiments facing each other in battle ... so that by putting our ideas into a common pool we can bring out ... legislation and administration which will be of substantial benefit to the nation as a whole.[7]

As a token of goodwill towards the Liberals, MacDonald followed this overture by announcing that an enquiry into electoral law would be instituted. This offered the Liberals some hope that Labour might be prepared to concede either proportional representation or the alternative vote, in exchange for Liberal support of the government. Yet the history of the second Labour government is one of attempts at co-operation which were successful only in limited areas of policy but failed either to resolve the central issue of unemployment or to ensure the long-term survival of the government.

There was collaboration between the parties on policy towards India, and the principle of encouraging India's progress towards self-government was accepted by the Labour, Liberal and Conservative Parties, with the exception of Churchill and the Conservative Right. Baldwin, the Conservative leader, was particularly anxious that India should not prove a source of partisan conflict as Ireland had been, and the development of Indian policy offers a good illustration of the benefits of all-party co-operation.

Disarmament was another field in which co-operation proved possible.

[7] H.C. Debs, vol. 229, cols. 64–5, 2 July 1929.

In March 1931, a three-party sub-committee of the Committee of Imperial Defence was established which proved, according to Sir Samuel Hoare, 'a remarkable example of inter-party co-operation on a vital question of Imperial policy'. The sub-committee's main conclusion was that disarmament could not be carried any further. 'Any further reduction of British armaments', it declared, 'could only be undertaken as part of an international agreement containing comparable reductions by other Powers and after taking into account the particular obligations and dangers of each country.'[8] This conclusion furnished the basis for the policies both of the second Labour government and of the National Government which succeeded it.

Another three-party committee was set up to consider how to contain the spiralling costs of unemployment insurance. This was less successful since the government took no notice of its recommendations, but proceeded with its own plans as if the committee did not exist. Since this committee, like that on disarmament, enjoyed the status of a Cabinet Committee, details of its discussions could not be revealed in the Commons. This led the Opposition parties to feel that they had been deceived by MacDonald, and had been inveigled into supporting the government whilst still unable to influence the precise content of policy proposals. In arguing this, however, they probably gave a Machiavellian interpretation to what was nothing more than muddle and confusion.

These committees, however, had little bearing on the problem of the government's long-term survival. For that, an agreement with the Liberals was necessary. In December, inter-party discussions were held between the leaders of the Labour and Liberal Parties on the government's Coal Bill, but agreement could not be reached, and the Bill only just passed its Second Reading. Yet an arrangement with the Liberals should not have proved too difficult to achieve. For relations between the Liberals and Labour in the second Labour government were, by contrast with the first, 'increasingly friendly, and the Whips worked together in considerable amity'.[9] In February 1930, discussions between the Labour and Liberal leaders were resumed, and the outlines of a bargain between the two parties began to emerge. Labour would concede electoral reform – the alternative vote rather than proportional representation – and the Liberals would agree to sustain Labour in office. In this way, Labour would secure 'two years of office from the Liberals and give them in return a permanent corner on our political stage'.[10] MacDonald,

[8] R. Bassett, *Nineteen Thirty One: Political Crisis* (Macmillan, 1958), p. 41.
[9] John D. Fair, 'The second Labour government and the politics of electoral reform, 1929–1931', *Albion* (Fall 1981), p. 282.
[10] Ibid., p. 283.

however, preferred informal discussions with Lloyd George, the Liberal leader, and was against making any bargain 'definite or committing it to writing'.[11] In any case, neither leader would have been able to carry his party with him in any formal agreement. MacDonald was under continuous pressure from the Labour Left, while Lloyd George faced the increasing hostility of the Liberal Right led by Sir John Simon who regarded the Labour government as an unmitigated disaster, and preferred to seek an accommodation with the Conservatives.

Discussions between the Labour and Liberal Parties became more formalised in June 1930, after the resignation of Sir Oswald Mosley from the government in protest against the timidity of its unemployment proposals. The government was widely accused of lacking ideas and drive, and perhaps the search for closer relations with the Liberals was intended as a way of countering this accusation. MacDonald invited Lloyd George to confer with him on the problems of unemployment and agriculture. Lloyd George accepted this invitation, although without consulting his party, and asked Lord Lothian and Seebohm Rowntree, neither of whom were MPs, to join him. A series of two-party conferences to deal with the problems of unemployment and agriculture were established. These were to be merely advisory in nature, but the Liberals were promised access to government files and to civil service advice. This promise, however, was hardly kept. In August 1930, the private secretary to Christopher Addison, the Minister of Agriculture, told the latter that he had selected for one of the joint meetings 'a considerable number of documents ... after consultation ... without including anything that would be very embarrassing'.[12] This was indicative of the spirit in which the government entered the negotiations, and it is hardly surprising that they made little contribution to a resolution of the difficult problems which they were discussing.

The meetings appeared to bind neither party. The government continued making new proposals on unemployment and agriculture without even bothering to inform those attending the conferences, while the Liberals continued to vote for or against government legislation on an ad hoc basis. In the autumn of 1930, however, with unemployment rising inexorably, and the government seemingly condemned to electoral disaster if it were forced suddenly to go to the country, the discussions became more serious. Lloyd George told MacDonald that 'the co-operation of the Liberals in the coming session would be dependent upon a definite understanding that the Government would introduce and pass legislation for Electoral Reform'. He also told the Prime Minister that if he did not

[11] Ibid., p. 284.
[12] Vandepeer to Addison, 28 August 1930, Addison Papers MS 19.

secure such a concession from Labour, he would be open to a bargain with the Conservatives. As a result, the Cabinet agreed to enter further discussions on the alternative vote. At a Cabinet meeting on 17 November 1930, the Cabinet recognised that the price of Liberal co-operation would in fact be electoral reform. 'It was suggested that the task of Ministers would be facilitated if, instead of consultation in regard to each Bill, some general understanding could be reached. In this connection it was pointed out ... that before any general arrangement could be made, the Liberals would require an understanding in regard to Electoral Reform, and on this subject they had not defined their attitude.'[13] In December, however, Labour actually committed itself to the alternative vote, and a bill was introduced in 1931. In March 1931, further joint committees were established to deal with other policy areas: telephones, town planning and the housing of farm labourers. They made little progress.

In his memoirs, Philip Snowden implies that an agreement was reached between the Labour and Liberal Parties. Labour would concede the alternative vote, while the Liberals would keep the government in office for the two years needed to pass the legislation over the expected opposition of the House of Lords – at that time, the Parliament Act required a bill to be passed three times by the Commons to surmount the Lords veto. However, there is no evidence of any formal agreement, nor were the Liberals committed to supporting government legislation. Reminiscing in the 1950s, Lord Thurso, formerly Sir Archibald Sinclair, said that the Liberals were not committed 'to the support of any other legislation which the Government might introduce, nor [had they] given them any pledge that we would keep them in Office until the Electoral Reform Bill was passed into law. The most that can be said is that there was a reasonable, and practicable, if vague understanding between the Labour Government and the Liberal Party about the plain facts of the political situation at that time'. If there was a bargain, Thurso continued, 'it must have been the loosest bargain in political history', since it 'left us so much freedom of action'.[14] In the event, the Labour government introduced a bill providing for the alternative vote in February 1931, but it was rejected by the Lords, and before it could be re-introduced into the Commons, the government had fallen. Most probably the Liberals kept Labour in office until August 1931 not because of any formal agreement, but because of 'the half-promise of electoral reform',[15] fear of electoral

13 Fair, 'The second Labour government', pp. 292, 295.
14 Lord Thurso to D.E. Butler, 1 March 1951, 26 February 1951, Butler Papers, reprinted in Fair, 'The second Labour government', pp. 293, 301.
15 Campbell, *Lloyd George*, p. 274.

The constitutional consequences

losses and fear of protection. The action of the Liberals is to be seen not as the 'fulfilment of an agreement but as recognition of immediate political necessity'.[16] It may be however that Lloyd George privately offered rather more knowing that he could not publicly commit his party. 'It was', said Sir John Simon, 'Lloyd George's pact, not the party's'.[17]

The history of the second Labour government, then, was hardly one of successful inter-party co-operation in a hung Parliament. The Liberal leadership continually sought a wider understanding which the government was unwilling to offer. Indeed, the government sought less a parliamentary alliance to aid its legislation, for it had few ambitious measures which it wished to pass, than a working agreement to ensure its parliamentary survival, something which could be bought far more cheaply. Attempts were made to obtain Liberal support on a short-term basis for various government bills, but even when agreement seemed to be reached, the Liberals would not support the government in a disciplined way in the division lobbies, partly because this would mean accepting responsibility for government measures which they had been unable to influence. Not only was there to be no policy agreement sustaining the government, but even the attempts at ad hoc co-operation were far from successful. 'What emerges', as one historian has noted, 'is an unattractive picture of political manoeuvering, calumny, and subterfuge where the potential allies worked at cross-purposes – the object of the Government being to create conditions favourable to retaining office while the Liberals desired some greater prospect for attaining office in the future. Despite their interdependence, the party leaders were never able to reach an agreement on the vital issue of electoral reform, which would involve some possible sacrifice of their individual ends. The result was a process of mutual destruction which contributed to the fall of the Second Labour Government and opened the way for a Conservative bid for power.'[18] Such co-operation as existed amounted to no more than entirely informal understandings which could not be revealed even to some of the Labour and Liberal leaders, let alone back-benchers. Yet it is hard to conclude that the absence of a more formal agreement was in the interest of the Labour or Liberal Parties. Instead of merely negative manoeuvering, a more positive attempt to seek policies which could unite the two parties might well have ensured a full term of office for a government of the Left as well as contributing to a bolder approach on unemployment. Instead, the second Labour government chose to commit

[16] D.E.Butler, *The Electoral System in Britain Since 1918* (2nd edition, Oxford University Press, 1963), p. 65.
[17] Simon Papers, 27 November 1930.
[18] Fair, 'The second Labour government', p. 277.

political suicide rather than compromise its followers' hostility to the capitalist parties.

VI

The next minority government in Britain did not occur until March 1974 when Harold Wilson unexpectedly formed his second administration after the inconclusive general election of the previous month. The ghost of Ramsay MacDonald still haunted the Labour Party and the events of 1931 had given the Party an aversion to coalitions or deals of any kind with other parties. Indeed, at the 1973 Labour Party Conference, Wilson gave a pledge against any such arrangement in terms which it would have been difficult even for him to evade:

Let this be clear: as long as I am Leader of the Party, Labour will not enter into my coalition with any other Party, Liberal or Conservative or anyone else. (*Prolonged Applause*)

As long as I am Leader of this Party there will be no electoral treaty, no political alliance, no understanding, no deal, no arrangement, no fix, neither will there be any secret deal or secret discussions. Whatever the results of the election, a Labour Government will go forward boldly on its policy, challenging any manoeuverers to make their position clear in vote after vote. If, as they never dared to do between 1964 and 1966, they make it impossible for us to implement that programme, then the issue will be taken openly back to the people of this country for a final decision. (*Applause*) And let the danger light upon those who thought they could exercise an electorally unearned control over a constitutional government.[19]

In this speech, Wilson was clearly relying, as MacDonald had done in 1923/4, upon two constitutional conventions facilitating minority government at the expense of a majority coalition. There was first the convention that Labour, if the largest party, would be allowed to form a single-party minority government before the possibilities of a majority coalition had been explored; and secondly that a minority government would be entitled to a dissolution at a moment of its own choosing, thereby freeing it from the need to conciliate opposition parties in Parliament.

In the event, Wilson's predictions were almost wholly realised after the general election of February 1974. Edward Heath, the Conservative Prime Minister, attempted to construct a coalition with the Liberals, which although it would not have commanded a majority of seats in the Commons, would have been the largest single grouping in the House. The Liberals, however, rejected such a coalition, offering the Conservatives only support from outside the government on an agreed pro-

---

[19] Labour Party Conference Reports, 1973, p. 197.

gramme, an offer somewhat similar to that made subsequently by David Steel to James Callaghan in 1977 when it formed the basis of the Lib–Lab pact. But Heath rejected this offer as inadequate and resigned, and Wilson formed a minority government.

The Labour government, as we have seen, faced immediate defeat in the debate on the Address, and this was avoided only by threatening the Conservatives with an immediate dissolution. The government was safe between March and June, but as soon as the danger of a June election had passed, an election which the Conservative leaders believed Labour would win with a handsome majority, the government began to suffer defeats in the Commons. The first defeat came on 19 June, on a clause in the Finance Bill seeking to restore relief to trade unions de-registered under the 1971 Industrial Relations Act. From then until the end of the session in late July, the government was defeated another sixteen times. Wilson went to the country in October, and secured a narrow overall majority of only three. His tactical judgment had been vindicated in two respects, firstly in his view that the other parties would not be able to combine together to stop him either forming a minority government or defeating it in the House before he was ready to go to the country; and secondly that he could obtain an overall majority after only a few months in office as leader of a minority government. Had he needed more time to gain an overall majority, his strategy might not have worked.

VII

The narrow overall majority won by Labour in October 1974 did not last long. By April 1976, it had been whittled away through the loss of a by-election and the disappearance and defection of John Stonehouse. The government was to suffer six further by-election losses and three more defections during its term of office. Since the Conservatives enjoyed a huge lead in the opinion polls for most of the period, Labour had to avoid being forced to the country before the promised economic recovery had materialised.

The loss of its overall majority in April 1976 did not immediately worry the Labour government. For one of the items in the legislative pipeline was devolution, and the Scottish and Welsh Nationalists would not turn the government out until they were assured that assemblies in Edinburgh and Cardiff would be established. Unfortunately, however, the government found itself unable to steer the Scotland and Wales Bill through the Commons. Faced with a revolt by its own back-benchers as well as opposition from the Conservatives, the government decided to introduce a guillotine motion in February 1977. It did so, however, without consulting with the other parties sympathetic to devolution, since it assumed that the Nationalists and Liberals would not dare to defeat the legislation. But this judgment proved a miscalculation, as the Liberals were by now tired of being taken for granted. They had put forward a number of proposals seeking to improve the Scotland and Wales Bill, but these had been ignored. They now decided, with the two Welsh Liberal MPs dissenting, to vote against the guillotine. 'I persuaded the parliamentary party', wrote David Steel in 1980, 'that we should oppose the guillotine and make our continuing support for the measure dependent on proper consultation and attention to Liberal views'.[20] This emboldened Labour back-benchers opposed to devolution also to vote against the guillotine, and on 22 February the motion was defeated by 29 votes. The government was forced to abandon the legislation.

This cost the government the support of the eleven Scottish Nationalist MPs. Since the evidence of opinion polls showed that they were, at that time, the most popular party in Scotland, the Nationalists declared that they would do all that they could to force an immediate general election. On 17 March, the government, knowing that it would be defeated, refused even to contest an adjournment motion on its 1977 Public Expenditure plans and was defeated by 293 votes to 0. The Conservatives immediately put down a motion of no-confidence, to be debated on 23 March. It was clear that unless an understanding with one of the minority parties could be achieved, the government would be forced to go to the country at a time when the Conservatives were 16½% ahead in the opinion polls.

Labour first tried to reach an accommodation with the Ulster Unionists, but when this proved impossible, the Prime Minister, James Callaghan, summoned David Steel, the Liberal leader, to ask whether the Liberals would support the government in the no-confidence vote. Steel replied that the Liberals were not interested in the kind of ad hoc agreement on particular items of legislation characteristic of the years 1929–31. What he wanted was a general understanding so that there could be agreed co-operation on a wide range of issues between the government and the Liberal Party. He then sent the Prime Minister a letter declaring the basis on which the Liberal Party would 'be prepared to consider sustaining the Government in its pursuit of national recovery...'. The letter mentioned six points. Of these, three were connected with items of legislation. The first was that the government should not proceed with the Local Government Direct Labour Bill which had been announced in the Queen's Speech, nor were there to be any further

20 David Steel, *A House Divided: The Lib–Lab Pact and the Future of British Politics* (Weidenfeld and Nicolson, 1980), p. 28.

measures of nationalisation. Secondly, the government would have to resume the legislation on devolution, and take account of Liberal proposals on that subject. No government whip should be applied against proportional representation for the devolved assemblies. Thirdly, the government would 'undertake to introduce and commend to the House a Bill for direct elections to the European Parliament based on a proportional system'.

The first two conditions did not embarrass the government. Indeed, they would have to be met, whether or not there was an understanding with the Liberals. Because it was in a minority position, the government could not hope to pass further measures of nationalisation or the Direct Labour Bill. If the government sought support from the minority parties, it would have to legislate on devolution; while Harold Wilson had already committed the government to direct elections to the European Parliament.

The central difficulty, which almost prevented the pact coming into existence, was over the commitment to proportional representation for the European elections. This was something to which Callaghan was unable to commit himself, because he knew that such a commitment could not be honoured. Even if the Cabinet would accept it – and that in itself was highly unlikely – the Parliamentary Party as a whole would not, even if a three-line whip was imposed. In the end, Callaghan agreed to offer a choice of electoral systems, between the regional list system of proportional representation and the 'first past the post' system and promised to take account of the Liberal Party's views on the subject while giving a private assurance that he himself would vote for proportional representation.

These legislative matters were of considerable importance to Liberal MPs and activists but they did not represent the priorities of the average voter. Nor were they of central importance to David Steel. His concern was less with specific legislative gains than with the institutional machinery which would give reality to the idea of a pact and to Liberal participation in government. The other three points in his letter to the Prime Minister were thus directed to ensuring that Liberal influence on the government was formalised. There would have to be an immediate meeting between the Chancellor of the Exchequer and the Liberal Party's economic spokesman (John Pardoe) before the pact was finalised, to confirm that there was agreement upon an economic strategy based on a prices and incomes policy and reductions in personal taxation. Secondly, the terms of the agreement were to be published as a formal exchange of letters. Finally – and most important from Steel's point of view – a formal consultative committee between the two parties would be established. This committee would meet regularly to discuss joint strategy, and act as a court of appeal to resolve disagreements. It would be supplemented by informal meetings between government ministers and Liberal 'shadows', while Callaghan and Steel would act as ultimate arbiters on any issues which could not be settled by these informal meetings or the joint consultative committee.[21]

After some negotiation, agreement was eventually reached on these points, and Callaghan put the pact to his Cabinet which accepted it with four dissentients – Tony Benn, Albert Booth, Stanley Orme, and Bruce Millan. The government thus gained a comfortable victory in the no-confidence debate on 23 March and the 13 Liberal MPs, when added to the 310 Labour members, ensured that the government was (in a House of 635 members) safe from defeat while the pact lasted. The pact, which was duly inaugurated by an exchange of letters between Callaghan and Steel, was to be renewed for a year in July 1977, and it ended in July 1978, giving the government the assurance of a parliamentary majority until the autumn session of Parliament began in October 1978.

The pact – or 'agreement' as the Liberals preferred to call it – was a novel and curious constitutional experiment. It was certainly not a coalition agreement. The Liberals did not join the Cabinet; indeed they remained on the Opposition benches. There was no commitment by the Liberals to support every item of government legislation, nor on the part of the government to accept particular Liberal proposals. In the exchange of letters between Callaghan and Steel inaugurating the pact, it was explicitly stated that the agreement 'does not commit the Government to accepting the views of the Liberal party, nor the Liberal party to supporting the Government on any issue'.[22] The joint consultative committee, although staffed by civil servants, was in no sense a part of the official machinery of government, and if agreement could not be reached on a matter under discussion, the Liberals were entirely free to vote against government legislation in the Commons. During the life-time of the pact, they in fact voted against government measures on income tax levels, the dock labour scheme, National Insurance contributions and the devaluation of the green pound. Indeed, the Liberals threatened to vote against increases in the tax on petrol in the budget which Denis Healey introduced on 29 March, only six days after the pact had been agreed. The threat had to be withdrawn but the government nevertheless decided not to implement the increases.

[21] Ibid., pp. 36–7 gives the letter which Steel wrote to Callaghan laying out the six conditions.
[22] Alistair Michie and Simon Hoggart, *The Pact: The Inside Story of the Lib–Lab Government 1977–8* (Quartet, 1978), pp. 139–40.

Yet if the pact was not a full coalition, it was more than an ad hoc agreement on particular items of legislation of the type negotiated by Ramsay MacDonald and Lloyd George between 1929 and 1931. For the core of the agreement was that the Liberals would gain participation in the legislative process in exchange for a commitment to ensure the government's survival during the period of the pact; and regular negotiations were instituted between the Chief Whips of the two parties so that the government should not be in danger of losing any votes which it deemed vital.

Liberal participation in government legislation was secured through negotiations between government ministers and their Liberal 'shadows'. This gave the Liberals influence on all government legislation, not only those measures specifically mentioned in the pact. The commitment in the pact to particular legislative proposals was, therefore, to prove less important than the agreement on joint discussions between Cabinet ministers and their shadows; and the legislation which resulted from the pact derived more from the consultative process itself than from the original commitment. Alan Beith, Liberal Chief Whip at the time of the pact, has said that 'Many of the most valuable policy achievements of the agreement were ... gained through the process of negotiation.' The Liberals were granted the privilege, in Beith's words, of 'many detailed discussions on legislative priorities', and 'the nominal secrecy was a shroud concealing extensive consultation'.[23] On particular clauses in the 1978 Finance Bill, John Pardoe and his adviser were given access to privileged Whitehall documents, and were allowed to see government amendments before publication; indeed Pardoe's adviser helped to re-write that part of the legislation dealing with tax incentives for worker co-ownership schemes. In addition, the renewal of the pact in July 1977 gave the Liberals the privilege of consultation with the government 'with a view to determining the priorities in the Queen's Speech'. They were able to discuss government legislation with ministers before the Cabinet had taken a final decision on its commitments for the coming year.

Clearly, the success of an agreement of this type would depend upon the spirit in which it was operated. Where relations between ministers and their Liberal shadows were good, as between Roy Hattersley and Lady Seear, or William Rodgers and David Penhaligon, much could be accomplished. Where relations were bad, as between ministers who opposed the pact, and their Liberal shadows – Tony Benn and Jo Grimond, Albert Booth and Cyril Smith – little of value could be achieved. Central to the success of the pact was the personal rapport achieved

---

[23] Alan Beith, 'The working of the Lib-Lab arrangement', in *Probleme von Koalitionsregierungen in Westeuropa* (Friedrich-Naumann-Stiftung, 1978), pp. 31, 34.

between Callaghan and Steel. It is doubtful if the pact would have been workable if Harold Wilson had still been leader of the Labour Party, given his public commitments against understandings with minority parties; nor if John Pardoe rather than David Steel had been elected Liberal leader in 1976. Indeed, Pardoe's relations with Healey were always tense, and difficulties frequently had to be resolved by the two party leaders.

It was to prove symbolic, therefore, that the pact was inaugurated by an exchange of letters between Callaghan and Steel. It had been negotiated by these two men, with the assistance of their deputies – Michael Foot, who could provide an assurance that not all of the Left would be opposed to it, and John Pardoe. Although Denis Healey was also involved to a lesser extent, the Cabinet as a whole was not consulted. The pact was thus presented to the Cabinet as a *fait accompli* which it would have been difficult to alter or reject. 'It wasn't so much a Lib–Lab pact, as a Steel–Callaghan pact accepted by our respective colleagues with widely varying degrees of enthusiasm or lack of it.' It was for this reason that the strategic decisions were taken less by the joint consultative committee than by Steel and Callaghan negotiating directly. 'In practice', according to Steel, the joint committee 'dealt mainly with matters of important detail rather than principle. On major issues it tended to get by-passed in favour of Privy Council terms discussion between the Prime Minister and myself, or, for example, the Chancellor and myself.'[24]

Steel has called the pact 'a parliamentary but not governmental coalition',[25] but this description is perhaps misleading since the agreement was not one between the parliamentary Labour and Liberal parties, but between the parliamentary Liberal Party and the Cabinet. The Parliamentary Labour Party was not involved in the agreement. The absence of a formal party commitment was to prove of particular importance when the issue of proportional representation for direct elections to the European Parliament came before the Commons in December 1977. The government recommended proportional representation, and there was a free vote on the issue. Despite Liberal insistence on the importance of proportional representation to the continuation of the pact, however, 115 Labour MPs voted against it, and 46 abstained. Admittedly, more Labour MPs – 147 – voted for proportional representation than against it, while the pact ensured that such unlikely figures as Michael Foot and John Silkin were to be found in the pro-PR division lobby. Nevertheless, the defeat of proportional representation almost led to the collapse of the pact. Liberal activists insisted upon a Special Assembly of the Party in January 1978, to consider whether it should be continued, and it

[24] Steel, *A House Divided*, p. 153; Steel in *Probleme von Koalitionsregierungen*, p. 7.
[25] *A House Divided*, p. viii.

required all of David Steel's skill to prevent its rejection. The lack of a Labour Party Commitment was, in Steel's view, 'one of the fundamental weaknesses of the whole agreement, and I determined that if ever we were negotiating again after a general election with one of the major parties the prior formal assent of that parliamentary party as a whole to any agreement would be essential'.[26] Nor of course did the pact have any effect on the parties outside Parliament where they continued to oppose each other at the polls. An electoral pact, even a by-election pact, was never seriously contemplated.

<h1 style="text-align:center">VIII</h1>

Any overall assessment of the Lib–Lab pact is inevitably complicated by the changing fortunes of the Labour and Liberal Parties since it ended. At that stage, the general view was that Labour had managed to win Liberal support extraordinarily cheaply, and that Steel had been out-manoeuvered by a shrewder and more experienced politician. The Liberals did not secure significant legislative gains from the pact; and their success in amending such legislation as the Post Office and the Electricity Bills was hardly likely to excite the electorate. The Liberals failed to secure any significant improvements to the devolution legislation and since they supported devolution even more than the government, they could not allow it to be defeated in the Commons a second time.

Their failure to secure significant legislative gains did not, however, prevent the Liberals from being associated with the unpopularity of the Labour government. The pact made it difficult for them to attack the government without being accused of hypocrisy for keeping it in power for so long. The Liberals, therefore, seemed to have obtained the worst of both worlds – responsibility without power.

Labour seemed the sole beneficiary of the pact. In exchange for conceding only a minimal degree of influence over policy – and a minority government could in any event not have survived much longer without making a number of concessions – Callaghan assured himself of a majority in the Commons, and also gained the benefit of being able to choose when to dissolve Parliament. The fact that he did not take full advantage of these gains can hardly be attributed to the pact.

The Liberals claimed credit for preventing the passage of left-wing measures, but of course a minority government would not in any case have succeeded in getting such legislation passed by the Commons, even if there had been any inclination to introduce it. The Liberals also

[26] Ibid., p. 156.

claimed that the pact gave the country economic stability, but this too is questionable. It certainly made for a more stable arrangement than a minority government propped up from issue to issue by ad hoc agreements. But as the result of a general election in March 1977 would almost certainly have been the return of a Conservative government with an overall majority, this would of itself have brought stability in the sense at least of a government with full control of the Commons. At best, the Liberals could claim that they had delayed the coming to power of a government of the Right, and helped to ensure that the Labour government moved to the centre.

For David Steel the significance of the pact did not lie in the legislative gains which it achieved, but rather in the opportunity it offered of bringing the Liberals into association with government for the first time, excluding the war, since 1932. The pact, in Steel's view, would illustrate the benefits to be gained from party co-operation, coalition government and realignment. 'I want', he told Liberal candidates when the pact was in danger in January 1978, 'to be able to argue the case for a better way of running Britain and illustrate it as we've never been able to before by pointing to a successful period of political co-operation.'[27] The root cause of the divergence between Steel and other Liberals was that while they looked to it for specific gains, and particularly the winning of proportional representation for elections to the European Parliament, he 'was far more concerned with the general idea of a pact and the idea of consultations than he was in any policies which it might bring about'.[28]

It is now possible to look upon the events of 1977–78 with a more independent perspective from that fashionable at the time. The benefits which the Labour Party received from the pact turned out to be short-lived. Callaghan did not make good use of the central advantage which the pact gave him, the chance to choose for himself the timing of a general election rather than having that choice forced upon him by the minor parties. For, instead of dissolving in September 1978, immediately after the end of the pact, he continued until 1979, relying upon the support of the Ulster Unionists and the nationalist parties. Unfortunately, the result of the devolution referendums in March 1979 deprived him of the support of the Scottish Nationalists and he was forced to go to the country in May. After Labour's election defeat, the divisions between Left and Right in the Party intensified, Callaghan resigned, and, with the dramatic defection of the Social Democrats, Labour came to look less and less like a party of government.

[27] Ibid., p. 115.
[28] Michie and Hoggart, *The Pact*, p. 50.

The Liberals, on the other hand, did rather better than expected in the general election of 1979, securing 14% of the vote and 11 seats. Steel's strategy of seeking co-operation with other parties led eventually to the Alliance with the Social Democrats in 1981. The pact gave the Liberals exposure as a party of government and made their claims to political credibility more realistic than they had previously been. The pact, indeed, can be seen as a precursor of the new type of politics which the Alliance now seeks to introduce; and if the Alliance is successful, the pact will be seen ultimately to have benefited the Liberals rather than the Labour Party. *The Times* claimed on 24 May 1978 that the pact was 'a brave attempt to establish the conditions in which minority government can be made to work' and that was perhaps the fairest short-term assessment. But it could also turn out to have been the forerunner of a new style of multi-party, coalition-style politics in Britain, a politics still at that time only a distant dream in the eyes of those Liberals who negotiated the pact.

IX

The Lib–Lab pact is the only example in British twentieth-century experience of a minority government operating through an explicit agreement with another party on a long-term basis. It can be regarded as a half-way house between a full coalition and an ad-hoc agreement on particular issues – sharing some of the features of both, yet not to be identified with either. It is not typical of the experience of minority governments in Britain, which have generally been content to live from day to day relying upon a favourable opportunity to secure a tactical dissolution. Since periods of minority government have been brief and intermittent, there has been little inclination to consider how a minority government can be made to work on a long-term basis.

One central reason for this, as we have seen, is the Prime Minister's ability to secure a dissolution even if his government does not command a majority in the Commons. Were hung parliaments, however, to become a regular occurrence the convention that the Prime Minister of the day can automatically secure a dissolution might come to be questioned. By his actions in 1924 in sending Lord Stamfordham to sound out the opinion of the Liberal and Conservative leaders, George V showed that he did not regard the granting of a dissolution to a minority government as automatic. Harold Wilson's doubts in March 1974, and the hopes of some Conservatives that a defeat of the Labour government on the Address might be followed by the Queen summoning Edward Heath, also shows that not all leading politicians believed that the Prime Minister of a minority government had an automatic right to a dissolution. In April 1974, a group of Labour MPs wrote to Edward Short, the Leader of the House, to argue that the Sovereign was bound to grant a dissolution whenever the Prime Minister wanted it: 'In our opinion', they declared, 'the Prime Minister of the day has an absolute right to decide the date of the election following discussion with his Cabinet colleagues. In such circumstances, we believe, the Queen is both morally and constitutionally obliged to accept the advice given'. Short, however, replied that 'Constitutional lawyers of the highest authority are of the clear opinion that the Sovereign is not in all circumstances bound to grant a Prime Minister's request for a dissolution' (*The Times*, 8 April 1974). Under what circumstances, then, could the Sovereign refuse a dissolution to a minority government? Could she, for example, refuse if the Commons did not want to be dissolved? Should she consider whether an alternative administration can be formed without dissolving Parliament?

In 1950, when the question arose of whether a government with a majority, albeit a small one, could be refused a dissolution, *The Times* (2 May 1950) published a letter by 'Senex', later revealed to be Sir Alan Lascelles, Private Secretary to the King, in which he declared:

It is surely indisputable (and common sense) that a Prime Minister may ask – not demand – that his Sovereign will grant him a dissolution of Parliament; and that the Sovereign, if he so chooses, may refuse to grant this request. The problem of such a choice is entirely personal to the Sovereign, though he is, of course, free to ask informal advice from anybody whom he thinks fit to consult.

In so far as this matter can be publicly discussed, it can be properly assumed that no wise Sovereign – that is, one who has at heart the true interest of the country, the constitution, and the Monarchy – would deny a dissolution to his Prime Minister unless he was satisfied that: (1) the existing Parliament was still vital, viable, and capable of doing its job; (2) a General Election would be detrimental to the national economy; (3) he could rely on finding another Prime Minister who could carry on his Government, for a reasonable period, with a working majority in the House of Commons. When Sir Patrick Duncan refused a dissolution to his Prime Minister in South Africa in 1939, all these conditions were satisfied: when Lord Byng did the same in Canada in 1926, they appeared to be, but in the event the third proved illusory.

What might be called the Lascelles doctrine has proved extremely influential, and a similar formula has been used by S. A. de Smith in his well known text-book, *Constitutional and Administrative Law:*

Perhaps the following proposition would command a wide measure of support: the Queen may properly refuse a Prime Minister's request for a dissolution if she has substantial grounds for believing (i) that an alternative Government, enjoying the confidence of a majority of the House of Commons, can be formed without a General Election, and (ii) that a General Election held at that time would be clearly prejudicial to the national interest.[29]

Yet such views probably credit the monarch with too active a role. Except in highly pathological or revolutionary circumstances, it is hardly the Crown's responsibility to decide whether a general election would or would not be prejudicial to the national interest, or 'detrimental to the national economy'. That is an issue upon which the political parties may well be deeply divided, and it could be dangerous for the Sovereign to take sides upon it. The rule that the Sovereign can properly refuse a dissolution if an alternative government able to command the support of the House of Commons is available, seems more plausible, but the Sovereign will rarely be in a position to evaluate the likely durability of alternative coalitions or promises of support. The example cited by Lascelles of Lord Byng in Canada in 1926 is a good illustration of the dangers. Byng, the Governor-General of Canada, had refused a dissolution to the Prime Minister, Mackenzie King, whose party enjoyed only minority support in the Commons. He believed that Meighen, the Leader of the Opposition, could form a government commanding the confidence of Parliament. Meighen, indeed, gave assurances to this effect on the basis of informal promises which he had received from members of one of the minority parties. In the event, however, Meighen's government was defeated in the House only four days after his government was formed, and Byng granted his request for a dissolution.

The Sovereign, if she is to take the risk of refusing a dissolution, must have a cast-iron public guarantee that a government can be formed commanding the confidence of the Commons. Otherwise her action in refusing a dissolution can appear partisan. The only way in which such a guarantee can be obtained is through a public statement on the part of the Opposition parties committing them to work together. The onus is on them to prove beyond all reasonable doubt that an alternative government is possible.

But, even if the Sovereign has the assurance that an alternative government commanding a majority in the House is available, it by no means follows that she should refuse a dissolution. For it can still be argued that in many circumstances an election would be the best way to resolve the situation. This is particularly the case if 'the alternative Ministry would have little or no popular backing, or if it proposed to act, or was dependent upon the support of members who were proposing to act, in flagrant disregard of pledges to the electors'.[30] It is perfectly possible,

[29] S.A. de Smith, *Constitutional and Administrative Law* (3rd edition, Penguin, 1977), p. 104.
[30] Eugene A. Forsey, *The Royal Power of Dissolution in the British Commonwealth* (Oxford University Press, Toronto, 1943), p. 10.

after all, for the alternative majority ministry to be far less popular in the country than the minority government which seeks a dissolution. If government and Parliament cannot work together, there is a case for saying that the dispute should be resolved by the real political sovereign, which in a democracy is the electorate. A change of government which occurs without an election can, as the West German example in 1982 has shown, provoke resentment that democratic norms are being ignored, and it would be dangerous for the Sovereign to allow herself to be exposed to criticism on this score. 'In acceding to a minority Prime Minister's request for a dissolution, the Crown is implicitly acknowledging the superior claim of the electorate to arbitrate among the parties and to try to produce a majority.'[31] Where there is some doubt as to what course the Sovereign should pursue, she is best advised to take the course most strongly supported by precedent, and that would involve giving the Prime Minister of the day the benefit of the doubt and acceding to his request to dissolve. There can never be a guarantee that any specific decision will not have unfortunate consequences. But if the decision to grant a dissolution has bad results, the Sovereign is absolved from blame because she has acted according to precedent; but if the refusal to agree to a dissolution leads to difficulties, the Sovereign could be blamed for departing from precedent. The Sovereign, therefore, should normally accede to the request made by the Prime Minister of a minority government to grant a dissolution.

It is nevertheless in the public interest that the personal prerogative of refusing a dissolution should be retained. For it could be of great value in pathological circumstances if a Prime Minister seeks flagrantly to abuse the privilege of securing a dissolution. This could occur if, for example, a Prime Minister asked for a second dissolution immediately after a general election, or if there were a danger of a whole series of frequent dissolutions; or if a Prime Minister asked for a dissolution while he was in the process of being rejected by his party. But the prerogative of refusing a dissolution should not in normal circumstances be used to prevent the Prime Minister of a minority government obtaining a dissolution.

The situation could change, of course, if repeated hung Parliaments made it appear unlikely that further dissolutions would lead to a majority government. In such circumstances, the weapon of dissolution has less value, for it only postpones the need for co-operation between the parties. In countries with proportional representation, therefore, where majority single-party governments are rare, the right to dissolve has become less important than in Britain. It could well be that, if Britain adopted a proportional system of election, the politicians might agree

[31] Anthony King, *The Times*, 10 May 1969.

amongst themselves that the Prime Minister should be denied the right to dissolve unless he had the support of a majority in Parliament for such a course. But the adoption of a new convention of this kind would be a matter for the political leaders alone, and it would be for them, rather than the Sovereign, to take the initiative in developing it.

The logical outcome of this process might well appear to be fixed-term parliaments. Fixed-term parliaments are favoured by many advocates of proportional representation precisely because they believe that by depriving the Prime Minister of the possibility of a tactical dissolution, it will force the government to negotiate with other parties, so encouraging compromise in politics. Yet the dangers of such an innovation probably outweigh the advantages. For, if dissolution is impossible, the result can just as easily be immobilism and weak government rather than constructive compromise. It by no means follows that in every parliamentary situation, a viable government capable of securing the confidence of Parliament can necessarily be formed. The argument of those favouring fixed-term parliaments is that this will impose enough of a constraint upon the parties to ensure agreement on a government, but, if relations between the parties are bad, deadlock is an equally likely alternative. 'If', said David Ben-Gurion, the Israeli Prime Minister, 'I have to choose between a bad government or elections, I would choose the lesser evil – elections.'[32]

It would be unwise, therefore, to hamper the ability of the Prime Minister to secure a dissolution, although if multi-party politics were to become permanent, there would be a case for adopting the convention that the Prime Minister should only be able to secure a dissolution if Parliament is willing to grant it; while a coalition government, as the next chapter shows, will lead to a modification of the convention that a Prime Minister can secure a dissolution without the consent of his Cabinet. But, in other circumstances, it remains true that, in Waldeck-Rousseau's words, 'the ability to dissolve ... is not a menace to universal suffrage, but its safeguard. It is the essential counterbalance to excessive parliamentarism, and for this reason it affirms the democratic character of our institutions.'[33]

IX

As compared with a majority government, whether of a single party or a coalition, a minority government might be expected to increase the

---

[32] Quoted in E. Likhovski, *Israel's Parliament: The Law of the Knesset* (Oxford University Press, 1971), p. 34 fn.
[33] Quoted in B.S. Markesinis, *The Theory and Practice of Dissolution of Parliament* (Cambridge University Press, 1972), p. 234.

power of Parliament *vis-à-vis* the executive. For, without a majority in the Commons, a government will also lack a majority in Standing Committees, since these must reflect the balance of the House as a whole. If it wishes to secure the passage of legislation, therefore, it must consult with other parties. A prudent government would 'test the water' before introducing legislation into the Commons, and Parliament would enjoy a genuine pre-legislative and consultative role in the scrutiny of legislation. Standing committees which Professor J. G. Griffith, in his detailed study of the subject, *Parliamentary Scrutiny of Government Bills*,[34] found to be almost entirely futile, might devote themselves to improving legislation, rather than merely replicating the party dogfight on the floor of the House.

Yet this has not occurred with past minority governments. Both the first and second Labour governments were highly cautious, with little contentious legislation. The Wilson minority government in 1974, although it had quite ambitious legislative plans, appreciated that the other parties would be unlikely to support such measures as the nationalisation of the docks and shipbuilding, the prohibition of pay beds in National Health Service hospitals, and the elimination of selection in secondary education; nor could the government afford to offer extensive compromises on such legislation, lest it be accused of betrayal by left- wing MPs and the extra-parliamentary party. Therefore it subordinated its desire to secure the passage of its legislation to the necessity of obtaining a majority.

The Lib–Lab pact diverged from this pattern in that it made possible the passage of the government's legislative programme. David Steel has treated the period of the pact as one in which the power of the Commons was augmented. 'The House of Commons', he claims, 'did enjoy a period when it actually controlled the executive. Unless the government could muster by argument a majority its measures could not pass.'[35] But this is not quite an accurate description of the relationships between government and Parliament during the period of the pact. For the consultation on legislation was not so much between government and Parliament as between the government and the Liberal Party in bilateral negotiations between Cabinet ministers and their Liberal 'shadows' and in the joint consultative committee. If agreement was reached in these forums, or between Callaghan and Steel personally, the Commons would have little influence on legislation, since the Liberals would be committed to secure its passage, and, together with Labour, they enjoyed a majority in the House. Indeed, if Callaghan and Steel were able to reach agreement, this would as good as bind not only Liberal back-benchers in the House

[34] J.G. Griffith, *Parliamentary Scrutiny of Government Bills* (Allen and Unwin, 1974).
[35] *A House Divided*, p. 153.

but even the Cabinet, which could hardly repudiate the negotiations. The discussions between Callaghan and Steel, therefore, performed a similar function to those of a steering committee in a coalition government, and they had the effect of downgrading the importance of the Cabinet. For the Cabinet would be making decisions on matters which had already been extensively discussed between the two party leaders.

During the period of the pact, the influence of the House as a whole was little greater than if there had been a majority government, although Liberal MPs, of course, enjoyed greater influence because of the pact. But in direct contrast to other periods of minority government, the pact provided for a certain continuity of policy. In his speech to the Liberal Assembly in 1977, Steel quoted the Director-General of the CBI as saying, 'at least businessmen have returned to operating in a climate in which they can plan ahead – instead of reacting to circumstances on a week-by-week basis'. Moreover, the pact gave the civil service the assurance that it was working for a government which was not liable to be defeated in the Commons at any moment. Such an effect could not have been achieved by a minority government forced to rely upon different coalitions of support for different issues. 'A Government, if it is to work fruitfully, needs to know not only that it will survive the following night or the following week, but that it can continue for months at a stretch...'[36] In the absence of a formal coalition, only the pact could give such an assurance.

The period of the pact coincided with a gradual increase in confidence and a reduction in inflation. There was also more legislative achievement than has been attained by other minority governments, which remain almost entirely bereft of significant legislative success. Nor were earlier minority governments successful in other respects. The first Labour government was far too timid to satisfy its supporters, and its touch was too uncertain to satisfy the electorate; the second Labour government showed itself helpless in the face of the slump and fell to pieces after two unsatisfactory years in office. The Wilson minority government failed to take effective steps to control inflation, and its pre-electoral promises served merely to store up trouble for the future. The pact therefore made for continuity in government at the cost of back-bench power. These two desiderata are essentially conflicting ones rather than complementary under minority as much as under majority government.

Where a pact or understanding allows a government to plan ahead with some assurance that its legislation will pass the Commons, there is no reason why back-bench MPs should enjoy more influence than under a minority government. Where there is no such understanding, and

[36] Ibid., p. 82; Michie and Hoggart, *The Pact*, p. 174.

legislation is at the mercy of Opposition parties, there is unlikely to be much continuity of policy.

Whether the back-bencher enjoys influence upon the executive depends less upon whether the government represents a majority in the Commons than upon deeper assumptions concerning the role of the MP. These assumptions have already been changing during the 1970s, as party cohesion has come to be undermined. MPs have seen themselves less as party delegates and more as representatives of particular opinions or constituency attitudes. There has been far less willingness to defer to party leaders, and this has greatly increased the incidence of cross-voting in the Commons. Between March 1974 and May 1979, about one-third of Labour MPs and around one-tenth of Conservatives cast at least 20 votes against their own party in the Commons. Indeed, the total number of government defeats between March 1972 and 1979 equalled 65 as compared with only 34 in the 66 years between 1905 and March 1972.[37]

There is no reason why multi-party politics should necessarily weaken cohesion any further. Indeed, it could strengthen cohesion. For, if hung Parliaments require party leaders to enter into agreements for viable government to be secured, then they will need to rely upon the support of their followers in carrying out the agreements which they have reached. Party leaders will have to be given the authority to commit their followers and majority endorsement of a particular course of action must commit the minority, if agreements are to be effective. In the case of the Lib–Lab pact, for example, Jo Grimond, David Penhaligon, and later Cyril Smith, although against the pact, found themselves unable to vote against their colleagues in crucial divisions lest they be accused of helping to bring the government down. Indeed, one of David Steel's complaints against the pact was that it left Labour back-benchers too much freedom to vote against proposals, such as proportional representation for elections to the European Parliament, upon which he and Callaghan were agreed. Steel wanted the agreement to bind the Parliamentary Labour Party as well as the Cabinet precisely so that left-wingers would be unable to dissent. No better example could be given of the way in which coalitional politics requires strong party cohesion if it is to work. It is for this reason that coalitions between like-minded parties are so much easier to construct in Continental countries using list systems of proportional representation than in Britain; for in such countries, the party leadership frequently has the power to deny re-nomination to dissenting back-benchers. Thus neither multi-party politics nor proportional representation can necessarily be expected to lead to an increase in the power of Parliament.

37 Philip Norton, *Dissension in the House of Commons 1974–1979* (Clarendon Press, 1980), pp. 434, 441.

A qualification to this generalisation must be made, however, for the single transferable vote method of proportional representation might indeed lead to an increase in the influence of the back-bench MP through its effects upon party cohesion. For, under STV, MPs would be competing with colleagues from the same party, as well as with MPs from other parties. They would therefore have an incentive to differentiate themselves from their colleagues representing the same multi-member constituency, and one way of doing this might be to display a record of legislative independence in the Commons. Such individualistic action might win constituency votes; and even if it led to the MP falling foul of the leadership, this might not matter, since a party rebel can hold his seat against the disapproval of his party leadership, the national machine of his party, or even his local constituency association.

Admittedly, executive dominance in the Irish Republic where STV is used is probably greater than in Britain. But this is perhaps due as much to the localist political culture upon which STV is superimposed as to the electoral system. In Britain, where MPs and constituents are more policy-orientated, and divisions within the parties deeper and more ideological, STV could well have the effect of enhancing back-bench power. But this, looked at from the point of view of stability and continuity of policy-making, could prove a mixed blessing.

X

There is, then, no inherent reason why multi-party politics should shift the balance of executive-legislative relations towards the back-bench MP. Nevertheless if hung Parliaments were to persist and the strength of minority parties continued to increase, this could affect Parliament in a different way. For it would undermine the special status of the Opposition and of its Leader. The Opposition would lose the privileges which it enjoyed *vis-à-vis* the minority parties, and the Leader of the Opposition would become merely the leader of one of the Opposition parties. The Commons would cease to be a forum in which the allocation of time was determined bilaterally between government and Opposition; instead the time of the House would come to be allocated on a more proportional basis. Thus not only would a minority government lose its ability to control the Commons timetable, but the opposition would no longer enjoy a near-monopoly of the debating time of the House. Instead, the Commons would be organised by a number of political groups of roughly equal status. It would come to resemble a Continental legislature, since it would comprise a number of mutually competing political groups. Parliamentary politics would be coalitional rather than adversary.

Britain and Ireland are the only countries amongst the ten member states of the EEC whose parliamentary procedure does not recognise the existence of political groups. Britain is the only EEC member state which offers the opposition party a special status, designates by statute a Leader of the Opposition and pays him a salary. In Britain, there is no statutory provision regulating the parties in Parliament, and the only recognition given to them by the standing orders of the Commons is the requirement that committee membership should, so far as possible, reflect the balance of parties in the House. But the official Opposition – the largest Opposition party – is accorded considerable privileges in organising the House. Since 1937, a salary has been paid from the Consolidated Fund to the Leader of the Opposition, and since 1965 to the Opposition Chief Whip and Assistant Whip also. The Opposition has been given the right to choose the subject for debate on supply days, but could, at its discretion, allocate some of its time to minority parties. This provision, which was purely customary until July 1982, is now regulated by the standing orders of the Commons. This for the first time enshrines the right of the Leader of the Opposition to control the debating time of all the Opposition parties; 19 days are set aside as Opposition days and these 'shall be at the disposal of the leader of Her Majesty's Opposition' (Standing Order 6 (2)). There is no requirement to consult with the leaders of other Opposition parties. In recent years, however, the Opposition, by convention, has granted the Liberals one half-day per session (although at the time of writing the SDP is granted no such benefit). The Scottish Nationalists and Plaid Cymru have also been given supply days occasionally in the past.

Procedure in the Commons is thus determined on the basis of a division of labour between government and Opposition. When the government has a majority, it dominates the legislative time of the House, while the Opposition dominates the debating time. It is, therefore, peculiarly difficult for minority parties to use the Commons to put across their own distinctive point of view. They have to take a position on legislation promoted by the government, or on a motion put forward by the Opposition. They cannot themselves define the issues for debate and this seriously limits their opportunities for influencing the political debate in the country.

This division of labour is only possible, of course, because of the great discrepancy in size between the government and Opposition on the one hand, and the minority parties. If this discrepancy were to lessen, and (as occurred in 1923/4) three parties, each with over 100 seats, were regularly to secure representation in the House, it would become difficult for current conventions to continue. The time of the House would have to be divided more evenly between the parties, and the leader of the largest single Opposition party would not be able to retain his special status, nor indeed would there be an official Opposition enjoying special privileges at all. Governments would find it more difficult to control the time of the House, or to operate through 'the usual channels' with the Opposition. Power in the Commons would be more widely dispersed, not necessarily in the interests of back-benchers, but so as to give greater influence to the leaders of the minority parties. If multi-party politics and proportional representation led to the end of 'adversary politics' at the hustings then this would have to be reflected in the workings of the House. The physical layout of the Commons, with its sharp division between two sides on the floor of the House, would come to seem less appropriate than the semi-circular arrangement characteristic of Continental legislatures. If the electorate decided that it wished Parliament to reflect more accurately the main currents of political opinion in the country, the party leaders would have to take account of this preference. There could be quite extensive changes in the procedures and working of the Commons, and these could affect its role in the political system as a whole.

To carry the analysis any further, however, would be to enter too far into the realm of the speculative. What should be clear is that the working of minority government in a period in which multi-party government were to become the norm would be very different from anything Britain has yet experienced. Minority governments in Britain have not in the past been very successful. Part of the reason for this failure lies in the fact that they were seen as unnatural interludes, and there seemed no incentive for politicians to master the new habits necessary for minority government to work effectively. If there were now to be a long period of multi-party politics, however, politicians would either have to accustom themselves to minority government or, if majority government is to continue, learn how to operate a coalition. In the political systems of the Continent which use proportional systems of election, coalition is generally the preferred alternative to minority government. It is to an analysis of coalition government, therefore, that the final chapter is devoted.

8

Coalition government

I

In Britain, majority government has normally meant single-party government. On the Continent, by contrast, majority government is usually secured through coalition. For where multi-party politics produces a hung parliament, coalition is the alternative and generally the preferred alternative, to minority government. The head of state, when he asks a *formateur* to construct a government, often restricts his mandate to the formation of a majority government, and only when it has been shown that no candidate can construct a majority government, is minority government regarded as an acceptable alternative. Advocates of proportional representation in Britain also prefer coalition to minority government. For coalitions, precisely because they can command a majority in the Commons, are likely to prove more stable and long-lasting than minority governments. They are also likely to grant third parties greater influence than could be achieved by supporting a minority government from outside the Cabinet.

In a coalition, the minority parties will themselves assume responsibility for governmental decisions. This is likely to yield more control over legislation than a pact or understanding. For parliamentary activity is a far less important means of securing political influence than the gaining of a share in executive decisions. By the time a Bill is presented before Parliament, its main outlines have usually been agreed after extensive consultations between government departments and the relevant interest groups. Governments will generally be unwilling to re-open the package at the request of Parliament. But, with participation in government, the minority party gains influence at the formative stages of the legislative process.

The compensating disadvantage, however, is that the minority party may lose its separate identity and be submerged by the larger partner, as happened to the Liberal Unionists, National Labour and the Liberal Nationals. It is more difficult, therefore, for a minority party to preserve its integrity under a coalition than under a parliamentary arrangement.

Yet minority government and coalition should not be seen as polar opposites. Neither of these terms describes a single type of governmental arrangement, but a range of possibilities which can merge imperceptibly into each other. Minority governments, as Chapter 7 has shown, can operate in a number of different ways, and a general understanding such as that formalised in the Lib–Lab pact bears some resemblances to a coalition. Indeed, wherever there is a regularised procedure of consultation between a minority government and a party not represented in the government upon which it relies for its majority, there will be some similarities in the pattern of co-operation which must develop if coalitions are to function successfully. Where government depends upon an arrangement between one or more parties, the form which these arrangements take may be less significant than the simple fact of co-operation. The precise constitutional status of the agreement can easily obscure the political reality of practical co-operation.

II

Coalition governments in Britain have been the product of emergency – either war or economic crisis. Yet, just as minority government can take a number of different forms, so also 'coalition' is not a term denoting a single type of government but rather a series of possible variants. In Britain, coalitions have on the whole, been of two contrasting types. First, there has been the all-party coalition, or government of national unity formed when there is some single over-riding aim such as victory in war upon which all the parties are agreed. The coalition formed by Winston Churchill in May 1940 is an obvious example. Indeed, A. J. P. Taylor has described it as 'more than a coalition' since it was 'in the unique position of commanding the almost unanimous allegiance of both parliament and country'.[1] It was supported by all the parties represented in the Commons except the Independent Labour Party which had three MPs, and the solitary Communist who in fact came to support the Coalition after Germany's attack on the USSR in June 1941. The coalition formed by H. H. Asquith in May 1915 might also be regarded as a government of national unity. It included all the parties represented in Parliament except for the Irish Nationalists who, although they supported the war, refused to serve in any British government. There was no organised party opposition to either the Churchill or Asquith governments, and parliamentary opposition was confined to scattered backbench dissidents and ginger groups.

[1] A.J.P. Taylor, '1932–1945', in Butler (ed.), *Coalitions in British Politics*, p. 74.

Opposition to these coalitions, although scattered, could be highly effective; and in the case of the Asquith coalition it was actually responsible for the collapse of the government in December 1916 and its replacement by a new coalition under Lloyd George. The opposition to Churchill's government was wider than is generally imagined, and in the early stages of the war, Churchill was forced to take account of it in making appointments. He was, for example, eager to appoint Sir Stafford Cripps as Leader of the Commons in February 1942, to protect himself against the anti-government campaign which Cripps threatened to lead. But of course none of the back-bench rebellions came at all close to toppling the Churchill administration.

On other occasions, coalitions have been formed with the hope that they would be supported by all the parties, but that hope has turned out to be illusory. After Asquith's fall in 1916, political leaders were eager to construct a government within which Asquith would serve. But this proved impossible, and Asquith led the opposition to the Lloyd George Coalition. Asquith's opposition was, however, a highly patriotic one; and the only challenge which he mounted, a rather half-hearted attack in the Maurice debate of May 1918, was easily rebuffed.

The National Government formed in August 1931 was also intended by its leaders to match the ideal embodied in the Asquith and Churchill administrations – a government of national unity formed for a single purpose, in this case to support the programme for economic retrenchment and survival. Although the hope was that this programme would be supported by all of the parties, Labour came out in opposition to the National Government shortly after it was formed. Thus the government achieved the unity only of the anti-socialist parties rather than of the nation as a whole.

The second type of coalition which has been prevalent in Britain has been that which is a precursor of the fusion of a section of one party with another. The Conservative/Liberal Unionist coalition which ruled Britain between 1895 and 1905 was of this type, with the two parties fusing in 1912. The non-Conservative parties, other than the Liberals, comprising the National Government – the National Labour and Liberal National Parties – fused with the Conservatives: National Labour in 1945, and the Liberal National Party (which became National Liberal in 1948), as late as 1966. The coalition between the Lloyd George Liberals and the Conservatives which governed from December 1916 to October 1922 was seen by some as a step towards fusion, but the Conservatives broke with the Coalition in 1922 to fight the general election as an independent party, while the Coalition Liberals returned to the Liberal Party in November 1923 after Baldwin went to the country on the issue of

Protection. This second type of coalition, unlike the first, has realigned rather than eliminated, party opposition. Except in the years 1916–18, the Lloyd George Coalition faced vigorously organised Opposition in Parliament, as did the Conservative/Liberal Unionist Coalition and the National Government.

These coalitions were sustained by electoral pacts. The Conservatives and Liberal Unionists had agreed since 1886 that they would not oppose each other in the constituencies; and a similar agreement was made between the Lloyd George Liberals and the Conservatives in 1918, and the various parties comprising the National Government in 1931, but on both of these occasions, there were a few breaches of the agreement where government candidates split the vote. The Asquith and Churchill coalitions were buttressed by an electoral truce so that vacancies remained uncontested by the major parties.

Coalition governments have all commanded majorities in Parliament, and on the four occasions 1900, 1918, 1931 and 1935 – when coalitions have been endorsed by the electorate in the twentieth century (1906 and the two elections of 1910 saw the rejection of the Conservative/Liberal Unionist Coalition), they have been able to secure the votes of a majority of the voters. In this they contrast dramatically with single-party governments in Britain, none of which in this century has gained a popular majority – the nearest were the Liberals in 1906 with 49.0% of the vote, and the Conservatives in 1955 with 49.7% of the vote. Coalition governments have thus been able to secure popular majorities while single-party governments have not. They have also been longer-lasting and generally more secure than minority governments. The shortest was the Asquith government which lasted for only 19 months. The Lloyd George Coalition was not overthrown until it had governed for nearly six years. The 1931 National Government became, after September 1932 when the Liberals and Snowden resigned, in effect 'a Conservative government, headed by a non-Conservative, and with a number of other non-Conservatives dotted uneasily about';[2] in that form it lasted for nearly eight years, until May 1940, when it was superseded by a genuinely national (i.e. all-party) coalition.

III

Both the Lloyd George Coalition and the National Government were responsible for significant constitutional innovations, and their methods of working differed from those of single-party majority government.

---

[2] David Marquand, '1924–1932', in Butler (ed.), *Coalitions in British Politics*, p. 71.

Both were returned with large majorities in general elections, and greeted as saviours of the nation. Both collapsed with ignominy, and their failures were used to condemn the whole idea of coalition. The air of corruption which surrounded Lloyd George's government made coalition seem an unacceptable form of government during the 1920s; while the belief that the National Government had neglected the unemployed and failed to grasp the character of the Nazi menace left few lamenting its fall. As late as October 1974, when the Conservatives seemed to be proposing a coalition govern-ment if they won the election, they were met with reminders of the allegedly catastrophic record of the National Government in the 1930s. Yet the circumstances surrounding the fall of the Lloyd George Coalition and the National Government have perhaps obscured their real achievements.

During the Second World War, Lloyd George contrasted the structure of the Churchill government – 'a Coalition of Parties and their nominees' – with his own, which was 'a War Directorate in the real sense of the term'.[3] Lloyd George brought into his Cabinet men such as Smuts, Milner and Sir Eric Geddes, who, although lacking a strong party base, had the drive and energy to carry out the tasks necessary for victory and post-war recon-struction. To strengthen his own position in the policy-making process, he established a 'Garden Suburb' of advisers in 10 Downing Street, and these confidants enjoyed more influence than Cabinet ministers. Power depen-ded less on formal authority than on proximity to the Prime Minister. In fact the Lloyd George Coalition, both in war and peace, was more presidential in style than any other administration that Britain has ever known. The proceedings of the Cabinet were regularised by the establish-ment of the Cabinet Secretariat in 1916, and the Secretary to the Cabinet was made responsible to the Prime Minister of the day; while, in 1919, the Prime Minister also gained the right to make senior civil service appoint-ments on the recommendation of the Permanent Secretary to the Treasury who became Head of the Civil Service.

The central weakness of Lloyd George's presidential style of leadership lay in the fact that, as Beaverbrook put it, he was 'a Prime Minister without a party'.[4] The Coalition Liberals were a group united less on policy than on sustaining Lloyd George in office. They entirely lacked an ideological basis of their own. They had no strong roots in the country and their party organisation was non-existent except in Wales. The government was therefore 'less of a coalition between one party and another than one between a party and a prime minister whose party resources, outside his native land, were minimal'.[5]

---

[3] Taylor, '1932–1945', p. 85.
[4] Lord Beaverbrook, *The Decline and Fall of Lloyd George* (Collins, 1963), p. 9.
[5] Kenneth O. Morgan, '1902–1924', in Butler (ed.), *Coalitions in British Politics*, p. 45.

After the government had fallen, A. J. Balfour told Bonar Law that Lloyd George was 'absolutely impartial between the Parties which, for the head of a Coalition Government, was a great advantage'; but from the point of view of the Prime Minister's own position, it exposed him to acute danger. Until 1918, the Conservatives lacked a majority in the Commons, and were therefore dependent upon the Coalition Liberals; but the general election of 1918 gave the Conservatives a majority of their own, making the Coalition Liberals superfluous from their point of view. It might have been predicted that the Coalition would last only as long as Lloyd George retained sufficient prestige in the country to be an asset to the government. If he became a liability, the Conservatives would drop him, as they proceeded to do at the famous Carlton Club meeting in October 1922. The collapse of the Coalition was mourned by few outside the ranks of professional politicians, but K. O. Morgan, the historian of the Lloyd George government, has argued that: 'with hindsight, the record of the coalition may not seem so ignoble. It pursued far-sighted policies of social reform and reconciliation. The survival of democratic institutions in Britain during the inter-war years perhaps owes something to its efforts.' It was, he concludes, 'one of the very few truly successful coalitions in our history'.[6]

IV

The National Government was formed on 24 August 1931 for the specific purpose of carrying out the economic cuts which had split the Labour Cabinet. The original intention was that the coalition should then be dissolved, and the ensuing general election be fought on a normal party basis. For this reason, and to differentiate the National Government from the Lloyd George Coalition, its leaders insisted that it was not a coalition in the normal sense of the term. The official statement announcing the formation of the government declared that:

The specific object for which the new Government is being formed is to deal with the national emergency that now exists. It will not be a Coalition Government in the usual sense of the term, but a Government of Co-Operation for this one purpose.

When that purpose is achieved the political parties will resume their respective positions.

In a radio broadcast on 25 August, the day after the formation of the government, Ramsay MacDonald insisted that 'It is not a Coalition Government. I would take no part in that', and Baldwin, the Conserva-

[6] Ibid., pp. 43, 50, 34.

tive leader, said that there was 'no question of any permanent Coalition'. On 29 August he told his Conservative followers in the Commons that 'when the economies are carried and the Budget is balanced – you will have a straight fight on tariffs and against the Socialist Party'.[7]

But events conspired to render these promises obsolete. Contrary to expectations, the formation of the National Government did not produce economic stability. The drain on sterling continued, and, on 18 September, Britain was forced to leave the gold standard, a step which the National Government had been formed specifically to prevent. But even this was not sufficient to end the emergency.

The Labour Party, which was the largest in the House, came out in vitriolic opposition to the National Government, and it was believed in Establishment circles that fears of the return of a Labour government in the forthcoming general election were having an unfavourable effect on foreign confidence. On 5 September MacDonald wrote to Baldwin saying that if Labour 'were to have a majority or could even form a Government after the next Election, the country would again be faced with a financial crisis which would then in all probability break upon it and ruin it. Can we draw a line between this time of crisis and a normal condition which is to follow? I do not see any such line.'[8] Geoffrey Dawson, the editor of *The Times*, put to Baldwin the idea that the National Government should seek the endorsement of the electorate as a coalition, while, on 28 September, the Labour Party expelled those of its members who had joined or supported the National Government, thus removing MacDonald's escape route.

These pressures were reinforced by the Bank of England, and in mid-September the Acting Governor of the Bank, Sir Ernest Harvey, and a Director, Edward Peacock, told the Cabinet:

While disclaiming any right to an opinion on political events, the representatives of the Bank, when pressed as to their view of what the American and French banking interests would be likely to consider would provide sufficient security for further credits, had indicated that a general election in which the three parties were acting independently would not be regarded as providing sufficient certainty for the establishment of a stable government as the result. An appeal to the electorate by a National Government on a national policy devised to rectify the financial situation, was more likely to be regarded favourably abroad.[9]

If it was to fight an election, the National Government had to achieve a compromise on the issue of tariffs versus Free Trade; for while the

[7] Bassett, *Nineteen Thirty One*, pp. 167, 168, 180.
[8] David Marquand, *Ramsay MacDonald* (Cape, 1977), pp. 655–6.
[9] CAB 59 (31), quoted in D.J. Wrench, 'The National Government, 1931–1935' (Ph.D. thesis, Bangor, 1973), p. 36.

Conservatives were adamant for Protection, the Liberals and the Chancellor, Snowden, were determined Free Traders. After complex negotiations, the government decided to issue a brief manifesto asking for a 'doctor's mandate', while the parties comprising the government were to publish their own separate manifestos in which they could state their own individual positions on Free Trade. This was to cause difficulties later.

The National Government was returned with a crushing majority in the general election held on 27 October. It gained 554 out of 615 seats, of which the Conservatives won 473. The Labour Party was reduced to only 46 seats, and the Opposition as a whole had only 56 MPs in the new House. Such large majorities rarely augur well for a government, and, in the case of the National Government, it was bound to put its coalitional character under strain. For the Labour Party was clearly no longer a threat to the financial stability of the country, while the Conservatives were perfectly well able to govern on their own without the aid of their Labour and Liberal coalition partners. The Liberals with only 33 MPs were in danger of entirely losing their separate identity and being submerged by the Conservatives. Their bargaining position was therefore very weak.

The Conservatives regarded the election result as giving them a mandate to introduce a tariff, and, after a short-lived suspension of collective Cabinet responsibility, the 'agreement to differ' of January 1932, this led to the resignation of the Liberal ministers from the government, although the Liberal Party did not in fact move to the Opposition benches until November 1933.

It was evident that the Conservatives now regarded the National Government less as a coalition, than as a means towards the fusion of the National Labour and Liberal National elements. 'We shall put the tariff through', Baldwin told his friend Tom Jones in January 1932, 'and if it does well it will drop out of party politics very much like Free Trade did. Then leave suitable time to change the title of our Party to National, as there will be little which really divides us from the great bulk of the Liberals.' Neville Chamberlain also expected that there would be a 'move towards that fused Party under a National name which I regard as certain to come'.[10]

Baldwin's view that the National Government was a means of resolving contentious party issues such as the tariff is by no means without foundation. After the introduction of a revenue tariff in January 1932, the Ottawa Agreements in August establishing Imperial Preference, and

[10] Thomas Jones, *A Diary with Letters 1931–1950* (Oxford University Press, 1954), pp. 25–6; Iain Macleod, *Neville Chamberlain* (Frederick Muller, 1961), p. 161.

the resignation of the Liberal ministers, the Free Trade/Protection debate entirely disappeared from British politics. This would have been more difficult to achieve under a single-party government which would have met with stronger Labour and Liberal opposition. A tariff could only be introduced by a government with a large majority containing elements from the Labour and Liberal Parties prepared to support Protection. There was a Protectionist majority scattered amongst the three parties, but it could not be mobilised against the doctrinaire Free Traders who dominated the Labour and Liberal Parties in the 1920s. It could be mobilised only by a coalition.

Similarly, the National Government managed to contain disagreements on India more easily than a purely Conservative government would have done. The opposition of the Conservative right led by Churchill could be discounted since the government was pushed towards the centre on this issue not only by the Prime Minister, MacDonald, who in 1930 had called a round-table conference to examine how India could proceed to dominion status, but also by the Foreign Secretary, Sir John Simon, who had presided over a statutory commission on Indian self-government in 1927. The leaders of the National Government knew that its large majority had been obtained through the allegiance of electors who normally supported the Labour or Liberal parties, and it was eager to avoid alienating them.

As a corollary it may be argued that, precisely because it was so eager to seek compromise, the National Government was unable to give the country a clear lead, especially on issues of foreign policy. That was the criticism which Churchill made when he accused it of being 'decided only to be undecided, resolved to be irresolute, adamant for drift, solid for fluidity, all powerful for impotence'.[11] Yet, the failures of the National Government were due as much to the personalities of its leaders as to its coalitional character. It would be difficult, for example, to complain that the government of Neville Chamberlain failed to offer clear policies, even if they were in a direction which Churchill and other critics of the government regarded as disastrous. If MacDonald and Baldwin failed to offer a clear lead, this was less because they were at the head of a coalition government than because they were temperamentally more at home in a political world of half-lights, shadows and blurred edges. Even so, under the MacDonald and Baldwin administrations, Britain rearmed more rapidly than was generally realised, and it is possible that a more strident appeal in favour of British rearmament would, by frightening the electorate, have proved counter-productive.

Speaking on the Import Duties Bill in the Commons in February 1932,

11 H.C. Debs, vol. 317, col. 1107, 12 November 1936.

Walter Elliot argued that the National Government in resolving the issue of the tariff had cleared it from the political arena:

The things we are discussing tonight must be cleared out of the road before we can come to the great questions of the century – the reorganisation politically, socially and economically which the country will have to go through; the rising spirit of the younger generation; the contribution which youth has still to make to the future of the country. Our efforts in those directions, are being 'cribbed, cabin'd and confined' by these dusty and fusty remnants of nineteenth-century problems. Let us clear them out of the way. We have taken the first step, we must deal with the question speedily, in order that we may get on with the problems which will still remain an issue when this problem itself is no longer an issue in any part of the House.[12]

Seen in this light, the National Government helped to secure a genuine realignment of political forces, resolving issues which could otherwise have provoked dangerous divisions. One may contrast the success of the National Government in resolving the questions of Indian self-government and the tariff with the attitudes of politicians to Irish Home Rule, an issue which bedevilled British politics between 1885 and 1922. Both Gladstone in 1885 and Lloyd George in 1910 had sought an all-party approach to Home Rule, and it is difficult to believe that the issue would not have been handled more successfully if that could have been achieved. So too, in our own times, it might be argued that questions such as trade union reform and constitutional reform can be better resolved by a coalition than by a one-party government.

V

So far we have considered two types of coalition government, an all-party government of national unity, and a coalition which is a step towards the fusion of a section of one party with another. The formation of such coalitions in Britain has been the product of crisis circumstances. Coalition government is not seen as a normal response of the political system to multi-party politics, as it is in Continental countries with proportional electoral systems. For there is a third type of coalition in which two or more parties, unable to gain a majority on their own, agree to share power by combining together. There is no intention of merging, and the coalition partners assume that they will fight the next general election as separate parties without an electoral pact.

In Britain, constitutional conventions have, as Chapter 7 showed, militated against co-operative coalition in situations where no single party enjoys a majority in Parliament; while in the 1970s, the discre-

12 H.C. Debs, vol. 261, col, 392, 4, February 1932.

pancy in size between the Liberals and the major parties has made coalition an unattractive option. In 1977, the Liberals preferred a pact to a coalition – not that a Labour government would have countenanced coalition in any case – since a party of 13 can hardly avoid being submerged if it enters a coalition with a party commanding 310 seats. The electoral system which magnifies the discrepancy between the two large parties and the smaller parties has played its part in making coalition government more difficult to achieve in multi-party situations. Indeed the plurality system of election serves to collapse a multi-party political system into a two-party one.

Acceptance of coalition government as a normal response to multi-party politics probably depends, therefore, upon proportional representation. As David Steel has put it, 'Against participation inside coalition, which is attractive on policy grounds, I must say that so long as the Liberal Party has so few MPs and we have an electoral system which denies us fair representation I would find it extremely difficult to see how we could contribute fully to coalition.'[13] With proportional representation, on the other hand, the parties would be more nearly equal in strength, and coalition might come to be accepted as a normal method of government, rather than as something reserved for special circumstances. Coalitions might cease to be regarded as undesirable exceptions to the norm of single-party rule, and be seen as the natural way for the political system to accommodate itself to hung Parliaments. If that happened, although some of the lessons of past British coalitions might well be relevant, historical experience would be of limited value in explaining how they would work since their purpose would be so different from that of past coalitions. The more relevant experience is that of the Continental democracies of north-western Europe where stable coalition has long been regarded as the normal form of government.

VI

The central problem of a power-sharing coalition is how to combine Cabinet solidarity which requires common policies, with the preservation by the independent parties comprising the coalition of their separate identities. The smaller party in a coalition must be particularly alert to ensure that it is not regularly outvoted in Cabinet discussions, or held responsible for Cabinet policy while being unable to exert any real influence over it. Inevitably, coalitions cause strains amongst the parties composing them, and tensions between the party leaders who have to

---

[13] David Steel, in *Probleme von Koalitionsregierungen*, p. 7.

compromise in Cabinet, to the anger of their parliamentary and extra-parliamentary organisations who may come to feel a sense of acute disappointment if not betrayal. It is for this reason that coalitions are so peculiarly liable to disintegrate through internal disagreement. Therefore special institutional arrangements have to be made to secure inter-party agreement at every stage in the life of a coalition government from its formation to its dissolution. The general effect of these arrangements is to weaken the position of the Prime Minister and make him less powerful than he would be in a single-party government.

The formation of a coalition will involve negotiations on both the personnel and the programme of the government. The representation of individual parties in the Cabinet will depend not only upon their parliamentary numbers but also upon the strength of their bargaining position. This factor in turn will vary with the position of a party within the political spectrum. A party which is operationally in the centre such as the FDP in West Germany, the Christian Democratic Appeal in Holland, or the Liberal and Centre parties in Sweden, will have a stronger bargaining position than a captive party such as the Swedish Conservatives or the Dutch Liberals, which are both on the Right of the political spectrum, and have no effective choice of options. It is for this reason that pivot parties tend to be over-represented in coalition governments. This has certainly been true of West Germany where the FDP, with a vote varying from between 5.8% in 1969 to 10.6% in 1980, has regularly secured four out of the 17 cabinet posts. So also, the smaller parties were over-represented in the National Government in Britain in August 1931, since it was their allegiance which gave the government its 'national' character.

The formation of a coalition government involves two stages. In the first, there are negotiations about which posts go to which parties, and how many posts each party is entitled to. In the second, there is the allocation of cabinet posts to particular individuals. At this second stage, the power of the Prime Minister is especially limited, since he cannot choose for himself who his cabinet colleagues are to be, but must, in general, accept the nominations of his coalition partners. The Prime Minister can generally veto a nomination, but not choose which ministers from another party he is willing to accept. In the coalition formed in West Germany in 1982, between the CDU/CSU and the FDP, for example, the CDU/CSU supported by the Prime Minister refused to accept the Free Democrat nominee for the Ministry of the Interior, Gerhart Baum, because they believed that he was too liberal. Insofar as the choice of his cabinet is concerned, the Prime Minister of a coalition is clearly in a weaker position than the Prime Minister of a single-party government; yet giving him the power of veto offers, perhaps, an acceptable compromise between the stability and homogeneity of a single-party government, and the need to allow a coalition partner to decide upon its own ministerial appointments.

Further, the Prime Minister will lose the exclusive freedom to reshuffle his cabinet and will have to secure agreement with his coalition partners on government changes. He will not be able to require the dismissal of a minister from another party, if that minister has the support of his party.

A communication from the prime minister to one of the coalition parties to the effect that a cabinet minister is, for example, no longer *politically* suited to be the head of the ministry would indeed in most cases be interpreted as an open challenge to that party and consequently to one and all of its cabinet ministers in the coalition government.[14]

This is likely to give individual ministers of a smaller party a more than proportionate influence over the policy-making process. For if a dissenting minister from a coalition partner threatens to resign, he threatens also to bring the coalition down if he gains the backing of his party. Thus, a minister might succeed in getting his own way in a coalition government even if opposed by a majority of the cabinet, and perhaps a majority of the legislature as well.

The need to secure inter-party agreement is bound also to affect the working of the mechanism of cabinet government. For a coalition government requires some machinery by which the views of the partners can be made known, and disagreements resolved. In general, contentious issues in coalitions are decided *outside* the formal machinery of cabinet government, and inter-party arrangements of an informal kind are established. In West Germany, for example, there was during the SPD/FDP coalition a weekly *Koalitionsgesprach* between the two party leaders, Helmut Schmidt and Hans-Dietrich Genscher, and the leaders of the parliamentary groups, Herbert Wehner and Wolfgang Mischnick; while to secure parliamentary co-ordination, Wehner and Mischnick were accustomed to attend cabinet meetings. In Sweden, the three-party Fälldin coalition which governed between 1976 and 1978, and 1979 and 1981, organised a *Sammlingskansla* (joint committee) at which disagreements could be settled by the party leaders. In Norway, the four-party coalition led by Per Borten, which governed between 1965 and 1971, established a four-party committee to work out compromises. In Israel, by contrast, co-ordination is secured in a more formal manner through representation on cabinet committees. For example, the foreign affairs committee, after the 1981 general election, consisted of the four ministers

---

[14] Arve Solstad, 'The Norwegian coalition system', *Scandinavian Political Studies*, 4 (1969), p. 161.

concerned with foreign affairs, and four representatives of the National Religious Party, who, although having no specialist connection with foreign affairs, were coalition partners whose agreement needed to be secured if government was to operate effectively. In Britain, it might be possible to secure co-ordination through a formalised Inner Cabinet within which coalition partners were represented as of right. Certainly, the partners would have to agree to a balance of representation not only in the cabinet, but on cabinet committees as well.

The net effect of these various arrangements whose purpose is to secure inter-party agreement amongst coalition partners, is to weaken the formal machinery of cabinet government in favour of the steering body in which the party leaders resolve contentious issues. The cabinet is no longer a strategic body laying down the direction of government policy, since that function is undertaken by the steering committee of the coalition. Instead, the cabinet becomes a ratifying body, its function being reduced to one of registering and implementing the decision of the coalition leaders. For it would take a very bold minister to attempt to untie a package agreed after laborious negotiations between the partners to the coalition.

As well as the settling of disagreements between the coalition partners, coalitions must also ensure that the component parties actually carry out agreements reached. In general the steering committee responsible for the one function also performs the other. Normally, party discipline in a coalition government will have to be firmer than in a single-party government, since the stability of a coalition depends upon the belief on the part of its members that agreements will be honoured. Back-bench dissent, even when it does not threaten the government, is dangerous for a coalition since it threatens the mutual confidence upon which the compromise and accommodation needed to keep a government going are based.

It is therefore a mistake to argue, as some proponents of proportional representation do, that coalition government would lead to greater back-bench power. Coalitions might ensure that a wider range of views were brought into the policy-making process, and that political power would be dispersed more widely amongst the parties represented in the legislature; but this would not benefit back-bench members. Precisely because they ensure greater party discipline, the list systems of proportional representation used in all Continental countries except France ensure a greater degree of coalition loyalty than either the plurality system or the single transferable vote method of proportional representation. Because list systems tend to weaken the power of local constituency organisations and back-benchers *vis-à-vis* party leaders, they make it easier for party leaders to enforce discipline. Therefore coalition partners can enter into negotiations with the confidence that agreements made will also be honoured.

The arrangements made for the dissolution of a coalition are also likely to be different from those pertaining to a single-party government. For, the partners in a coalition would be unwise to join without securing an agreement on when Parliament can be dissolved. If the Prime Minister were to retain the unilateral right to recommend a dissolution, even against the wishes of his coalition partners, he could use it to put pressure on them, and this might disturb the spirit of power- sharing which is the essence of a coalition. In general, therefore, the timing of dissolution is a matter for decision by the cabinet in coalition governments. Lloyd George was not allowed by the Conservatives to dissolve in January 1922, the only occasion in the twentieth century when a Prime Minister has been unable to secure a dissolution at a time of his own choosing. In Israel, the Prime Minister cannot dissolve unless the Knesset agrees, so that when in 1982 Menachem Begin threatened a dissolution in an attempt to show that the electorate had confidence in his policies in the Lebanon, his coalition partners were able to block him. In West Germany, the Chancellor can dissolve the Bundestag only if he loses a vote of no-confidence. Helmut Schmidt was thus deprived in 1982 of a weapon which he might have used against the FDP, deterring them from undermining his government. For, if he had been able to threaten a dissolution he might have been able to persuade the FDP not to switch alliances to the CDU/CSU, and it could be argued that because the Chancellor lacked the power to dissolve, the FDP was able to change sides without an election. In Denmark, there is an informal rule that some months have to elapse between one election and another; and when coalition agreements are drawn up between the parties, they invariably include a promise by the Prime Minister that he will not seek a dissolution before a certain date.

The machinery by which coalitions attempt to secure co-ordination of policy and the resolution of disagreements is necessary to give effect to the will to agreement where that exists but it cannot of itself ensure inter-party harmony. What is central to the successful working of coalition is a spirit of co-operation between the partners, rather than particular institutional mechanisms. There has to be an awareness of the limits of practicable compromise and a willingness not to force divisive issues to breaking point. Where such an awareness is present, the precise machinery by which it is made concrete is of merely subordinate importance. For machinery itself cannot create the attitudes necessary for successful coalition.

VII

In addition to securing agreement on the allocation of posts and the method of executive decision-making, coalitions must decide upon a programme. Here too the Prime Minister will enjoy less power than in a single-party government. He will no longer be free to sum up the sense of cabinet meetings in his own way without ensuring that his views are in accordance with those of his coalition partners; nor will he be able unilaterally to interpret government policy, even if the constitution gives him the right to do so. In West Germany, for example, the constitution gives the Chancellor *Richtlinienkompetenz* – the power to lay down the guidelines of government policy. But in coalition governments this has been limited by the practical fact that Chancellors have had to clear major policy statements with coalition partners beforehand.

Any programme, inevitably, will be a compromise. It is usually published, or when not published, leaked to the press, and can vary in length from a small number of items to the 83 items contained in the formal coalition agreement between the four parties comprising the Israeli government in 1981, and including such highly detailed matters as in no. 30: 'Maintenance and development standards for general military boarding schools will also apply to the religious military boarding school, from the ninth grade upwards'. Where agreements are published, the items in them are often regarded as having a special status binding ministers to accept them, while on issues not included in the agreement, the parties may be allowed to go their own way. In Israel, the publication of the coalition programme has the force of a covenant or pledge binding its signatories, while other issues are sometimes held to be free ones on which the components of the coalition can go back to their members to decide upon their position. This convention is known as one of 'mutual' rather than collective responsibility. In the Netherlands, likewise, coalition governments agree to regard some issues as 'free issues' on which collective responsibility will not be enforced, while in Norway between 1965 and 1971, the Borten coalition agreed to suspend collective responsibility on non-central issues.

VIII

Coalition government in Britain would be likely to alter the workings of Cabinet government in a variety of other important ways. It is difficult to predict what institutional machinery would be developed to ensure co-ordination between the coalition partners, but whatever the machinery, the result of coalition would probably be, as on the Continent, to increase significantly the power of the Cabinet *vis-à-vis* the Prime Minister. This increase in power would, however, probably accrue not to the Cabinet as a collective body, but to the coalition partners which compose it. For it is to be expected that coalition government would considerably weaken the status if not of collective responsibility, of collective Cabinet unanimity.

There have been three occasions in British twentieth-century politics when the convention of collective unanimity has been broached. One of these was under the National Government in 1932, but the other two examples – in 1975 and 1977 – occurred under a single-party Labour government, albeit a government which was itself a heterogenous coalition of competing elements.

In January 1932, the National Government agreed to allow the advocates of Free Trade within the Cabinet to speak and vote against government legislation. In 1975 the Labour government allowed the anti-Marketeers in the Cabinet to speak outside the Commons against the government's recommendation that Britain should vote 'Yes' in the forthcoming referendum on continued membership of the EEC; and in 1977 the same government allowed ministers to vote against its recommendation that there should be direct elections to the European Parliament. In addition, there have, of course, been numerous unilateral breaches of the rule of collective unanimity through leaks, newspaper articles and injudicious public remarks by Cabinet ministers. It has not been difficult for anyone interested in public affairs in recent years to learn both the details of major divisions in Cabinet, and to discover which ministers hold particular views on the various matters dividing the Cabinet. The maintenance of collective unanimity in its pristine form requires perhaps a respect for privacy which is hardly possible in an age of mass communications and investigative journalism.

The 'agreement to differ' in 1932 offers an example of a coalition government collectively deciding to suspend collective unanimity. The decision by the National Government to fight an election as a coalition led, as already described in Section IV, to the publication of three separate manifestos, contradicting each other on the issue of Protection versus Free Trade, as well as one national manifesto signed by the Prime Minister. 'We are now committed', Neville Chamberlain wrote to his sister-in-law, 'to the extraordinary proceeding under which we go to the country as a united Government, one section of which is to advocate tariffs while the other declares it has an open mind but is unalterably convinced of the virtues of Free Trade ... I never fought an election under such a difficulty ... I do foresee a pack of troubles as soon as the election is over, first in the formation of the Government and then in the formulation of policy.'[15]

[15] Macleod, *Neville Chamberlain*, pp. 153–4.

Chamberlain's prediction was to prove perfectly accurate and the device of issuing separate manifestos served only to postpone trouble not to avert it. For, only three months after the election, the Cabinet accepted a revenue tariff with four dissentients – the three Liberal members of the Cabinet (Samuel, Maclean and Sinclair) and Lord Snowden, who was also an uncompromising Free Trader. When, on 21 January the Cabinet accepted the revenue tariff, the four ministers duly offered their resignations. The next day, however, Lord Hailsham produced a formula by which the dissentient ministers would be allowed to stay in the government while retaining their Free Trade convictions. They could 'remain, with full liberty, both of votes as well as of speech, on the matter on dispute'[16] which would be the subject of a whipped vote in the Commons.

After some hesitation, the Free Trade ministers accepted this proposal and were therefore allowed, as Cabinet ministers, to retain all the freedoms of a private member. 'What the Ministers have done', Tom Jones, a former Deputy Secretary to the Cabinet, told Baldwin, 'is really to carry the expression of their dissent a step further than the practice of placing it on record in the Cabinet Minutes. And just as you drop your dissent once you record it, so they should drop it after stating it to the House.' 'Quite so', Baldwin replied.[17]

The government then issued the following statement:

The Cabinet has had before it the report of the Committee on the Balance of Trade, and after prolonged discussion it has been found impossible to reach a unanimous conclusion on the Committee's recommendations. The Cabinet, however, is deeply impressed with the paramount importance of maintaining national unity in presence of the grave problems that now confront this country and the whole world. It has accordingly determined that some modification of usual Ministerial practice is required and has decided that Ministers who find themselves unable to support the conclusions arrived at by the majority of their colleagues on the subject of import duties and cognate matters are to be at liberty to express their views by speech and vote. The Cabinet, being essentially united on all other matters of policy, believes that by this special provision it is best interpreting the will of the nation and the needs of the time. (*The Times*, 23 January 1932)

When the Import Duties Bill was introduced into Parliament, the unusual spectacle was to be seen of ministers arguing that their colleagues on the Treasury bench were about to bring ruin to the country. Perhaps the 'agreement to differ' was made in the belief that the Free Traders would content themselves with a merely formal dissent in the Commons; but if

[16] Lord Hailsham, as quoted by Samuel, in Samuel Papers, Box 87 (7), Course of Political Events, Jan 18–23 1932.
[17] *A Diary with Letters 1931–1950*, p. 26.

that was the hope, Samuel, the Home Secretary, soon destroyed it by campaigning in the country, and by speaking firmly and indeed contemptuously in the Commons against his colleagues. Vansittart, the Permanent Secretary at the Foreign Office, who heard the speech, told Baldwin of his objection to it:

It ain't exactly what 'e sez
It's the nasty way 'e sez it.[18]

Meanwhile Snowden in the Lords accused his Cabinet colleagues of seeking to take the country back into the hungry forties. 'The generation which knew from experience the horror and starvation of Protection is gone. The new generation must learn what Protection is from its own experience and sufferings', and Snowden denounced 'the patent fallacies, the unfounded claims and the contradictory assumptions upon which this measure is based'.[19] Such vitriol hardly made for amity in Cabinet relationships.

The 'agreement to differ' was the subject of a motion of censure in Parliament, but the Opposition attacked it in a rather half-hearted way. For the Labour Party was deeply suspicious of·collective unanimity which it associated with Cabinet secrecy. Labour leaders had been particularly anxious to dissociate themselves from the accusation that, in the second Labour government of 1929–31, they had agreed to economies of the kind which the National Government was in the process of carrying out, and they had not hesitated subsequently to describe in the Commons the nature of proceedings in Cabinet and in Cabinet committees at that time. In moving the censure, therefore, George Lansbury, the Labour leader, was forced to declare, 'I want now to say that we are not opposing this procedure because we think that such procedure should not take place on occasion, or because we are opposed to Members of the Government having freedom of action.'[20] Inevitably, therefore, his citation of Morley and Dicey on the need for Cabinet unity was bound to appear a little unconvincing.

Baldwin offered a rather more sophisticated defence when it fell to him to justify the course which the National Government had taken. Collective responsibility, he declared, had grown with the rise of party, in order that the government would be able to present a united front to the King, and later so that the government could maintain its position in Parliament without individual ministers being picked off one by one by the Opposition for particular policy failures. 'As party government grew and

18 Middlemas and Barnes, *Baldwin*, p. 662. fn.
19 H.L. Debs, vol. 83, col. 697, 29 February 1932.
20 H.C. Debs, vol. 261, col. 516, 8 February 1932.

strengthened in this country, so that rule became essential for the maintenance of party government. Party discipline is necessary to party survival.'

The National Government, however, was not a party government, but a coalition, and so the survival of party was not in question. 'Had the precedent been made for a party Government', Baldwin went on, 'it would have been quite new and it would have been absolutely dangerous for that party.' 'Is our action constitutional?', Baldwin asked in conclusion. 'Who can say what is constitutional in the conduct of a national Government? It is a precedent, an experiment, a new practice, to meet a new emergency, a new condition of things, and we have collective responsibility for the departure from collective action.'[21]

Whatever the merits of Baldwin's defence, the 'agreement to differ' did not hold the Cabinet together for long. For in September 1932, Samuel, Sinclair and Snowden resigned from the government because they could not accept the Ottawa Agreements which buttressed Protection with a scheme of Imperial Preference; they felt that the agreement to differ could not be maintained. 'You cannot do it a second time', Lord Lothian told Tom Jones. 'The dirty dogs', was Baldwin's response, 'They always behave like this when rough weather approaches.'[22]

The 'agreement to differ' failed to retain Cabinet unity. Yet the reasons usually given as to why it failed are wide of the mark. It did not fail because it breached the doctrine of collective Cabinet unanimity, but because it did so on what had become an issue of central importance for the government. The purpose of the 'agreement to differ' in January 1932, as with the separate manifestos in October of the previous year, was to prevent a subordinate issue from breaking up a government of national recovery. The central purpose for which the government was formed was, after all, in the view of its leaders, the need to secure economic recovery through the passage of emergency measures, not to impose a tariff. Indeed, the more vigorous tariff reformers in the Conservative Party such as Amery and Page-Croft, were rather sceptical of the benefits of the National Government since they believed that it would inevitably water down the Conservative commitment to Protection. Partly for this reason those who were Protectionists *à l'outrance* were not included in the government since they could not be expected to share the 'national' spirit of compromise.

During the general election campaign and again in January 1932, the leaders of the National Government believed that the coalition should be maintained and were willing to compromise. The defection of the Liberal

---

[21] H.C. Debs, ibid., cols., 534, 535.
[22] *A Diary with Letters 1931–1950*, p. 55.

ministers of the government would, it was thought, undermine confidence in the government, and therefore weaken the country's prospects of economic recovery. By September 1932, however, that belief was no longer so strongly held, the economic situation was rather more stable, and the government could continue perfectly happily without the Liberals. The Conservatives, therefore, were unwilling to make any further concessions to keep the Liberals in the Cabinet, while the Liberals were unwilling to sacrifice their beliefs any longer in order to maintain the coalition. The Liberals 'also felt that the essential emergency of 1931 was over, that the parliamentary position of the Government would not be weakened in the eyes of the foreign world, that the three-party co-operation over India should be maintained, and that they could really do more to promote the ends they cared about, disarmament, low tariffs, progress over India, etc. by criticism and support from an independent but friendly position outside than from within.'[23]

The 'agreement to differ', then, failed because an instrument which can properly be used to resolve differences on subordinate issues in a Cabinet, was being employed in an attempt to resolve an issue which the Cabinet was coming to regard as central rather than subordinate. If, on the other hand, the Import Duties Bill introduced into Parliament in February 1932 had been the final instalment of a Protectionist policy, and the issue had not arisen again in Cabinet, there is a chance that the 'agreement to differ' might have helped maintain the unity of a coalition whose members did not, on other issues, disagree along party lines.

The other two agreed suspensions of the doctrine of collective unanimity – in 1975 and 1977 – were both adopted under a single-party Labour government, in the Commons. The purpose was, however, the same as in 1932, to allow a government to contain an irresolvable difference on a subordinate issue. The guidelines in 1975 and 1977 were more restrictive than those of 1932. In April 1975, Harold Wilson in a written answer in the Commons published the Guidelines for the Agreement to Differ which had been approved by the Cabinet in March 1975:

... those Ministers who do not agree with the Government's recommendation in favour of continued membership of the European Community are, in the unique circumstances of the referendum, now free to advocate a different view during the referendum campaign in the country.

This freedom does not extend to parliamentary proceedings and official business. Government business in Parliament will continue to be handled by all Ministers in accordance with Government policy. Ministers responsible for European aspects of Government business who themselves differ from the Government's recommendation on membership of the European Community will state

---

[23] Lord Lothian to Thomas Jones, 9 September 1932, ibid., p. 53.

the Government's position and will not be drawn into making points against the Government's recommendation. Wherever necessary Questions will be transferred to other Ministers.

I have asked all Ministers ... not to allow themselves to appear in direct confrontation, on the same platform or programme, with another Minister who takes a different view on the Government recommendations. (7 April 1975. Written Answer 351)

In addition, dissenting ministers would be required to follow government policy at all meetings of the Council of Ministers of the European Community and at similar meetings. Seven Cabinet ministers took advantage of this provision.

It will be seen that these guidelines were more restrictive than the freedom accorded to dissenting ministers in 1932, in that those opposing the government's recommendations in 1975 were prohibited from stating their position in the Commons. The reason for this difference, according to Wilson, was that in 1932, 'the only possibility of agreement to differ in a Conservative, Liberal and minuscule Labour Coalition was through debate in the House. In the present situation there is a referendum campaign, which is of a totally different order, because all Members who have availed themselves of the unprecedented offer of agreement to differ are free to campaign in this referendum. I therefore believe that the 1932 precedent is totally inapplicable in this situation.'[24] However, one junior minister, Eric Heffer, refused to accept these guidelines, and actually spoke in the Commons against the government's recommendation. He was summarily dismissed, without even being allowed the privilege of resignation.

In other respects, however, the 1975 agreement to differ worked well, in that by allowing the dissenting ministers to remain in the government, it made possible its survival. Nor can it be pretended that it led to any disquiet in the country outside the narrow ranks of the strict constitutionalists. The same was true of the suspension of collective unanimity on the occasion of the European Assembly Elections Bill in July 1977, when six cabinet ministers and 26 junior ministers voted against direct elections. When Margaret Thatcher as Leader of the Opposition asked the Prime Minister, James Callaghan, whether collective responsibility applied to his government, the latter offered the jocular reply, 'I certainly think that the doctrine should apply, except in cases where I announce that it does not.'[25] Mrs Thatcher's response was to accuse him of turning cabinet government into a farce.

Yet Callaghan's comment, despite its flippancy, lays bare the reality of the convention of unanimity. It is a rule of prudence rather than a doctrine

[24] H.C. Debs, vol. 889, col. 1014, 8 April 1975.
[25] H.C. Debs, vol. 933, col. 552, 16 June 1977.

of the Constitution. Sir John Hunt, as Cabinet Secretary, declared that he understood collective responsibility to be more than a convention, but 'a reality and an important part of the constitution'. Yet he did not regard the agreement to differ in 1975 'as breaching collective responsibility because this was a decision by the Cabinet as a whole to waive collective responsibility on one particular issue for a limited time. It was not a decision which any Minister took unilaterally ... '[26] There is no reason why collective responsibility should necessarily mean collective unanimity, and, in the case of a coalition, an agreement to differ can well serve the purposes of cabinet government by ensuring that contentious issues are not pressed too far.

Collective responsibility, as Baldwin noticed, arose with the growth of party. It was an instrument designed to ensure party solidarity. In the days before the 1867 Reform Act when parties were much more loosely organised, it was quite customary for there to be "open questions" upon which the Cabinet made no collective decision, but left it open to ministers to decide as they wished. Alpheus Todd in his *Parliamentary Government* (1892 edition) declared that 'unanimity in the cabinet has become an acknowledged rule' but noticed nevertheless that 'such great questions as parliamentary reform, the ballot, the abolition of the slave trade, hours of labour in factories, marriage with a deceased wife's sister, women's disabilities, household franchise in counties, and the Public Worship Regulation Bill, with other minor matters, have severally been considered as 'open questions' by some administrations, though not by others'.[27] Other examples can be cited for the years after 1892. The 1905 Liberal Cabinet decided to follow the practice of Gladstone's 1880 ministry in regarding women's suffrage as an open question; and when Asquith returned to Parliament in 1920, he found that under the Lloyd George Coalition 'collective responsibility seemed to have vanished, and with it had gone Treasury Control and other things which he thought to be the imperatives of good government ... The head of the government was seldom in the House of Commons, and in his absence, it was difficult to ascertain whether ministers who answered questions spoke for the government or could commit it to anything.'[28] This, of course, was not due to a deliberate suspension of collective responsibility, but a lack of

[26] Cross-examination of Sir John Hunt, in *A-G v Sunday Times*, cited in Hugo Young, *The Crossman Affair* (Hamish Hamilton and Johathan Cape, 1976), p. 84.

[27] Alpheus Todd, *Parliamentary Government in England: Its Origin, Development and Practical Operation* (1892 edition, edited by Spencer Walpole, Sampson, Low, Marston and Co.), vol. 2, p. 79.

[28] J. Spender and C. Asquith, *Life of Herbert Henry Asquith, Lord Oxford and Asquith* (Hutchinson, 1932), vol. 2, p. 331. I am grateful to Dr Brian Harrison for drawing my attention to this quotation.

coherence in the government generally, a result of Lloyd George's personality, the peculiarities of the political situation and the disruption of normal party ties.

If collective responsibility developed with the growth of party, it is only to be expected that the weakening of party should also weaken the force of the convention. The two major parties, which once seemed to stand for coherent social philosophies, have become in reality exceptionally quarrelsome coalitions. The electorate has come to accept that the parties comprise a wide spectrum of political opinion, and is thus prepared to tolerate ministers who openly differ from their Cabinet colleagues. Indeed, the open expression of such differences may appear more honest than the pretence that Cabinet ministers find themselves in agreement on all of the major issues with which they deal.

Whether the supposed convention of collective unanimity is observed or not is more a matter of political prudence than morality. A government would, no doubt, be punished by the electorate if it abandoned the convention too frequently. Yet there is no reason to believe that the electorate disapproved of the agreements to differ under Wilson and Callaghan. Perhaps they welcomed the fact that the realities of political disagreement could emerge from behind the constitutional screen which usually serves to hide them.

A coalition government may find it particularly useful to be able to abandon collective unanimity from time to time. For the central problem faced by a coalition is that it is likely to break up through disagreement on subordinate issues. That is what happened, for example, to the anti-socialist coalition in Sweden in 1978 on the issue of nuclear energy; and in 1981 on tax reform. The Borten coalition in Norway also collapsed through internal disagreement in 1971 when, unlike the Wilson and Callaghan governments in Britain, it was unable to contain Cabinet conflicts on the EEC issue.

But if coalition governments in Britain decide to allow agreements to differ on specific issues, they will have to accept the corollary that MPs cannot be whipped when Cabinet ministers are free. It would be odd to allow ministers, the majority of whom, are after all, MPs, rights in the Commons which back-bench MPs do not enjoy. If ministers are to be allowed to differ, MPs must be allowed a free vote. Issues where collective unanimity is abandoned, therefore, would become very like the 'open questions' prevalent at an earlier period of British politics when the party system was in flux.

Coalition government, if it is to be successful, requires not only a positive striving for agreement, but also the willingness not to press issues on which the parties comprising the coalition cannot agree. Methods must therefore be found of defusing contentious but subordinate issues, of so dealing with them that they do not cause the break-up of the coalition. Suspension of collective unanimity is one way in which this might be achieved. Use of the referendum, as in 1975 on the EEC and in 1979 on devolution, might be another. Both are likely to prove useful weapons for coalitions. Nor is the use of such weapons reprehensible. For collective unanimity can easily serve to muzzle policy differences which should be openly ventilated. The electorate, after all, was perfectly aware that in the 1974–79 Labour government, James Callaghan and Tony Benn differed on a wide range of issues, just as they are aware that in the Conservative government elected in 1979, Mrs Thatcher and James Prior disagreed on such issues as incomes policy and trade union reform. Yet for presentational purposes both governments had to appear unanimous.

There is nothing blameworthy if honourable politicians, united on fundamentals, openly admit to honest disagreement on important if subordinate issues of policy. It is not less honest openly to avow such disagreement than to speak and vote in support of views which one does not hold. If coalition government were to lead to a loosening of the conventions governing the operation of the Cabinet, and a greater willingness to acknowledge differences of view, that would be a benefit and not a disadvantage. For it would bring the conventions of government more into accord with the preconceptions of the electorate.

Yet there must of course be limits to the extent to which the conventions of cabinet government can be loosened by a coalition. If the government is to survive, there must be some issues upon which ministers agree to stand together. There are bound to be questions which are so central to the continuing policies of the government that the coalition will fall apart if ministers are seen to be publicly at odds with one another. That, perhaps, has been the commonest cause of the collapse of coalitions in the Fourth Republic in France, and in contemporary Italy.

The existence of separate parties in a government will inevitably add to the strains of cabinet government, and so it will be vital to construct machinery which provides the maximum opportunity to resolve differences and reach accommodations on the central questions while allowing for the defusing of subordinate issues. Ministers will be aware that the appearance of serious disunity is damaging to their standing; yet they will also appreciate that coalitions must operate upon a looser basis than single-party government. To secure the necessary balance between consensus and conflict in a coalition cabinet will not be easy. But the art of coalition government is precisely to reconcile these conflicting aims.

IX

'England', said Disraeli in 1852, 'does not love coalitions.' This supposition, as a number of recent opinion polls have shown, can no longer be taken for granted. Indeed, one of the reasons which many electors give for favouring proportional representation is that it will lead to coalition government. If multi-party politics persists in Britain, then single-party government becomes impossible. The country must be ruled either by a minority government or by a coalition. It would be difficult to dispute, either from British or Continental experience, that coalitions are likely to prove more effective than minority governments both in securing continuity of policy and ensuring that a wider range of views are taken into account in the policy-making process. If multi-party politics proves to be enduring, then coalitions will become the only way by which majority government can be secured.

Conclusion

The first part of this book described the development of multi-party politics in Britain. Multi-party politics, it was suggested, is unlikely to prove a temporary phenomenon, but will endure. It is less likely to lead to a realignment of parties, as occurred in the 1920s, than to a system of tri-polar competition between three major political groupings. At the same time, the very role of party will alter so that political parties will become less cohesive and less able to satisfy the demands of the electorate. This will inaugurate a period of political uncertainty and volatility unlike anything experienced in Britain since the end of the Second World War.

Sooner or later, multi-party politics is likely to lead to a hung Parliament. Indeed, changes in electoral behaviour would have increased the likelihood of this outcome even without the formation of the SDP. Yet, as the second part of this book shows, British constitutional norms have hardly adapted to the norms of multi-party politics. Although coalitions and minority governments have played an important role in the history of twentieth-century Britain, the Constitution still assumes the continued existence of a stable two-party system with single-party governments alternating in office.

There is thus a serious conflict between the realities of electoral life and the presuppositions of the Constitution. In a world of multi-party politics, politicians are still required to operate a constitution designed for a two-party system. This is bound to lead to a period of considerable constitutional strain. For no constitution can ignore political reality for long. It must reflect the political conditions of the day if it is to survive. Yet the adaptation of the Constitution is likely to prove a process of great difficulty. For, as Chapter 5 and 6 investigating the process of government formation show, it is hardly possible to lay down precise constitutional rules and conventions where the agreement on fundamentals which would give them life is lacking. Constitutions, whether written or unwritten, can be effective only if based upon consensus. Yet in Britain there is no longer a shared consensus on constitutional matters, and so it is not possible to provide constitutional norms regulating the behaviour of political actors under multi-party politics.

Electoral reform is regarded by many of its advocates as a means of producing such a consensus. The influence of proportional representation, so it is suggested, will be felt both in the political system, where it will exert a gravitational pull drawing the parties towards the centre; and also in wider social relationships where it will encourage power-sharing and compromise. The supporters of electoral reform hope that it will change attitudes so that, in place of an adversary culture whose deleterious effects can be seen in politics and industry alike, more harmonious social relationships will develop.

The conventional critique of this approach claims that the politics of compromise is a suitable response only to the economics of expansion. With the disappearance of prospects of economic growth, politics becomes a zero-sum game in which conflicts can no longer be resolved by the incremental methods of bargaining and compromise. Social conflict becomes sharper and political life more polarised. In a period of economic crisis, therefore, proportional representation and coalition government are luxuries which society cannot afford. They are likely to lead only to deadlock and stalemate. Yet it is possible to turn this critique on its head and suggest that precisely because the tensions in modern society are so deep, it must be the function of the political system to do all it can to moderate them, instead of contributing to the polarisation of opinion. In a zero-sum society, any mechanisms which can help to contain the forces of conflict will also contribute to the strengthening of social ties. Indeed, the countries which have adapted best to the pressures of social change and economic recession have been those which have developed powerful institutional mechanisms for producing consensus and moderating conflict. Seen in this perspective, the development of multi-party politics and the reform of the electoral system can serve to strengthen, not weaken, the British Constitution.

Appendix: Coalition and minority governments in Britain since 1895

Coalition governments

Dates	Prime Minister	Composition of coalition	No. of MPs	Distribution of Cabinet seats by party	Nature of coalition
1895–Dec 1905	Lord Salisbury (Con) 1895–July 1902 A.J. Balfour (Con) July 1902–Dec 1905	Conservative and Liberal Unionist	(1895) 341 Con 70 LU	(1895) 14 Con 5 LU	Step to fusion, achieved 1912
May 1915–Dec 1916	H.H. Asquith (Lib)	Conservative, Liberal and Labour	(May 1915) 286 Con 263 Lib 35 Lab	(May 1915) 8 Con 12 Lib 1 Lab 1 non-party	Wartime three-party
Dec 1916–Oct 1922	D. Lloyd George (Lib)	Conservative, part of Liberal Party and Labour	(Dec 1916) 285 Con 263 Lib 34 Lab (Dec 1918) 368 Con 133 Coal Lib 10 Coal Lab 25 Irish	(Dec 1916) 13 Con 7 Lib 2 Lab (Oct 1919) 11 Con 8 Lib 1 Ind Lab	Wartime coalition continuing after war ended. Attempts at fusion having failed, coalition dissolved by Conservatives Oct 1922.

Aug 1931–May 1940	J. Ramsay MacDonald (Nat Lab) Aug 1931–June 1935	Conservative, Liberal National, Liberal (until Sept 1932) and National Labour	(Aug 1931) 243 Con 53 Lib 12 Lab 3 Ind	(Aug 1931) 4 Lab 4 Con 2 Lib	Intended as all-party coalition, but opposed by bulk of Labour Party and, after Nov 1933, by Liberals, who had resigned from the government in Sept 1932. Liberal National and National Labour eventually fused with Conservatives.
	S. Baldwin (Con) June 1935–May 1937		(Nov 1931) 473 Con 35 Lib Nat 33 Lib 13 Nat Lab	(Nov 1931) 11 Con 3 Lib 2 Lib Nat 4 Nat Lab	
	N. Chamberlain (Con) May 1937–May 1940			(Sept 1932) 13 Con 3 Lib Nat 3 Nat Lab	
May 1940–May 1945	W.S. Churchill (Con)	Conservative, Labour and Liberal	(May 1940) 415 Con 166 Lab 18 Lib	(May 1940) 3 Con 2 Lab 0 Lib	Wartime coalition ended by agreement May 1945

Minority governments

Dates	Prime Minister	Method of survival	Outcome
Jan 1910–May 1915	H.H. Asquith (Lib)	Government could rely on Liberal and Irish Nationalist support	Wartime coalition formed May 1915
Jan–Nov 1924	J. Ramsay MacDonald (Lab)	Some Liberal support	Defeated Oct 1924 in vote which it chose to regard as issue of confidence
June 1929–Aug 1931	J. Ramsay MacDonald (Lab)	Some Liberal support. Possibly buttressed by an informal agreement	Government broke up Aug 1931 having failed to agree upon economy measures
March–Oct 1974	H. Wilson (Lab)	Conservatives abstained, fearing early dissolution	Election victory, Oct 1974
April 1976–May 1979	J. Callaghan (Lab)	April 1976–March 1977 ad hoc support from different minority parties. March 1977–July 1978 pact with Liberals. Oct 1978–March 1979 Opposition disunited	Defeated in vote of confidence March 1979

Bibliographical note

The only book so far published on multi-party politics in Britain is Henry Drucker (ed.) *Multi-Party Britain* (Macmillan, 1979). This consists of a series of individual essays on the different parties, written before the 1979 general election. The essays vary in quality, but the chapter on the Liberal Party by Michael Steed is outstanding.

The background to the post-war consensus in Britain is given in Paul Addison, *The Road to 1945* (Cape, 1975), while Andrew Gamble, *Britain in Decline* (Macmillan, 1981), offers an intelligent Marxist's critique of party attitudes which sheds a good deal of light on the issues discussed here. On the problems of territorial politics, Tom Nairn, *The Break-Up of Britain* (2nd edition, Verso, 1981) and Richard Rose, *Understanding the United Kingdom* (Longmans, 1982), are full of insights. My own book, *Devolution* (Oxford University Press, 1979), traces the history of one attempt to resolve these complex problems.

On the relationships between the Liberal and Social Democratic traditions in the early part of the century, Peter Clarke's work is fundamental. Both *Liberals and Social Democrats* (Cambridge University Press, 1978) and the more special-ised *Lancashire and the New Liberalism* (Cambridge University Press, 1971) hark back longingly to a period when the two traditions were seen as com-plementary rather than conflicting. Clarke's essay in Vernon Bogdanor (ed.), *Liberal Party Politics* (Oxford University Press, 1983) looks at the history of the two traditions from the perspective of the Liberal/SDP Alliance. Martin Pugh, *Electoral Reform in Peace and War 1906–1918* (Routledge and Kegan Paul, 1978) shows how the failure to achieve electoral reform helped to break up the Progressive Alliance.

Three of the leaders of the SDP have published books setting out their political programmes: David Owen, *Face the Future* (Cape, 1981), Shirley Williams, *Politics is for People* (Penguin, 1981) and William Rodgers, *The Politics of Change* (Secker and Warburg, 1982). The best account of the genesis of the SDP is probably Ian Bradley, *Breaking the Mould* (Martin Robertson, 1981). There is also a valuable book of essays which reprints Roy Jenkins' 1979 Dimbleby Lecture, entitled *The Rebirth of Britain*, ed. Wayland Kennet (Weidenfeld and Nicolson, 1982). Vernon Bogdanor, 'The Social Democrats and the Constitution' in *Political Quarterly*, 52 (1981) discusses the central role played by consti-tutional reform in the programme of the SDP.

Much less has been written on the Liberal Party. Arthur Cyr, *Liberal Party Politics in Britain* (John Calder, 1977) remains the most recent general account of the Party. Peter Bartram, *David Steel: His Life and Politics* (W. H. Allen, 1981) is also useful. The essays in Vernon Bogdanor (ed.), *Liberal Party Politics* attempt a more comprehensive coverage of the Party's political attitudes, organisation and electoral strategy.

On recent electoral trends, the best guides are Ivor Crewe, 'Is Britain's two-party system really about to crumble?' in *Electoral Studies* (1982), Richard Rose, *Class Does Not Equal Party: The Decline of a Model of British Voting* (Studies in Public Policy, no. 74, Centre for the Study of Public Policy, University of Strathclyde, 1980) and John Curtice in Vernon Bogdanor (ed.), *Liberal Party Politics*. G. Gudgin and P.J. Taylor, *Seats, Votes and the Spatial Organisation of Elections* (Pion, 1979) show how the first-past-the-post system makes the relationship between votes and seats unpredictable and highly volatile in a multi-party system. John Curtice and Michael Steed, 'Electoral choice and the production of government: the changing operation of the electoral system in the United Kingdom since 1955' in *British Journal of Political Science*, 12 (1982), analyses trends in the electoral system which make it less likely to produce single-party majority governments in the future.

S.E. Finer (ed.), *Adversary Politics and Electoral Reform* (Anthony Wigram, 1975) is the *locus classicus* of the 'adversary thesis', while his book *The Changing British Party System, 1945–1979* (American Enterprise Institute, 1980) is an attempt to carry the argument further. Vernon Bogdanor, *The People and the Party System: The Referendum and Electoral Reform in British Politics* (Cambridge University Press, 1981) discusses the contemporary arguments for electoral reform, and attempts to relate them to the historical debate.

Giovanni Sartori, *Parties and Party Systems: A Framework for Analysis*, vol. 1 (Cambridge University Press, 1976), is the basic work on party systems. André Siegfried, *Géographie Électorale de l' Ardèche sous la IIIe République* (A. Colin, Paris, 1949) and François Goguel, *Géographie des Élections Françaises sous la troisième et la quatrième République* (A. Colin, Paris, 1970) are classics of electoral geography showing the historicity of voting patterns. Seymour M. Lipset and Stein Rokkan, 'Cleavage structures, party systems and voter alignments: an introduction', in Lipset and Rokkan (eds.) *Party Systems and Voter Alignments: Cross-National Perspectives* (Free Press, New York, 1967) show how party systems develop from historic cleavages. The analysis in Rokkan and Lipset is derived from Stein Rokkan's theory of the evolution of parties in Western Europe expounded in his brilliant book of essays, *Citizens, Elections, Parties* (Universitetsforlaget, Oslo, 1970). I have tried to show that this theory over-emphasises the stability of party systems in the West in my concluding essay in Vernon Bogdanor and David Butler (eds.), *Democracy and Elections: The Political Consequences of Electoral Systems* (Cambridge University Press, 1983).

Otto Kirchheimer's essays collected in *Politics, Law and Social Change* (Columbia University Press, 1969) analyse the theory of the 'catch-all' party, while Kevin Phillips, *Post-Conservative America: People, Politics and Ideology in a Time of Crisis* (Random House, New York, 1982) offers a thought-provoking account of radical and populist trends in modern parties of the Right.

On the problems discussed in Part 2, the best work has been done in Scandinavia. Henrik Hermerén, *Regeringsbildningen i Flerpartisystem* (Studentlitteratur, Lund, 1975) offers the most complete account of the principles of government formation in six constitutional monarchies in north-western Europe. There is an English summary of Hermerén's ideas at the end of his book; and an article, 'Government formation in multiparty systems' in *Scandinavian Political Studies* (1976). Olof Rúin, 'Patterns of government composition in multi-party systems:

Bibliographical note

the case of Sweden', in *Scandinavian Political Studies* is also of great value, while Olof Petersson's *Regeringsbildningen 1978* (Rabén and Sjögren, Stockholm, 1979), offers a detailed account of the government-formation process under the new rules in Sweden. André Molitor, *La Fonction Royale en Belgique* (CRISP, Brussels, 1979) is an excellent study of the role of constitutional monarchy in Belgium.

On Britain, very little has been published. Sir Ivor Jennings, *Cabinet Government* (3rd edition, Cambridge University Press, 1959) is the classic text, but it does not offer much help on the problems likely to arise in a multi-party system. Chapters 2 and 3 of Bagehot's *The English Constitution* offer a utilitarian analysis of the monarchy, but Harold Nicolson's incomparable *King George V: His Life and Reign* (Constable, 1952) is still the best source for the practical operation of constitutional monarchy. Rodney Brazier, 'Choosing a Prime Minister', in *Public Law* (1982) offers a useful if idiosyncratic study of the problems. Philip Laundy, *The Office of Speaker* (Cassell, 1964) is the most thorough analysis of the Speakership, and shows how inapplicable the Swedish solution would be in the British context. S. A. de Smith, *The New Commonwealth and its Constitutions* (Stevens, 1964) contains useful information on how the New Commonwealth countries have sought to codify the unwritten understandings of the British Constitution. On the dissolution of Parliament, Eugene A. Forsey, *The Royal Power of Dissolution in the British Commonwealth* (Oxford University Press, Toronto, 1943), and B.S. Markesinis, *The Theory and Practice of Dissolution of Parliament* (Cambridge University Press, 1972) offer useful if formalistic accounts.

Richard W. Lyman, *The First Labour Government 1924* (Chapman and Hall, 1957) and Robert Skidelsky, *Politicians and the Slump: The Second Labour Government 1929–1931* (Macmillan, 1967) provide valuable accounts of the first two minority Labour governments, and there is some material in Harold Wilson, *Final Term: The Labour Government 1974–1976* (Weidenfeld and Nicolson and Michael Joseph, 1979) and Barbara Castle, *The Castle Diaries 1974–1976* (Weidenfeld and Nicolson, 1980) on the third.

The best account of the tortuous negotiations between Labour and the Liberals in the second Labour government is John D. Fair, 'The second Labour government and the politics of electoral reform, 1929–1931', in *Albion* (Fall 1981). Very little has been published on the problems of minority government, but Linda Geller-Schwartz, 'Minority government reconsidered', in *Journal of Canadian Studies* (Summer 1979) and Erik Rasmussen, 'Les relations du parlement et du ministre dans les gouvernements de minorité', in *Parlement et Gouvernement: Le Partage du Pouvoir* (Actes du Colloque de Florence, October 1977) contain many valuable insights. On the Lib–Lab pact, David Steel, *A House Divided: The Lib– Lab Pact and the Future of British Politics* (Weidenfeld and Nicolson, 1980) and Alistair Michie and Simon Hoggart, *The Pact: The Inside Story of the Lib–Lab Government 1977–8* (Quartet, 1978) are the accounts of insiders which manage to reveal a good deal about the workings of British government.

Much has been published on coalitions, but most of the literature is concerned with formal theories of coalition, rather than with how coalitions actually work in practice. Of the former, Lawrence C. Dodd, *Coalitions in Parliamentary Government* (Princeton University Press, 1976) is probably the most useful. Eric C. Browne and John Dreijmanis (eds.), *Government Coalitions in Western Democracies* (Longman, 1982) offers a judicious mixture of coalition theory tested against the reality of coalitions in eleven modern democracies. The short booklet: *Probleme von Koalitionsregierungen in Westeuropa*, published by the Freidrich-Naumann-Stiftung, the research foundation of the West German Free Democrats, contains more valuable insights into the problems of coalition government than many books with much larger pretensions.

On coalitions in Britain, David Butler (ed.), *Coalitions in British Politics* (Macmillan, 1978) offers an excellent survey. Lord Beaverbrook, *Politicians and the War 1914–1916* (Collins, 1960) shows how the failure to offer the Conservatives their fair share of places in the Asquith coalition of 1915, 'made the whole edifice ... shaky from the very beginning and ultimately prepared the way for the overthrow of Mr Asquith as Prime Minister' (p. 130). The best source on the working of the National Government is the unpublished Ph.D. thesis by D.J. Wrench, 'The National Government, 1931–1935' (Bangor, 1973). There are two good accounts of the working of the Borten coalition in Norway, Jan Henrik Nyheim, 'Norway; the co-operation of four parties', in *Scandinavian Political Studies* (1967); and Arve Solstad, 'The Norwegian coalition system', in *Scandinavian Political Studies* (1969). A good deal has been written on collective responsibility. The best modern discussions are in John P. Mackintosh, *The British Cabinet* (Stevens, 1962) and Patrick Gordon Walker, *The Cabinet* (revised edition, Fontana, 1972). There is a typically provocative article by S.E.Finer, 'One out, all out', in *New Society*, 25 August 1977, while Hugo Young's account of the prosecution of the *Sunday Times* in *The Crossman Affair* (Hamish Hamilton and Jonathan Cape, 1976) contains much valuable material on the conventions of cabinet government.

Index